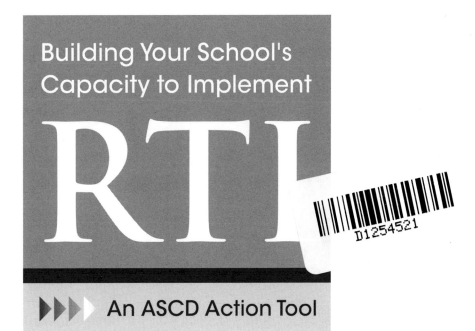

Building Your School's Capacity to Implement

RTI

An ASCD Action Tool

Patricia Addison
Cynthia Warger

Building Your School's
Capacity to Implement

RTI

an ASCD
Action*TOOL*

1703 North Beauregard St. • Alexandria, VA 22311-1714 USA

Phone: 1-800-933-2723 or 1-703-578-9600 • Fax: 1-703-575-5400

Website: www.ascd.org • E-mail: member@ascd.org

Author guidelines: www.ascd.org/write

Gene R. Carter, *Executive Director*; Judy Zimny, *Chief Program Development Officer*; Gayle Owens, *Managing Director, Content Acquisitions and Development*; Nancy Modrak, *Publisher*; Debbie Brown, *Content Development*; Mary Beth Nielsen, *Manager, Editorial Services*; Katie Freeman, *Project Manager*; Gary Bloom, *Managing Director, Creative Services*; Catherine Guyer, *Senior Graphic Designer*; Mike Kalyan, *Manager, Production Services*; Marlene Hochberg, *Desktop Publishing Specialist*

All web links in this book are correct as of the publication date below but may have become inactive or otherwise modified since that time. If you notice a deactivated or changed link, please e-mail books@ascd.org with the words "Link Update" in the subject line. In your message, please specify the web link, the book title, and the page number on which the link appears.

PAPERBACK ISBN: 978-1-4166-1168-4   ASCD Product #111007   n01/11

Quantity discounts for the paperback edition only: 10–49 copies, 10%; 50+ copies, 15%; for 1,000 or more copies, call 1-800-933-2723, ext. 5634, or 1-703-575-5634.

Library of Congress Cataloging-in-Publication Data

Addison, Patricia.
  Building your school's capacity to implement RTI / Patricia Addison and Cynthia L. Warger.
      p. cm.
  Includes bibliographical references.
  ISBN 978-1-4166-1168-4 (pbk. : alk. paper) 1. Remedial teaching. 2. Response to intervention (Learning disabled children) 3. Slow learning children—Education. I. Warger, Cynthia L. II. Title.
  LB1029.R4A33 2010
  371.9'043—dc22
                                        2010051200

17 16 15 14 13 12 11   2 3 4 5 6 7 8 9 10 11

Building Your School's
Capacity to Implement

RTI

Introduction 1

How This Action Tool Is Organized 5

PART 1: STARTING THE RTI PLANNING PROCESS

About Part 1 11

Section 1: Launching an RTI Initiative 13

Establishing a School-Based RTI Leadership Planning Team 15

Planning Support for the RTI Leadership Planning Team 19

Deciding What to Look For in an RTI Coordinator 22

Section 2: Getting Started with RTI 25

Building the RTI Leadership Planning Team 28

Taking a Look at How Other Schools Have Implemented RTI 32

Understanding the Roots of RTI 42

Reviewing Web-Based Resources 49

Selecting or Reviewing an RTI Definition 53

Crafting a Vision for RTI in the School 57

Exploring Connections: How RTI Fits with Other School
and District Initiatives 61

PART 2: UNDERSTANDING RTI COMPONENTS

About Part 2 67

Section 1: Ensuring Effective Core Instruction 71

Reviewing Student Data in Relation to Core Instruction 76

Reviewing Core Instruction in Relation to Standards:
Focus Questions 82

Looking at Differentiated Instruction 85

Understanding Research-Based Instructional Practices 89

Conducting Observations of Research-Based Instructional Practices . . . 92

Considering a Proactive, Schoolwide Approach
to Behavioral Interventions 96

Strengthening Core Instruction via Classroom
Management Practices 101

Ensuring Cultural Responsiveness as Part of the Core
Instructional Program 106

Indentifying Curriculum Resources for Tier 1 Interventions 110

Identifying Supplemental Instructional Materials 113

**Section 2: Understanding a Multitiered Response
to Intervention Approach** 117

   Organizing for Intervention 121

   Creating a Library of Interventions 125

   Examining Research-Based Academic Interventions
   at Tier 2 and Tier 3 128

   Identifying Behavioral Interventions at Tier 2 and Tier 3 132

   Building a Tiered Approach to Intervention:
   Inventorying Resources and Interventions 136

   Identifying Gap Services 139

   Tracking the Success of Interventions 143

   Understanding How RTI Fits with Special Education
   Eligibility for Learning Disabilities 146

**Section 3: Establishing the Problem-Solving Process
and RTI Intervention Team** 150

   Considering RTI Intervention Team Tasks: Details, Details, Details 154

   Forming the RTI Intervention Team: "Must-Have" Characteristics 158

   Reviewing Current School-Based Teams:
   Opportunities for RTI Expansion 162

   Establishing a Problem-Solving Process 165

   Creating a Request for Assistance Form 168

   Determining a Problem-Solving Model for Identifying
   Student Interventions at Tier 2 and Tier 3 171

   Looking at Data Sources to Document Student Difficulties 177

   Developing the Intervention Planning Template 180

   Ensuring Fidelity of Implementation 183

   Developing Forms 189

   Addressing Logistics 193

   Helping the RTI Intervention Team Troubleshoot
   Possible Challenges 195

Section 4: Establishing a Progress Monitoring Process 199

   Considering Curriculum-Based Measurement
   at the Elementary Level 204

   Considering Progress Monitoring Measures at the Secondary Level 209

   Reviewing Commercial Progress Monitoring Tools 214

   Planning for RTI Assessment: Data Sources 218

Section 5: Establishing a Universal Screening Process 221

   Planning for Universal Screening 225

   Understanding Universal Screening Assessments Currently in Use 228

   Reviewing Commercial Screening Instruments 231

Informing Instruction: Universal Screening in the Classroom 234

Looking at Screening Results: Are There Sufficient Interventions
for Students who Demonstrate Difficulties? 237

PART 3: DEVELOPING AND IMPLEMENTING THE RTI PLAN

About Part 3 243

Section 1: Putting It All Together—Developing the RTI Framework and Implementation Plan 245

Preparing a Flowchart of the RTI Process 247

Planning for Parent Communication and Involvement 249

Communicating About RTI 254

Drafting the RTI Plan and Timeline 260

Planning and Monitoring Implementation of the RTI Framework 266

Section 2: Introducing RTI to School Staff Members 289

Starting with an Overview: A PowerPoint Presentation on RTI 292

Using Nonlinguistic Representations to Foster Reflection,
Understanding, and Discussion of RTI 294

Presenting the RTI Definition 298

Understanding Changing Roles: Staff Survey 301

Searching Web-Based Resources and Summarizing Findings 306

Providing Staff with an Understanding of RTI Components 310

Understanding Interventions in the RTI Pyramid 312

Sharing the Draft RTI Implementation Plan 317

Showing the Relationship of RTI to Other School Initiatives 321

Eliciting Ideas, Reactions, and Questions via a Frayer Diagram 325

Section 3: Developing the RTI Intervention Team 329

Orienting the RTI Intervention Team: A Team-Building Activity 332

Developing the RTI Intervention Team: Roles and Responsibilities 336

Reviewing RTI Intervention Team Tasks Related
to Identifying and Monitoring Interventions 340

Planning Professional Development for the RTI Intervention Team 345

Using a Protocol for RTI Intervention Team Meetings 349

Organizing for Data Use During RTI Intervention Team Meetings 353

Facilitating Fidelity of Implementation 356

Section 4: Monitoring and Supporting RTI Implementation 362

Understanding and Implementing RTI: Self-Assessment
and Identification of Additional Supports 364

Assessing RTI Implementation Progress via Focus Groups 368

Monitoring Implementation: Looking at Program Data 372

Reflecting on Next Steps and Planning Enhancements 376

DOWNLOADS

Electronic versions of the tools are available for download
at **www.ascd.org/downloads**.

Enter this unique key code to unlock the files:
GF2DE 0DEFD DC514

If you have difficulty accessing the files, e-mail webhelp@ascd.org
or call 1-800-933-ASCD for assistance.

▶▶▶▶ INTRODUCTION

Response to Intervention, or RTI, is a school improvement system characterized by effective core instruction, a multitiered system of supports, data-based problem solving, progress monitoring, and universal screening. Once a school or district's interest moves beyond the "talking about" stage and into the "careful consideration" or "let's move forward" stage, the individual or group of individuals championing the RTI concept in a school will be faced with two major tasks—to develop the RTI framework for the school, and to develop the RTI implementation plan. This action tool is designed to help school leaders navigate those two tasks.

This action tool provides the school administrative team and a team of educators—referred to throughout as the RTI Leadership Planning Team—with tools to help them plan how RTI will look and how it will be implemented in their school. It does not promote a particular model or approach to RTI. Rather, the assumption is that schools should develop or adopt a framework that fits what they need and then develop the capacity to put the framework into place. As the following vignettes demonstrate, educators develop interest in RTI for a variety of reasons.

▲▲▲▲▲

The School Improvement Team at Buffalo Hills Middle School has been studying student achievement patterns, and there is concern. During the past several years, there has been a steady decline in student achievement on the state assessments. During that same period of time, student demographics have changed as well. In particular, about 20 percent of students from one of the feeder schools entered the middle school with significant literacy difficulties, whereas for several years that number had hovered around 6 percent. Team members want a way to intervene as soon as possible—especially with reading issues—and in a consistent manner. They know that resources are limited, and as a result they will need to organize carefully to maximize use. The School Improvement Team has been reviewing the potential of an RTI framework to help organize how the school addresses the reading difficulties of entering 6th grade students.

▲▲▲▲

Like many other principals in the district, Dr. Allen, the principal at Howell Elementary School, has attended several workshops on RTI sponsored by the State Department of Education. Three years ago, the school implemented a schoolwide positive behavioral support approach that has been successful in keeping students in their classrooms and engaged in their work. Dr. Allen is intrigued about how an RTI approach might expand upon this work and address students' academic difficulties.

▲▲▲▲

The Owen County School District has decided to implement an RTI framework throughout the district in response to state statutes that define how students are identified as having specific learning disabilities. Although the district has identified certain parameters for the initiative, administrative teams in each school are being asked to develop a plan for implementing RTI with staff. Principals are being encouraged to enact the following timeline:

- Year One: Conduct a thorough analysis of the instructional program and develop a viable RTI framework.
- Year Two: Focus on strengthening the core instructional program.
- Year Three: Implement a data-based, problem-solving approach that includes a multitiered system of supports.

▲▲▲▲

Within their professional learning community, 1st and 2nd grade teachers at Beach Elementary School have been investigating how an RTI approach might be used to intervene early with students who struggle with reading or mathematics. Teachers have conferred with the administrative team and have been asked to prepare a plan for how RTI might operate in the school. In addition to the first and second grade teachers, the planning team will include the assistant principal, the reading coach, and a third grade teacher.

▲▲▲▲

Just as these educators became interested in RTI for different reasons, there are numerous definitions, models, and approaches—not to mention entry points and strategies for implementation—from which to choose in planning for and implementing RTI. The purpose of this action tool is to help educators who are interested in establishing an RTI approach in their school do so in a way that addresses the preparation levels and capacity of the staff while maintaining the integrity of most RTI frameworks. The action tool helps planning teams navigate their way through several steps:

- Getting started, including forming the RTI Leadership Planning Team and deciding how RTI aligns with the school's vision and school improvement goals.
- Understanding the major RTI components—an effective core instructional program for all students, a multitiered system of support for struggling students, data-based problem solving, progress monitoring, and universal screening—and assessing the capacity of school staff to implement each.
- Planning the RTI framework and creating the RTI implementation plan.
- Introducing RTI to school staff and conducting and monitoring implementation activities.

A FEW ASSUMPTIONS

As with any set of planning tools, there are assumptions that are inherent in their design. That does not mean that the planning tools cannot be modified, only that they were designed with certain considerations in mind:

- Although there are numerous benefits to an RTI approach—such as providing an early intervention structure to address student learning and behavioral needs—this action tool assumes that individuals reading it already have an interest in RTI, have considered its potential for addressing school needs, and are ready to move forward with implementation.
- The school administrator will provide leadership for the RTI initiative and be involved throughout the planning and implementation process. This assumption does not mean that others—such as the assistant principal or the RTI Leadership Planning

Team chair—should not be entrusted with leadership roles. Rather, it underscores the importance of the principal's leadership in the change effort.

- A school-based team—referred to throughout the action tool as the RTI Leadership Planning Team, or simply the planning team—will develop the RTI framework and RTI implementation plan. Team members should have the skills and knowledge to develop an RTI framework. They also should have an understanding of the change process, including professional development, in order to develop a viable implementation plan.

- As with any change initiative, it takes time to plan, build capacity, obtain staff support, implement, and fine tune. This action tool assumes a multiyear commitment.

- The tools in each section are not presented as linear steps that teams must follow. Rather, each tool addresses issues related to the topic at hand, allowing planning teams to decide whether or not to address them. Further, tools may be modified or adjusted to meet the preferences and needs of team members.

▶▶▶ How This Action Tool Is Organized

This action tool consists of a series of activities that the RTI Leadership Planning Team members may use in developing their school's RTI framework and RTI implementation plan. The RTI Action Tool is organized into the following three parts, with varying numbers of sections.

Part 1: Starting the RTI Planning Process. The purpose of Part 1 is to help the principal and the RTI Leadership Planning Team begin the planning process. There are two sections in Part 1:

- **Launching the RTI Initiative**. The tools in this section are designed to help the principal and administrative team choose planning team members and organize support and resources for the team.
- **Getting Started with RTI**. The tools in this section are designed to help the planning team begin to operate as a unit while becoming oriented to RTI. The tools provide team members with various ways to determine the school's capacity for RTI planning and implementation.

Part 2: Understanding RTI Components. The purpose of Part 2 is to provide the RTI Leadership Planning Team members with background information on the most common RTI framework components. The five sections in Part 2 correspond to these components—effective core instructional program, multitiered system of support, data-based problem solving, progress monitoring, and universal screening. At the end of Part 2, team members should have sufficient knowledge of RTI—as well as school staff members' capacity to implement it—to develop their RTI framework and implementation plan.

Part 3: Developing and Implementing the RTI Plan. The sections in Part 3 help the RTI Leadership Planning Team develop the draft RTI plan and see it through to implementation and monitoring. There are four sections in Part 3:

- **Putting It All Together—Developing the RTI Framework and Implementation Plan**. The tools in this section are designed to help the planning team create the proposed RTI framework and implementation plan.
- **Introducing RTI to School Staff Members**. The tools in this section are designed to help the planning team introduce RTI to staff members and to assess their willingness to support the initiative. These tools are designed as professional development activities that can be presented to the entire staff or to small groups.
- **Developing the RTI Intervention Team**. The tools in this section are designed to help the RTI Leadership Planning Team form the RTI Intervention Team, which is the group that receives staff requests for assistance, develops an intervention plan to address the problem, and monitors progress. The tools also include suggestions for providing professional development for the RTI Intervention Team and for helping the team get up and running. The tools in this section can also guide the RTI Leadership Planning Team in establishing the problem-solving process.
- **Monitoring and Supporting RTI Implementation**. The tools in this section provide the planning team with strategies for monitoring implementation, assessing effect, and responding to challenges.

Tools are designed either as conversation starters, reflection probes, activities, or forms. In addition to the activity itself, each tool contains the following sections:

- Purpose of the tool. This section presents an orientation to the topic featured in the tool.
- How to use this tool. [*Note*: Each tool includes suggested processes, but teams may find other ways to use each tool.] At the end of this section is a "Decision Point" that identifies a particular aspect of the planning process that requires the planning team's attention.
- Tips and variations. This section presents suggestions for modifying the tool and lists issues that may arise in the course of completing the tool.

Some tools reference other resources, but the tools may be completed without them.

HOW TO USE THIS ACTION TOOL

The administrative team and RTI Leadership Planning Team should familiarize themselves with the action tool. Together, they should decide on a schedule for working through the tools. If teams choose to complete only some of the tools, the administrator or the RTI Leadership Planning Team chair should ensure that team members have access to the information on the topics covered in the tools they do not complete.

ELECTRONIC TOOLS AND RESOURCES

The tools are available for download. To access these documents, visit www.ascd.org/ downloads and enter the key code found on page viii. All files are saved in Adobe Portable Document Format (PDF). The PDF is compatible with both personal computers (PCs) and Macintosh computers. The main menu will let you navigate through the various sections, and you can print individual tools or sections in their entirety. If you are having difficulties downloading or viewing the files, contact webhelp@ascd.org for assistance, or call 1-800-933-ASCD.

MINIMUM SYSTEM REQUIREMENTS

Program: The most current version of the Adobe Reader software is available for free download at www.adobe.com.

PC: Intel Pentium Processor; Microsoft Windows XP Professional or Home Edition (Service Pack 1 or 2), Windows 2000 (Service Pack 2), Windows XP Tablet PC Edition, Windows Server 2003, or Windows NT (Service Pack 6 or 6a); 128 MB of RAM (256 MB recommended); up to 90 MB of available hard-disk space; Internet Explorer 5.5 (or higher), Netscape 7.1 (or higher), Firefox 1.0, or Mozilla 1.7.

Macintosh: PowerPC G3, G4, or G5 processor, Mac OS X v.10.2.8–10.3; 128 MB of RAM (256 MB recommended); up to 110 MB of available hard-disk space; Safari 1.2.2 browser supported for MAC OS X 10.3 or higher.

GETTING STARTED

Select "Download files." Designate a location on your computer to save the file. Choose to open the PDF file with your existing version of Adobe Acrobat Reader, or install the newest version of Adobe Acrobat Reader from www.adobe.com. From the main menu, select a section by clicking on its title. To view a specific tool, open the Bookmarks tab in the left navigation pane and then click on the title of the tool.

PRINTING TOOLS

To print a single tool, select the tool by clicking on its title via the Bookmarks section and the printer icon, or select File then Print. In the Print Range section, select Current Page to print the page on the screen. To print several tools, enter the page range in the "Pages from" field. If you wish to print all of the tools in the section, select All in the Printer Range section and then click OK.

PART 1

Starting the RTI Planning Process

▶▶▶▶ ABOUT PART 1

RTI may come about for a variety of reasons. For example, the School Improvement Team may determine that RTI is a vehicle for improving identified student achievement. Or, a principal may see RTI as a means to organize academic and behavioral supports and resources. In some cases, RTI may be a districtwide agenda in response to state and federal statutes (e.g., Individuals with Disabilities Education Improvement Act). In any case, the principal and the administrative team will have a major role in initiating the RTI process with staff members.

In RTI approaches, the principal draws on staff members to provide planning and leadership. Often, an RTI Leadership Planning Team is formed to work with the principal and administrative team to assess the school's readiness for RTI, plan the RTI framework, provide leadership for the initiative, help orchestrate staff professional development relative to RTI, establish the problem solving process, and monitor progress.

The sections in Part 1 help the principal and RTI Leadership Planning Team get started.

Launching the RTI initiative. The tools in Section 1 are designed to help the principal and administrative team choose RTI Leadership Planning Team and organize support and resources for the team. At this time, the principal and administrative team should make decisions related to selecting an RTI coordinator.

Getting started with RTI. The tools in Section 2 are designed to help the planning team begin to operate as a unit while becoming oriented to RTI. The tools provide team members with various ways to determine if RTI is a good fit with the school.

The principal is encouraged to work closely with the RTI Leadership Planning Team, especially through the tools in Section 2. The principal and RTI Leadership Planning Team should assess the team's level of knowledge and skills when deciding whether to complete all or some of the tools in this section. Keep in mind, however, that although team members may have knowledge and skills relative to RTI, the tools offer an opportunity for team building—that is, fostering a common perspective and helping to ensure that all team members are on the same page.

The RTI Leadership Planning Team will use the information in Section 2 to develop an understanding and shared definition of RTI, to determine whether RTI is a good fit with the school, and to identify what steps are needed to proceed.

SECTION 1 OVERVIEW: LAUNCHING AN RTI INITIATIVE

Initially, the building principal is certain to assume a strong leadership role in launching the RTI initiative. As with all school improvement initiatives, principal leadership and support are necessary for success.

When launching an RTI initiative, schools typically form a small, school-based team to support the principal in planning and providing leadership for the RTI initiative. In this Action Tool we refer to this team as the RTI Leadership Planning Team, although it has been called by other names (e.g., RTI School Improvement Team, RTI Team, etc.). The challenge is to select team members who not only represent various school constituencies, but also possess skills and knowledge relevant to RTI.

Often the principal will work with the RTI Leadership Planning Team to ensure that the members have the resources and support they need to carry out their tasks. Once the planning team has begun its work, some principals may not be as directly involved in day-to-day activities. However, principals should continue to monitor progress and provide support as needed. Their role as school leaders is essential to the success of RTI.

Some schools have created an RTI coordinator position to manage the day-to-day RTI activities. As part of RTI planning and implementation, the administration—with input from the RTI Leadership Planning Team—will want to consider the need for a staff member to serve in this role. Depending on the school's resources and needs, this may be a part-time or full-time position. In the absence of new resources, some schools may find it helpful to make adjustments in the responsibilities of a designated staff member in order for that individual to assume the RTI coordinator role.

PURPOSE OF THIS SECTION AND SUMMARY OF TOOLS

The purpose of this section is to provide the principal or leadership personnel with information about establishing the RTI Leadership Planning Team and providing support. The information can be used to determine team membership, identify resources and support specific to RTI, and decide what to look for in an RTI coordinator.

- Determine team membership.
- Identify resources and support specific to RTI.
- Decide what to look for in an RTI coordinator.

The tools are as follows:

- **Establishing the School-Based RTI Leadership Planning Team.** This tool is designed to help the principal and other building administrators think about factors related to developing the RTI Leadership Planning Team.
- **Planning Support for the RTI Leadership Planning Team.** This tool will assist the principal and members of the administrative team in identifying and planning for ways to support and communicate with the RTI Leadership Planning Team.
- **Deciding What to Look For in an RTI Coordinator.** Some schools have created the RTI coordinator position to manage day-to-day RTI activities. This tool provides a checklist of traits, knowledge, and capabilities that the RTI Leadership Planning Team or administrator might use to screen potential applicants.

After completing these tools, the principal and the administrative team will have chosen members for the RTI Leadership Planning Team, identified supports for the team, and decided on who to appoint as the RTI coordinator if it is determined that one is needed.

Launching an RTI Initiative

 # Establishing a School-Based RTI Leadership Planning Team

PURPOSE

Establishing an RTI framework will require a long-term commitment from school administrators and other faculty members to achieve the desired school improvement outcomes. Thoughtful and systematic planning will be essential during each stage of the process—from planning to implementing to sustaining. Forming an RTI Leadership Planning Team is highly recommended as the vehicle to support and advise the school principal in this work and to provide consistent oversight, guidance, and decision making consistent with the authority designated by the principal. The purpose of this tool is to help the principal and other building administrators think about factors related to the development of the RTI Leadership Planning Team.

HOW TO USE THIS ACTION TOOL

The principal and other building administrators who compose the school's administrative team should review and discuss the questions posed in the tool. A designated note taker should record pertinent information from the discussion that may serve as a helpful reference later.

Decision point: The principal or administrative team should decide which staff members will be invited to serve on the school's RTI Leadership Planning Team.

TIPS AND VARIATIONS

1. The tool may be completed by the building principal and used as a springboard for discussion with other members of the administrative team, such as assistant principals.
2. Each member of the administrative team (e.g., principal, assistant principals, director of guidance) might complete the tool individually as preparation for discussion and decision making about forming an RTI Leadership Planning Team.

3. The school principal or designee might use the tool to help generate questions and prepare for consultation with other schools regarding the composition of their planning team and other factors related to the team's functioning (e.g., frequency of meetings and decision-making authority).

Establishing a School-Based RTI Leadership Planning Team

Reflective Questions	Notes
Expectations of Others • Are there state Department of Education or central office expectations or recommendations for establishing a school-based RTI Leadership Planning Team? • How have school teams been established historically (e.g., independent principal decision, staff advisory committee recommendation, parent input)? • Are there expectations among faculty members or parents based on these historical practices?	
Assessment of Current Teams and Implications for RTI Leadership Planning Team • What types of school-based teams currently exist? • What are their overall responsibilities? • How frequently do they meet? • How representative are current teams relative to the entire faculty? • How representative is the leadership of these teams? • How would you assess the effectiveness of the current teams? • Given the size of your faculty and the structure of current teams, how many individuals should you consider for the RTI Leadership Planning Team composition? • Is there an existing team undertaking work that is similar to some of the components of RTI? What are the advantages/disadvantages of modifying their roles and/or membership so that they assume the responsibilities of an RTI Leadership Planning Team? • How will school administrators be represented on the team? What are the implications for their other team responsibilities?	

17

Identification of Characteristics Needed for RTI Leadership Planning Team

- What staff skills, characteristics, and experiences do you consider to be most important among RTI Leadership Planning Team members? For example:

    1. Communication skills

    2. Collaboration skills

    3. Differentiated instruction expertise

    4. Formative assessment expertise

    5. Behavior management expertise

    6. Technology expertise

    7. Research-based interventions knowledge

    8. Teaching experience

    9. Leadership experience

    10. Belief that all students can learn

    11. (Other)_____

- When considering your faculty and the identified skills, characteristics, and experiences, who are some of the potential candidates for the RTI Leadership Planning Team?

Next Steps and Projected Dates for Completion:

Launching an RTI Initiative

 Planning Support for the RTI Leadership Planning Team

PURPOSE

The RTI Leadership Planning Team will play an invaluable role in establishing an RTI framework for the school. Team members will need the ongoing encouragement and support of the school's principal and other building administrators as they take on this complex work. The purpose of this tool is to assist the principal and other members of the administrative team in identifying and planning for ways to support and communicate with the RTI Leadership Planning Team.

HOW TO USE THIS TOOL

The principal and other members of the administrative team should discuss the questions provided. A designated note taker should record pertinent information. Ideas generated as a result of this discussion should subsequently be shared by the principal with the RTI Leadership Planning Team. It may be helpful for the principal to obtain input from planning team members before finalizing the decisions.

Decision point: The principal and administrative team should determine the types of supports and expectations that will be established to help the RTI Leadership Planning Team function effectively and efficiently.

TIPS AND VARIATIONS

1. The principal might use the tool for individual reflection and note-taking. The notes and ideas might subsequently be used to develop agenda topics for the initial meeting with the RTI Leadership Planning Team.

2. The principal or designee might identify one or two school-based leaders experienced in implementing RTI and pose the questions outlined on the tool to them, reflect on their feedback, and consider its applicability.

3. Selected questions might be rephrased and posed by the principal to the members of RTI Leadership Planning Team so that their input is considered before the administration begins making decisions.

ASCD 19

Planning Support for the RTI Leadership Planning Team

Reflective Questions	Notes and Ideas
School Leader's Role in Planning with the Team and Decision-Making Authority • How will you share your vision of RTI with the proposed RTI Leadership Planning Team? • How will you communicate the team members' roles and responsibilities? • How will you obtain team members' input to further refine your vision and facilitate buy-in? • How will you identify the planning team's leader or coleaders? • What are the leader's specific responsibilities and how will they be communicated to the leader and to the team? • What communication vehicle will potential team members use to accept or decline the invitation to serve on the team? • Will you as the school leader serve as a standing member or ad hoc member? • What commitments can you or other building administrators make to meet regularly with the team to obtain feedback and to provide input and guidance? • What communication vehicle will you use when you are unable to meet with the team? • What decision-making authority will the team have? What types of decisions may it make in your absence?	
Outside Collaboration • What opportunities exist to collaborate in person, via telephone, or electronically with other individuals, schools, or districts with experience in implementing an RTI framework? • What RTI training and support opportunities are available within the school division? • What training and support opportunities are available through state or national organizations?	

Meeting Logistics • What schedule adjustments or assignment changes might be needed in order to create regularly scheduled time for the team to meet? • How often should the team meet? • What vehicles will be used to ensure that the necessary follow-up actions occur after meetings are held?	
Ongoing Communication • How will team members communicate with the faculty as a whole to share their progress, facilitate buy-in, obtain input, and respond to questions? How frequently will this communication occur? • How will the team communicate with the parent community to share updates, obtain input, and respond to questions? How frequently will this communication occur?	

Other Questions

Action Steps, Individuals Responsible, and Targeted Completion Dates

Deciding What to Look For in an RTI Coordinator

PURPOSE

Some schools have created an RTI coordinator position to direct and manage RTI implementation. This may be a full-time or part-time position, depending on the school's needs and funding availability. Typical tasks assigned to the RTI coordinator include the following:

- Scheduling RTI Intervention Team meetings. (Note: RTI Intervention Teams are discussed in Part 2, Section 3, "Understanding the Problem Solving Process.")
- Reviewing requests for assistance and assigning caseloads to RTI Intervention Teams.
- Providing professional development.
- Troubleshooting problems.
- Monitoring data collection activities and ensuring that data is kept safe and confidential.
- Serving as a liaison to faculty, administrators, and family members.
- Managing the monitoring process.
- Recommending changes in how RTI is implemented.

In some cases—especially in smaller schools—the RTI coordinator also may serve as the RTI Intervention Team facilitator. The purpose of this tool is to provide a checklist of traits, knowledge, and capabilities that the RTI Leadership Planning Team or administrator might use to screen applicants.

HOW TO USE THIS TOOL

The administrator or RTI Leadership Planning Team should review the tool and discuss the advantages and disadvantages of having an RTI coordinator on staff. Examples of discussion topics include the following:

- Should the position be part time, and if so, can an individual receive release time (e.g., reduced course load, reduced duties such as playground supervision, and so on) or a stipend to perform these duties?

- How should the position be posted and filled? What criteria will ensure fairness in hiring?
- Is there anyone already on staff who has the knowledge and skills to serve as an RTI coordinator (e.g., reading coach)? Would any of these staff members be interested?
- Is it possible to hire someone from outside the school to serve in this role? What are the advantages and disadvantages of having someone new to the school coordinate RTI efforts?
- Can the RTI coordinator role be shared among faculty members?
- What are the advantages and disadvantages of assigning these responsibilities to a faculty member who is the facilitator of an RTI Intervention Team, a department or grade level team chair, guidance counselor, etc.?

Decision point: The administrator or RTI Leadership Planning Team members should determine the viability of an RTI coordinator in the school. If the team members decide that one is needed, they should prepare a job description and application process that can be shared with the administration for further action.

TIPS AND VARIATIONS

1. Check with the administration to see if there are certain standard employment procedures that must be followed. If your school district has a union contract, check to see if there are any restrictions or considerations when assigning new responsibilities or offering compensation for additional responsibilities.

2. Solicit informal input from faculty members as to whether any of them might be interested in taking on this role. Find out what resources might be necessary.

3. Prioritize the list of knowledge, skills, and characteristics listed in the tool in the event that no one in your pool of applicants has all of them.

4. Use the list of knowledge, skills, and characteristics in the tool to develop a job description.

Deciding What to Look For in an RTI Coordinator

KNOWLEDGE AND SKILLS

____ An understanding of the RTI process and purpose

____ Progress monitoring tools and techniques

____ Universal screening tools and techniques

____ Data-based decision making

____ Effective core instruction

____ Interventions for struggling students

LEADERSHIP SKILLS

____ A belief in the validity of RTI to help all students learn

____ Providing professional development and an understanding of adult learning practices

____ Coaching skills

____ Organizational and managerial skills

____ Collaborative skills

____ Follow-through skills

____ Communication skills

____ Problem-solving skills

SECTION 2 OVERVIEW—GETTING STARTED WITH RTI

The RTI Leadership Planning Team is responsible for planning and overseeing implementation of the RTI framework. Once the planning team has been formed, team members will begin to lay the foundation for the RTI initiative:

- **Deciding how they will work as a team.** This task includes such things as setting ground norms for participation, establishing roles and responsibilities, and determining how the team will operate. Some teams also may find it useful for members to state their personal commitment to the RTI work.
- **Becoming oriented to the work.** This task includes reviewing the overall tasks and outcomes. It also involves setting a timeline for each phase.
- **Establishing a basic understanding of RTI.** This task includes researching the historical roots of RTI. It also involves reviewing definitions and adopting or creating definitions to guide the work.
- **Gauging the school's readiness for RTI.** This task includes reviewing other ongoing initiatives and resources.

PURPOSE OF THIS SECTION AND SUMMARY OF TOOLS

The purpose of this section is to provide the RTI Leadership Planning Team with an introductory look at RTI. The team will use this information as a starting point for deciding if RTI is right for the school and, if so, choosing the general approach that team members will take in developing their RTI framework. This section of the action tool contains tools that will assist team members in the following activities:

- Identifying their individual strengths related to RTI
- Considering different RTI definitions and frameworks
- Identifying resources
- Exploring how aspects of RTI already may be in place in the school

The tools are as follows:

- **Building the RTI Leadership Planning Team.** Once the planning team is convened, members may use this tool to identify specific roles and responsibilities.
- **Taking a Look at How Other Schools Have Implemented RTI.** Most schools will implement RTI to best fit their existing school organization and structure. The RTI Leadership Planning Team may use this tool to investigate how other schools have implemented an RTI framework.

- **Understanding the Roots of RTI.** The development and convergence of key research, legislation, and policy reports have fueled much of the current interest in RTI. The planning team may use this tool to consider RTI in the context of the school's response to historical trends.

- **Reviewing Web-Based Resources.** In familiarizing themselves with RTI, the planning team members may use this tool to review several websites and share findings.

- **Selecting or Reviewing an RTI Definition.** The planning team members should take time to review various definitions. This tool is designed to assist the team members in gaining a deeper understanding of RTI; to assist members in thinking about the relevance of the selected definitions to the school; and to assist members in considering the development or adoption of their own definitions.

- **Crafting a Vision for RTI in the School.** A first step in considering whether RTI will be a good fit with the school involves articulating how it supports the school's shared vision for education. The planning team can use this tool to discuss how RTI might support the school's vision as well as how the vision might be adjusted to incorporate an RTI perspective.

- **Exploring Connections: How RTI Fits with Other School and District Initiatives.** In gauging the school's readiness for RTI, the planning team will want to consider how RTI may fit with other ongoing initiatives in the school. This tool provides the team with a discussion template.

At the end of this section, RTI Leadership Planning Team members should have a basic understanding of RTI and be ready to deepen their knowledge about essential RTI components. Team members also should have begun a conversation about the school's capacity to implement an RTI initiative and the types of resources and professional assistance the school will need in order to be successful.

REFERENCES AND ADDITIONAL RESOURCES

ASCD. (2010). *Implementing RTI in secondary schools* [DVD Set]. Alexandria, VA: Author.

Fisher, D., & Frey, N. (2010). *Enhancing RTI: How to ensure success with effective classroom instruction and intervention.* Alexandria, VA: ASCD.

International Reading Association. (2010). *Response to intervention: Guiding principles for educators from the International Reading Association* [Brochure]. Retrieved March 30, 2010, from http://www.reading.org/Libraries/Resources/RTI_brochure_web.sflb.ashx

National Association of State Directors of Special Education. (2008). *Response to Intervention: Blueprints for implementation: School Building Level (p. 2)*. Alexandria, VA: Author.

Building the RTI Leadership Planning Team: Roles and Responsibilities

PURPOSE

Once the RTI Leadership Planning Team is convened, it is helpful to identify roles and responsibilities. The purpose of this tool is to provide planning team members with a guide for completing this task.

Meeting roles typically include the following:

- **Chair**. It should be clear how the chair will be chosen. In some schools, the chair is appointed. Usually the chair is responsible for facilitating the meeting, organizing the agenda, making sure any necessary materials are available, providing routine feedback to the administration, and inviting additional people to the meeting. Some chairs may choose to delegate some of these responsibilities to other team members. Or, if the school provides support staff for assistance, the chair may delegate some tasks.
- **Note taker**. Keeping minutes is necessary for documenting the planning process. This individual may be a team member or a support staff member. Sometimes, this individual also carries out the role of filing paperwork, sending out meeting reminders, and so on.
- **Time keeper**. This role is necessary to help the team stay on track and cover the agenda. This role may rotate from meeting to meeting.
- **Activity facilitator**. Some of the tools contain activities for the RTI Leadership Planning Team. Teams may want to identify different members to serve as activity facilitators to present the activity, lead the discussion, and so on.
- **Resource specialist**. Periodically, team members may require more information from outside sources. Team members serving in this role may be assigned to gather additional resources for the team.
- **Evaluator**. Teams often benefit from ongoing feedback and evaluation regarding progress on the planning task and on interpersonal process (i.e., team building) development. The team member serving in this role presents feedback and engages other team members in reflecting on their progress.

- **Staff liaison**. Some teams assign a staff liaison to communicate progress to school staff. The individual serving in this role also may be called upon to elicit information from staff members as needed.

Depending on the team composition, the same member may serve in multiple roles.

HOW TO USE THIS TOOL

The tool helps guide the discussion about potential roles and responsibilities and to engage team members in providing input and finalizing plans for the team's functioning. For example, the team might be asked their views about rotating some of the responsibilities or if they would prefer to maintain the same role for a designated period of time. This meeting also would provide an opportunity for individual team members to share their comfort level with assuming one or more specific roles. In addition, team members should identify other practices and procedures that may not align with specific roles but would contribute to their ability to operate effectively and efficiently. Agreements or decisions about the roles and responsibilities should be recorded on the tool form by a note taker or by the RTI Leadership Planning Team member who is guiding the discussion.

Decision point: The planning team will determine the specific roles and responsibilities that will be represented on the team and will assign members to fill these roles. They will also determine other processes that might help the team to function effectively and efficiently.

TIPS AND VARIATIONS

1. Prior to the meeting, team members might be given the tool and asked to record their ideas about specific roles and assigned responsibilities. The planning team chair could collect this information before the meeting and analyze it to identify commonalities and differences. The chair could begin the meeting with a summary of those views and subsequently lead a discussion to help reach consensus and make final decisions regarding designated roles and responsibilities and other meeting and support processes.

2. The planning team designee who is chairing the meeting might use this time to discuss the importance of engaging in processes that help the team members assess their effectiveness and efficiency, recommend changes, and identify their need for additional support. An additional section could be added to the tool, and team

members could complete it on a periodic basis (e.g., bimonthly) as a way to report on their team's overall functioning and their views about the effectiveness of the roles and responsibilities. This added section of the form might be titled Self-Assessment of Effectiveness and Efficiency and Recommended Changes and Supports.

3. Before discussing roles and responsibilities, team members may want to introduce themselves and to share their commitment to RTI. Even in cases where team members have worked together previously, it is helpful to engage in a discussion about why they are interested in RTI and how they believe an RTI approach will benefit students in the school.

Building the RTI Leadership Planning Team: Roles and Responsibilities

Roles	Responsibilities	Designated Individuals
Chair		
Note taker		
Timekeeper		
Activity facilitator		
Resource specialist		
Evaluator		
Staff liaison		
Other roles		
Other agreements regarding team functioning		

Taking a Look at How Other Schools Have Implemented RTI

PURPOSE

RTI is a framework that each school will interpret in its own way. There is no exact way to implement it. In fact, most schools will implement RTI to best fit their existing school organization and structure. RTI can be initiated schoolwide or it can have a particular focus (e.g., 1st and 2nd grade teachers, 9th grade algebra, and so on).

The RTI Leadership Planning Team may want to investigate how other schools have implemented an RTI framework. In some cases, team members may contact nearby schools to request a visit. When schools are not available for visits, team members may want to review case studies. The purpose of this tool is to illustrate some of the processes schools use as they engage stakeholders, make decisions, implement different components of RTI, and assess their progress and effect.

HOW TO USE THIS TOOL

There are three suggested ways to use the tool.

- If a visit with a nearby school can be scheduled, then the questions in the tool can serve as a basis for discussion. A designated recorder should take notes to capture the discussion. The notes may help team members revisit their discussions and outcomes as needed during subsequent meetings.
- If a visit with another school is not possible—or in cases in which the RTI Leadership Planning Team members would like to enhance their learning—team members might select one of the case studies included after the discussion guide and read it either prior to or during a team meeting. The questions in the tool can form the basis for the discussion. A designated recorder should take notes to capture the discussion. The notes may help team members revisit their discussions and outcomes as needed during subsequent meetings.
- Locate video clips that describe how schools have implemented RTI. For example, ASCD has produced a video, "Implementing RTI in Secondary Schools." The State of Colorado (http://www.cde.state.co.us/media/rti/rtivideo/rti.htm) and the State of

Pennsylvania (http://www.youtube.com/watch?v=IsAqh2Pxg0A) also have produced videos of RTI frameworks. After watching a video, use the questions in the tool as a basis for discussion.

Decision point: The members of the RTI Leadership Planning Team should determine in what ways information gleaned from studying other schools' experiences with RTI can be helpful in their own school's planning processes.

TIPS AND VARIATIONS

1. Graphic organizers related to each of the questions might be generated in advance of the discussion to assist team members in processing their ideas related to the case study schools. For example, a two-column chart with the headings "similarities" and "differences" might be used for discussion of the first question. A Venn diagram can be another graphic option for the first question.

2. Case studies might be shared with other school teams or with the entire faculty during a workshop as a way to facilitate understanding of RTI. Following is an example of how the case studies might be used as a professional development activity.

    • In advance of the workshop, the facilitator should select a case study and record the questions, along with related graphic organizers, on chart paper and post the charts around the room. The workshop participants should be asked to read the case study individually and then engage in discussion.

    • As a variation, the facilitator might use a gallery walk approach. Ask participants to form four groups—one for each question—and to stand in front of one of the charts. Give participants five minutes in which to discuss the question and record their responses on the chart. Upon command (e.g., a bell is rung), the groups rotate to the next chart. They are given seven minutes to read what the previous group has written and then to add their own thoughts. This process continues until all groups have responded to all questions. Upon conclusion of the rotations, a reporter for each small group should verbally summarize the notes on one of the charts and share them with the entire group.

    • Following the summary presentations for each chart, the facilitator should express appreciation for the work, comment on the overall findings, respond to questions, and share potential next steps. A next step might be that the ideas and questions posed by the case study examinations will be reviewed by the RTI

Leadership Planning Team with resulting outcomes shared via RTI electronic updates or other established communication vehicles.

3. Additional case studies might be identified for use at future team meetings. An Internet search might yield possible case studies. For example, some schools have been featured in publications, such as the ones that follow:

Elementary Case Studies

Brown-Chadsey, R. (2007). No more "waiting to fail." *Educational Leadership*, *65*(2), 40–46.

Kearns, D., & Center for Student Progress Monitoring. (n.d.). *Reading case study #2: Grade 4 comprehension.* Retrieved March 28, 2010, from http://www.studentprogress.org/library/CaseStudy/reading_grade4_comprehension_3-4-09.pdf

National Research Center on Learning Disabilities. (2006). *School examples, students case studies, and research examples.* Retrieved March 28, 2010, from http://www.ldaofky.org/RTI/RTI%20Manual%20Case%20Studies.pdf

Skow, K., Brown, J., & the IRIS Center. (n.d.). *RTI: Progress monitoring.* Retrieved March 28, 2010, from http://iris.peabody.vanderbilt.edu/case_studies/ICS-011.pdf

Secondary Case Studies

Burns, M. K. (2008). Response to intervention at the secondary level. *Principal Leadership*, *8*(7), 12–15.

Canter, A. (2004). A problem-solving model for improving student achievement. *Principal Leadership*, *5*(4), 11–15.

Canter, A., Klotz, M. B., & Cowen, K. (2008). Response to intervention: The future for secondary schools. *Principal Leadership*, *9*(2), 12–15.

Martin, J. (2007). *Implementing Response to Intervention at the high school level: Every student, every day!* Retrieved March 25, 2008, from http://www.nwrel.org/nwrcc/rti-webinar/materials/rti-dhs.pdf

The Center for Comprehensive School Reform and Improvement. (2008, June). *Response to Intervention: Possibilities for service delivery at the secondary school level.* Retrieved September 28, 2009, from www.cenerforcsri.org

Windram, H., Scierka, B., & Silberglitt, B. (2007). Response to intervention at the secondary level: Two districts' models of implementation. *NASP Communiqué, 34*(5), 1–7. Retrieved March 25, 2008, from http://www.nasponline.org/publications/cq/mocq355rtisecondary.aspx

Taking a Look at How Other Schools Have Implemented RTI

DISCUSSION GUIDE

- In what ways does the school appear similar to our school? In what ways does the school appear to differ from our school?
- What components of the RTI framework are represented in the school and how was each component implemented?
- What can we learn from the school's approach to implementation of RTI? In what areas do we agree with the school's approach? In what areas do we disagree?
- What actions might we consider or recommend as a result of taking a look at the school?

CASE STUDY: ELEMENTARY SCHOOL

Mrs. Perkins is a 1st grade teacher and team leader at Wheatley Elementary School. She became interested in RTI after she and other faculty members were introduced to the framework in March of last year by the principal and central office staff and informed about the opportunity for Wheatley to become an RTI pilot site. The principal explained that the central office staff approached Wheatley because its schoolwide test results and on-site visits suggest that a strong core program is already in place and teachers work collaboratively. However, despite the strong core program and collaboration, there are struggling learners.

Mrs. Perkins concurred with the feedback the central office staff provided. During 1st grade team meetings, she and her colleagues had been discussing their concerns about the low reading levels among some of the students they thought of as at-risk as well as the particularly challenging behaviors of a few students. After hearing the overview of RTI, Mrs. Perkins viewed it as a possible vehicle for addressing both the reading needs and behavioral needs of their students in a more structured and systematic manner.

Mrs. Perkins accepted the principal's invitation to represent the 1st grade teachers on the RTI Leadership Planning Team—which included the principal, assistant principal, RTI coordinator, special education teacher, reading teacher and other grade level representatives—and she immediately begin to participate in regularly scheduled meetings. As her team's representative, Mrs. Perkins helped to keep her 1st grade colleagues informed of the planning team discussions, and she obtained and shared their feedback with the planning team during decision-making processes. For example, when the planning team was deciding on ways to phase in RTI implementation, Mrs. Perkins reported on her team's support for beginning in the fall with implementation at the kindergarten and 1st grade levels.

By the middle of May, with the principal serving as chair, the RTI Leadership Planning Team decisions and actions included the following:

- Wheatley would begin RTI implementation in September at the kindergarten and 1st grade levels.
- The planning team identified a universal screening instrument for kindergarten and 1st grade. They made this decision following their initial review of assessment websites; their in-depth review of several possible assessments based on criteria such as reliability and validity, cost, availability of alternative forms, and administration time; their consultation with central office staff and two other schools in the fourth year of RTI implementation; and their consideration of feedback from kindergarten and 1st grade teachers.
- The planning team formed an assessment team composed of individuals who would administer the universal screening instrument in the fall, winter, and spring. The speech pathologist, school psychologist, reading teacher, RTI coordinator, and assistant principal agreed to participate on the assessment team and to administer the assessments. Following a review of the screening results and identification of at-risk students, the kindergarten and 1st grade teachers would begin using the assessment instrument to collect progress monitoring data on selected students. Classroom teachers and assessment team members were scheduled for June training on administering the assessment and using the results for instructional planning.
- The planning team drafted a fall master schedule with specific 30-minute blocks of time dedicated for small-group interventions. They also decided that the RTI coordinator would meet with the designated grade level teams (kindergarten and 1st) following universal screening to help create homogeneous student groupings for Tier 2 and Tier 3 interventions based on skills identified as below benchmark.
- The planning team decided that kindergarten and 1st grade classroom teachers and support staff (reading teacher, special education teacher, two instructional assistants, and the RTI coordinator) would serve as interventionists to provide small-group Tier 2 and Tier 3 instruction for selected students. For example, a classroom teacher and

the reading teacher might instruct intervention groups simultaneously in different parts of the classroom while some of the remaining students worked at stations and some worked with an instructional assistant. The principal would identify an alternative space for tiered interventions in case this initial arrangement proved distracting for some students.

- Using a combination of the protocol model and the problem-solving model, the planning team decided to purchase research-based supplemental instructional materials for early literacy.

Mrs. Perkins agreed to continue serving on the RTI Leadership Planning Team for the new school year. She was pleased that the team would meet less frequently, since the principal and RTI coordinator would periodically observe intervention groups and participate in data meetings with the kindergarten and first grade team to review the progress monitoring data and discuss the effectiveness of the interventions.

CASE STUDY: MIDDLE SCHOOL

Parks Middle School serves 820 students in grades 6, 7 and 8. Approximately 40 percent of the student population comes from families that are economically disadvantaged. The majority (65 percent) of students are Caucasian, with 20 percent African American, 12 percent Hispanic, and 3 percent Asian American. About 5 percent of students are English language learners.

For two years, the school did not meet adequate yearly progress (AYP) targets. One subgroup, students with disabilities, did not meet AYP standards three years in a row. The staff turned to RTI to improve test scores and raise the achievement level for all students.

School staff initially embraced RTI. It was perceived as a good fit because the school was already implementing Positive Behavioral Interventions and Support (PBIS), which uses a tiered model that combines positive school climate and a data-driven, problem-solving approach to address student needs. RTI was linked directly to the school's PBIS framework.

The following RTI components were implemented:

- **Identify universal screening**. The staff decided to use a standard protocol system to identify students for supplemental tutoring in math or reading. Students who scored Partially Proficient or Unsatisfactory on the state assessment were scheduled into a math or reading tutorial. The tutorial sessions were offered in addition to regular classroom instruction and were scheduled during students' electives or their essential skills course. The school received additional money from the district to hire a teacher for these classes.

- **Establish problem-solving team**. The PBIS team structure was expanded to include academics. The team—which was composed of general educators, special educators, related services personnel, administrators, parents, and others—met on a weekly basis.

- **Implement problem-solving process**. A structured format was used for problem solving. The teacher collected data about a student's performance and submitted it to the team. After analysis of the teacher-collected data as well as other data that the team may have gathered, the team developed an intervention plan. As part of the plan, the team established a progress monitoring system and assigned responsibilities and an implementation schedule.

- **Conduct professional development**. As the team developed the RTI framework, it became clear that core instruction was not as strong as it should be. Teachers agreed that just as they had as a staff committed to developing knowledge and skills in providing positive behavioral support to students, they should do the same with academics. The staff identified differentiating instruction as a focus. Because one subgroup, students with disabilities, required academic attention, staff also identified Universal Design for Learning as a professional development focus.

The principal set a timeframe of three years to get the RTI framework up and running. The first year would be devoted to professional development. The second year would be devoted to getting the framework in place, including significant professional development in data-based decision making and progress monitoring. The RTI framework would be piloted in the third year, with significant review and reflection.

CASE STUDY: HIGH SCHOOL ENGLISH LANGUAGE ARTS

Staff at Jefferson High School began noticing a distinct decrease in the number of 9th and 10th grade students who were passing English language arts classes. Student difficulties included not reading at grade level, writing incomplete sentences, and being unable to compose an essay that met district rubric standards. Staff decided to apply RTI principles to help achieve their goal of improving the level of achievement in 9th and 10th grade English language arts and the passing rate.

Jefferson's student demographics had changed dramatically over the past five years. Currently, 35 percent of students come from families who are considered to be economically disadvantaged. Approximately 25 percent of students come from families who are migrant workers.

Jefferson's Literacy Success Team included the assistant principal, two English language arts teachers, a special education teacher, and the school's reading coach. Team members began by looking at universal screening data. They reviewed baseline data on literacy achievement and passing rates comprised of records from five prior years. These records included the following:

- Nine-week and semester passing rates (grade *C* or better).
- Performance on the state literacy assessment (percentage at the proficient level).
- Scores on the benchmark tests used by all teachers every six weeks to track reading and writing performance.

Jefferson's literacy curriculum is organized into the broad competencies that are parallel to the state standards. Team members reviewed the curriculum, textbook, and instructional technology resources to ensure alignment with state standards.

Team members also looked at the curriculum maps that the entire English language arts department instructional staff had completed as part of a professional development initiative the previous year. Teachers had analyzed the maps and identified consistencies, gaps, and overages. They had just finished realigning their courses. To ensure multiple presentation modes for each of the competencies, the team identified supplemental instructional resources. They also identified and designed explicit instructional routines for students with lower levels of relevant, prerequisite knowledge. In addition, they placed supplemental, explicit instruction on key literacy competencies online so it would be accessible at school and at home.

The team decided to organize its RTI framework as follows: Based on screening results, students with high levels of prerequisite knowledge were placed in 9th grade English language arts classes. In those cases where students tested ready for more advanced courses, they were assigned appropriately. Those with moderate or low levels of knowledge and skills were enrolled in basic literacy classes that focused on critical prerequisite skills.

The overall goal was to improve the percentage of students reaching the proficient level in literacy by 5 percent per year until 90 percent of students were proficient. The team then set goals for achievement in 9th grade English language arts as follows: 90 percent homework completion at an accuracy rate of at least 80 percent; 90 percent pass rate on weekly quizzes (e.g., vocabulary, comprehension, and writing); 90 percent passing unit tests; and 90 percent achieving nine-week and semester grades of *C* or above. Overall progress would be assessed through comparison with the five-year baseline data on unit, semester, and end-of-course examinations.

The team then established the problem solving approach. All English language arts teachers were eligible to request assistance. The team met on a weekly basis during the first semester and subsequently every other week to review class and individual graphs reflecting results; to discuss curriculum, instruction, and student engagement; to provide mutual support and exchange ideas; and to celebrate when goals were met. The principal and the reading coach attended as many of the meetings as their schedules permitted.

More intensive instructional interventions were established for those students who were falling behind in achieving literacy goals. The team chose from a list of evidence-based practices when suggesting an intervention for a particular student. In all three of the regular 9th grade classes, as well as in the four basic courses, special education coteachers provided small-group classroom tutoring. This instruction typically included one or two students with disabilities and three or four low-achieving students who were not eligible for special education. The small-group tutoring followed explicit and systematic instructional procedures with weekly progress monitoring using curriculum-based measures. Individual graphs were established and progress was monitored against goals for each of the students in Tier 2.

Understanding the Roots of RTI

PURPOSE

Although RTI frameworks are relatively recent, many RTI components have been in practice for many years. Historically, RTI finds its roots in research, legislation, and policy. Trends in these areas have developed and converged into many current day RTI frameworks. Following are selected examples.

THE INFLUENCE OF RESEARCH

- **Tiered models of intervention**. Two early studies often are cited as precursors to present-day RTI work. Deno and Mirkin (1977) investigated the effectiveness of a three-tiered intervention model for students' reading difficulties that incorporated curriculum-based measures for progress monitoring. That same year, Bergan (1977) investigated the effectiveness of a problem-solving model focused on implementing behavioral interventions with students that included a progress monitoring component. These early studies provided a foundation for future research and the development of two recognized RTI problem-solving models—the Standard Protocol Model is based on the work of Deno and Mirkin and the Problem-Solving Model is based on the work of Bergan.

- **Findings of the National Reading Panel (2000)**. In 1997, the U. S. Congress asked the National Institute of Child Health and Human Development to work with the U. S. Department of Education in establishing the National Reading Panel (NRP). Members of NRP met for two years and considered research studies on reading. They used research screening criteria that required the use of experimental or quasi-experimental designs and minimal sample sizes to eventually select several hundred studies for review and analysis. Their process of studying the research was a significant contribution to the field, and this group is credited with coining the term "scientifically-based reading research," which is an essential element of most RTI approaches.

- **Use of a three-tiered model in reading research**. As a follow-up to the NRP report, a number of research studies were undertaken to examine the most effective ways to teach reading, assess progress, and remediate reading difficulties. For example,

Vaughn and her colleagues (for a summary see Haager, Klingner, & Vaughn, 2009) investigated the effectiveness of a three-tiered intervention model for at-risk students experiencing reading difficulties. Students received early intervention. Those students who did not respond to the early intervention were provided with increasingly more intensive instruction. Many early RTI frameworks focused on reading and incorporated the types of practices used with these students.

THE INFLUENCE OF LEGISLATION

- **The No Child Left Behind Act of 2001 (NCLB).** NCLB legislation included the NRP findings that focused on the need for literacy proficiency, funding, and resources. States were directed to establish reading instruction programs that utilized proven, research-based strategies. As a result of this focus, the use of research-based curriculum-based measures to assess the effectiveness of intervention instruction has become more widespread and has contributed to the movement toward RTI.

- **Individuals with Disabilities Education Improvement Act of 2004 (IDEA).** IDEA guides states in how to implement special education services. The specific term *response to intervention* is not stated in IDEA; however, Congress alludes to RTI by permitting the determination of how a child responds to scientific research-based intervention when identifying a learning disability and by prohibiting states from requiring the use of a discrepancy model. The statute states:

    When determining whether a child has a learning disability, a local educational agency shall not be required to consider whether a child has a severe discrepancy between achievement and intellectual ability…a local education agency may use a process that determines if the child responds to a scientific, research-based intervention as a part of the evaluation procedures. [20 U.S.C. §1414(b)(A) and (B)]

    IDEA also acknowledges the components of reading instruction as defined in NCLB:

    A child shall not be identified to be a child with a disability if determinant factor is lack of appropriate instruction in reading, including in the essential components of reading instruction (as defined in section 1208 (3) of the Elementary and Secondary Education Act of 1965). [20 U.S.C.§ 1414 (b)(5)(A)]

Early Intervening Services is another component of IDEA that supports the development of RTI. The law indicates that up to 15 percent of IDEA funds targeted for students with disabilities may be used to provide early intervention for at-risk students without individualized education programs (IEPs) who require additional support in order to make progress in general education.

THE INFLUENCE OF POLICY

- **Overrepresentation of minority students in special education**. In 2002, the National Research Council, commissioned by the National Academy of Sciences, presented their report, *Minority Students in Special and Gifted Education*, to Congress. This report included findings that children are most often referred for special education due to behavior and poor performance in basic reading skills and that the traditional approach to special education eligibility can be described as a "wait to fail model" due to the lack of early intervention and supports. The National Research Council recommended a model to identify students at risk of failure and to provide effective intervention that would precede and reduce the need for special education.

- **Changing relationship between general education and special education**. In recent years, there has been a call for the unification of special education and general education. Often, this is the context of inclusionary practices. Two of the major issues associated with this discussion relate to requiring that the student must fail before receiving help and the misdiagnosis of students as disabled. In an RTI framework, prevention and early intervention are provided to students as needed.

- **Access to academic monitoring tools**. In response to increased accountability requirements, schools have relied more and more on assessments. In recent years, schools have started to acquire monitoring assessments and tools for tracking academic progress. A cornerstone of RTI is progress monitoring.

The development and convergence of key research, legislation, and policy reports have generated broad ongoing discussion, debate, and action across many U. S. state departments of education, institutions of higher education, school divisions, and professional organizations. These influences have fueled much of the current interest in RTI.

The purpose of this tool is to provide the RTI Leadership Planning Team with an opportunity to consider RTI in the context of the school's response to historical trends.

HOW TO USE THIS TOOL

The tool is designed as a series of questions to guide discussion.

Decision point: The RTI Leadership Team should determine the extent to which an RTI initiative supports or enhances current thinking and efforts in the various areas.

TIPS AND VARIATIONS

1. In cases where an RTI approach does not support current efforts in an area, the RTI Leadership Team may want to reflect on whether the school's approach in that area is effective or requires further discussion. For example, if the school's vision of special education and general education is that they are separate systems (e.g., with their own policies and goals), then the team may want to spend some time focusing on how that perspective might need to be changed to embrace RTI fully.
2. Identify aspects of a trend that the school may find challenging. Discuss how RTI might provide an impetus for supporting improvement in that area.
3. Invite individuals who have considerable seniority in the school to share their perceptions of how the trends looked over the years. Discuss unique aspects of the school's community in relation to how the trends played out.

REFERENCES

Bergan, J.R. (1977). *Behavioral consultation.* Columbus, OH: Charles E. Merrill.

Deno, S., & Mirkin, P. (1977*). Data-based program modification.* Minneapolis, MN: Leadership Training Institute for Special Education.

Haager, D., Klingner, J., & Vaughn, S. (Eds.). (2009). *Evidence-based reading practices for response to intervention.* Baltimore: Paul H. Brookes.

Individuals with Disabilities Education Improvement Act, 20 U.S.C. Sec. 1400 (2004).

National Institute of Child Health and Human Development, NIH, DHHS. (2000). *Report of the National Reading Panel: Teaching children to read.* Washington, DC: U.S. Government Printing Office.

Donovan, M. S., & Cross, C. T. (Eds.). (2002*). Minority students in special and gifted education. Report of the Committee on Minority Representation in Special Education.* Washington, DC: National Academy Press, National Research Council, Division of Behavioral and Social Sciences and Education.

No Child Left Behind Act of 2001, Public Law 107-110, 5, 115 Stat. 1427 (2002), et seq.

Understanding the Roots of RTI

Discussion Questions Regarding Historical Influences	Notes
NCLB What aspects of NCLB has our school embraced? How might an RTI framework help us enhance our work on related issues and goals?	
IDEA What is our school philosophy regarding the education of students with disabilities? How might an RTI framework help us enhance our work on related issues and goals?	
Reading In what ways has our school made investments in improving reading skills? How might an RTI framework help us enhance our work in improving reading achievement?	
Addressing the Needs of Students from Diverse Cultural and Ethnic Backgrounds How has our school demonstrated a commitment to ensuring that all students, including those students from diverse cultural and ethnic backgrounds, achieve? How has our school addressed challenges related to this topic? How might an RTI framework help us enhance our work in ensuring effective and equitable educational experiences for all students?	
Use of Research-Based Practices How has our school made investments in ensuring that, to the extent possible, instructional practices are research based? How might an RTI framework help us enhance our work in this area?	

Use of Data for Instructional Decision Making In what ways has our school made investments in ensuring that, to the extent possible, staff members have access to instructional data for decision making? How might an RTI framework help us enhance our work in this area?	
Recommendations and Individuals Responsible	

Getting Started with RTI

Reviewing Web-Based Resources

PURPOSE

In recent years there has been a proliferation of websites that address RTI. There also are a number of websites that address some aspect of RTI (e.g., progress monitoring). Many of these websites contain resources and downloadable tools.

In familiarizing themselves about RTI, members of the RTI Leadership Planning Team may want to review several sites and share findings. Because it is possible to literally spend weeks reviewing all of the available websites, it is helpful for team members to streamline the process. It also is helpful to document aspects of each website that may be helpful to planning. The purpose of the tool is to provide a template for recording website content for sharing and future reference.

HOW TO USE THIS TOOL

Select several websites to review, either by conducting a search using a standard search engine using "Response to Intervention" or a component of RTI (e.g., "Universal Screening Response to Intervention"). Use the tool form to record features such as

- Purpose and focus of the website.
- Sponsorship of the website.
- How the website supports your approach to RTI.
- Available resources.

Decision point: After reviewing different websites, the RTI Leadership Planning Team should decide which are relevant for their planning work as well as which ones might be useful resources for the entire school community.

TIPS AND VARIATIONS

1. Keep in mind that websites change frequently. If you think that something is worth downloading, do it now because it may not be there at a later time. Also, check back periodically for updates and new postings.

2. Assign different team members to particular websites. After reviewing the websites, share findings.

3. Keep the information on the websites in a notebook or in a virtual notebook that can be shared with the school faculty.

4. Some team members may prefer to use a search engine to find websites that deal with RTI. Others may find it helpful to have a starting list of websites that tend to get a lot of traffic. The following list can help to get you started. Although it is not all-inclusive, it does represent the variety of sites that are available. [*Note*: At press time, the URLs were valid.]

LEADERSHIP AND STAKEHOLDER CONSENSUS BUILDING

- The Colorado Department of Education: www.cde.state.co.us/RtI/ ToolsResourcesRtI.htm
- National Association of State Directors of Special Education (NASDSE): www.nasdse.org
- National Center on Response to Intervention: www.rti4success.org
- RTI Action Network: www.rtinetwork.org

DATA USE: CURRICULUM-BASED MEASUREMENT, UNIVERSAL SCREENING, AND PROGRESS MONITORING

- National Center on Student Progress Monitoring (*Note:* Funding for the site has ended, but resources are still available): www.studentprogress.org/
- National Center on Response to Intervention: www.rti4success.org/chart/progress Monitoring/progressmonitoringtoolschart.htm

EXAMPLES OF SCREENING TOOLS

- AIMSweb: http://aimsweb.com/
- DIBELS data system: http://dibels.uoregon.edu/
- Yearly Progress Pro (McGraw Hill): www.mhdigitallearning.com/
- Intervention Central (RTI section): www.interventioncentral.org/

ACADEMIC INTERVENTIONS

- The Access Center (*Note:* Funding for the site has ended, but resources are still available): www.k8accesscenter.org
- Florida Center on Reading Research (Characteristics of effective supplemental and intensive instruction): www.fcrr.org
- Review of core reading programs: www.fcrr.org/FCRRReports/reportslist.htm
- University of Oregon (see Big Ideas in Beginning Reading for Early Literacy): http://reading.uoregon.edu/
- University of Nebraska at Lincoln (information on cognitive strategy instruction): www.unl.edu/csi
- Vaughn Gross Center for Reading and Language Arts (information on reading interventions): www.texasreading.org/utcrla/
- What Works Clearinghouse through the Institute for Education Sciences: http://ies .ed.gov/ncee/wwc

BEHAVIORAL INTERVENTIONS

- Positive Behavioral Interventions and Supports: www.pbis.org
- Florida's Positive Behavior Support Project: http://flpbs.fmhi.usf.edu/resources_newsletter.asp

Reviewing Web-Based Resources

Website name:	Website URL:
1. Purpose and focus of the website:	
2. Sponsorship of the website:	
3. How the website supports our approach to RTI:	
4. Available resources:	

Selecting or Developing an RTI Definition

PURPOSE

Because RTI is a framework, there is no one definition. As the RTI Leadership Planning Team begins to review preliminary information on RTI, it is helpful to review different definitions. Eventually, the team will want to suggest a definition or craft one with staff that reflects the vision and beliefs of the school and district. Definitions and guiding principles can play significant roles in helping to guide the work of schools and in helping to facilitate clear communication about the purpose of the work.

A number of major organizations, including state departments of education, have written or adopted RTI definitions or guiding principles. These definitions and principles reflect the philosophies and views of the organizations and emphasize different purposes and components of the RTI framework. This tool is designed to assist the RTI Leadership Planning Team in gaining a deeper understanding of RTI; thinking about the relevance of the selected definitions to the school; and considering the development or adoption of their own definition or principles.

Visit the following websites to find and review examples of other organizations' definitions of RTI.

- Council for Exceptional Children: http://www.cec.sped.org/Content/NavigationMenu/Newsissues/ CurrentSpecialEdTopics/default.htm (click on "Response to Intervention" in the navigation column)
- National Education Association: http://www.nea.org/tools/13038.htm and http://www.educationvotes.nea.org/wp-content/uploads/2010/05/ ResponsetoIntervention.pdf
- National Center on Response to Intervention: http://www.rti4success.org
- National Association of State Directors of Special Education: http://www.nasdse.org/Portals/0/SCHOOL.pdf
- The International Reading Association: http://www.reading.org/Libraries/Resources/RTI_brochure_web.sflb.ashx

- Virginia Department of Education: http://www.doe.virginia.gov/instruction/response_intervention/guidance/responsive_instruction.pdf

HOW TO USE THIS TOOL

The chair of the RTI Leadership Planning Team or a designated facilitator might present one or more of the definitions or sets of guiding principles to the team. This may be done by circulating copies of the definitions and principles or by showing the definitions and principles, on a preprinted chart or slide.

Ask team members to identify key words in each definition and set of guiding principles. As team members identify the key words, the facilitator or a note taker should underline them or record them on a separate chart.

Following discussion of the broad components of the definitions and guiding principles, the discussion leader should request ideas for immediate follow-up action and identify an individual or individuals responsible for the action. Possible follow-up actions include the following:

- Obtain additional information on any components of the definitions and guiding principles that team members questioned.
- Seek definitions from other organizations that may be of particular interest to the team or future audiences.
- Draft a definition of RTI based on the team's discussion and circulate it for feedback prior to the next meeting.
- Schedule a follow-up meeting to discuss subsequent actions taken and to adopt a working definition or set of guiding principles for your school.

Decision point: At the end of the discussion, decide on a draft definition that can help guide the school's RTI work and can help to facilitate clear communication with stakeholders.

TIPS AND VARIATIONS

- One or more definitions might be assigned to designated individuals or a subset of the team. Upon completion of the aforementioned processes, the subgroup might summarize its findings orally or in writing with the larger team.

- The discussion leader or recorder might use a Venn diagram or other graphic organizers during the discussion of definitions and principles to highlight similarities and differences.

- Team members might be asked to identify additional definitions based on their reading of other documents or to seek definitions on websites of organizations that may be of particular interest to stakeholders (e.g., parent organizations, state departments of education, professional organizations, and so on). It will be particularly important to obtain and review the definition articulated by the state in which your school is located.

- Begin a two-column chart to highlight what RTI is and what it is not. Discuss the components of the definition(s) and record the discussion points on the chart. The chart might be maintained and expanded in subsequent meetings as the team reviews additional information about RTI.

- Drafts of the definition identified by the RTI Leadership Planning Team may be shared with the faculty or groups (e.g., School Improvement Team) as a way to broaden the understanding of RTI and to obtain feedback on the drafts.

Selecting or Developing an RTI Definition

Visit the suggested websites or others that are appropriate to your group. Use the following questions to review RTI definitions:

What are the key words or phrases in the definitions and guiding principles? (Underline them as they are identified or record them on a separate chart or slide.)

In comparing the definitions and guiding principles, what common elements can you identify? What are the differences?

Which components of the definitions and guiding principles do you particularly agree with, disagree with, or have questions about? Are any of these components similar to our current practices? How do the components of these definitions and guiding principles differ from our current practices?

Crafting a Vision for RTI in the School

PURPOSE

Educators use RTI to expand their capacity to teach and support students with diverse learning and behavioral needs. A first step in considering whether RTI will be a good fit in your school involves articulating how it supports the school's shared vision for education. Although there are different RTI approaches, most share an underlying philosophy that all students are general education students and the goal is to coordinate and allocate resources across classrooms and programs to support student achievement. The purpose of this tool is to provide an opportunity to discuss how RTI might support the school's vision for education.

HOW TO USE THIS TOOL

The tool is designed as a conversation starter that the RTI Leadership Planning Team can use in exploring the compatibility between RTI philosophy and the school's shared vision for education.

Decision point: At the end of the discussion, decide if an RTI philosophy is compatible with the school's vision statement. If not, determine the next steps for pursuing compatibility.

TIPS AND VARIATIONS

1. Use this tool as a stimulus to revisit the school's vision statement. Consider any major changes to the school in the time between when the current vision statement was adopted and now (e.g., changing demographics of students attending the school, or a subgroup of students who have not met curriculum standards on statewide assessments). Discuss how an RTI approach might address these changes.

2. Before using the tool, reflect on the following vignette:

   Staff at Longfellow School adopted the tenets of ASCD's Whole Child Initiative. As part of the adoption process, staff participated in comprehensive professional development and planning in which they adopted a vision statement that reflected the philosophy underlying the Whole Child Initiative. Their vision statement follows:

> Each student enters school healthy and learns about and practices a healthy lifestyle. Each student learns in an intellectually challenging environment that is physically and emotionally safe. Each student is actively engaged in learning and is connected to the school and the broader community. Each student has access to personalized learning and to qualified, caring adults. Each graduate is prepared for success in college or further study and for employment in a global environment.

The RTI Leadership Planning Team wanted to make sure that an RTI philosophy was compatible with the school's vision statement. Through their discussion they determined that an RTI philosophy was congruent in the following ways:

- Addressed the needs of all students.
- Focused on helping students succeed in a high-quality curriculum.

The RTI Leadership Planning Team also discussed how RTI supported the vision statement. For example, RTI offers a philosophical approach to ensuring that students have access to personalized learning. This is established through a coordinated system in which students receive effective core instruction that is supplemented as necessary with additional supports and interventions. Team members also felt that, although school staff responsibility for all students in the school is assumed in the Whole Child Initiative, to better align with the RTI focus it would be preferable to state it clearly.

RTI Leadership Planning Team members felt that these philosophical tenets could be articulated within the current vision statement. They proposed editing the fourth vision statement sentence to read:

> Each student has access to personalized learning—including effective core instruction and instructional supports and interventions as needed to address learning challenges—and to qualified, caring adults who take responsibility for all students in the school.

Once team members were satisfied with the proposed revision to the school's vision statement, they set about making plans as to how they would present it to the administration and school staff.

Crafting a Vision for RTI in the School

1. Retrieve a copy of your school's vision statement. Discuss it in relation to an RTI philosophy. Ask, "In what ways is our vision statement compatible with an RTI philosophy?" For example, does it
   - Include references to *all* children?
   - Address teaching and supporting students with diverse learning and behavioral needs?
   - Make it clear that school personnel have responsibility for *all* students?
   - Emphasize helping students achieve in the general education curriculum?
   - Allow resources to be provided for *all* students who need them?
   - Ensure that *all* students receive effective, high-quality instruction that meets their needs?
   - Commit to providing research-based instruction and interventions to the extent possible?
   - Cite a belief in the validity of data when making decisions about student performance?

2. Ask how an RTI philosophy might support the school's vision statement.

3. List areas in which an RTI philosophy conflicts with the school's vision statement. If your school's vision statement presently is in conflict with certain elements of an RTI philosophy, is it feasible to revise it? If yes, what will it take to revise it?

4. List areas of RTI philosophy that are not represented in the school's vision statement. If your school's vision statement presently does not include key philosophical tenets of an RTI philosophy, is it feasible to revise it? If yes, what will it take to revise it?

5. If your school's vision statement is compatible with an RTI philosophy, how will you describe the intersections to school staff members? To parents?

Exploring Connections: How RTI Fits with Other School and District Initiatives

PURPOSE

Generally, schools are involved in one or more major initiatives (e.g., Professional Learning Communities, P–16, 21st Century Skills, ASCD's Whole Child Initiative, and so on). A question that often arises is, "How will RTI fit with our other initiatives?" The purpose of this tool is to provide an opportunity to discuss connections among initiatives.

HOW TO USE THIS TOOL

RTI is an approach to organizing and providing academic and behavioral support to students. The tool lists essential elements that are found in an RTI approach:

- Universal screening
- Data-based problem solving
- Effective core instruction
- Supports and interventions, preferably research-based, that are organized in tiers to reflect their intensity
- Progress monitoring
- Professional development

For each initiative, conduct a crosswalk with RTI. Discuss the following points:

- Similarities between RTI and the initiative
- How the initiative might incorporate RTI concepts
- How an RTI approach might be used to support the initiative

Decision point: The RTI Leadership Planning Team should determine if there is an effective fit between it and other initiatives in the school. In cases where there are few initiatives to support RTI, the planning team members should discuss the implications and what that might mean in terms of the school's readiness for RTI.

TIPS AND VARIATIONS

1. Convene a meeting with leaders and supporters of the various initiatives (e.g., transition to 9th grade, drop-out prevention, English as a second language, inclusion of students with disabilities in general education curriculum, and so on). Present an overview of RTI. Invite participants to identify similarities between RTI and the initiative. Explore how the two approaches might be used in conjunction to support students.

2. Before using the tool, reflect on the following vignette:

   Staff at Holcomb School had adopted the tenets of ASCD's Whole Child Initiative. As part of the adoption process, staff had participated in comprehensive professional development and planning in which they responded to the initiative's essential questions:

   - How can we ensure that each student enters school healthy and learns about and practices a healthy lifestyle?
   - How can we help each students learn in an intellectually challenging environment that is physically and emotionally safe?
   - How can we be certain that each student is actively engaged in learning and is connected to the school and broader community?
   - How can we ensure that each student has access to personalized learning and to qualified, caring adults?
   - How can we prepare each graduate for success in college or further study and for employment in a global environment?

   The RTI Leadership Planning Team wanted to make sure that RTI would support and further the school's efforts in addressing these questions.

   Team members began by comparing the key elements of RTI to the Whole Child Initiative tenets. Overall, they concluded that an RTI approach might help support the tenets. Specifically they reached the following conclusions:

   - The universal screening element in RTI could be designed to obtain data on student intellectual, emotional, and physical characteristics related to student achievement. This information would serve as a baseline. Progress on the Whole Child measures would be monitored regularly.

- An RTI approach could be used to help students who are struggling. The RTI framework would ensure that students received help before they failed. Teachers would identify students who continued to struggle, collect data describing the problem, and bring that information to the RTI Intervention Team. The RTI Intervention Team and teacher (and parents as appropriate) would develop a personalized intervention plan. Student progress would be monitored. This approach would help ensure that students are able to learn in an intellectually challenging environment that is physically and emotionally safe.

- Attention would be given to ensuring effective core instruction for all students. This approach would ensure that students have access to high-quality instruction in safe environments.

Exploring Connections: How RTI Fits with Other School and District Initiatives

Initiative: _____

RTI Element	Similarities and Overlaps	Suggestions
Universal screening		
Data-based problem solving		
Effective core instruction		
Tiered supports and interventions		
Progress monitoring		
Professional development		

PART 2

Understanding RTI Components

▶▶▶▶ About Part 2

Once the RTI Leadership Planning Team members have decided that RTI is a good fit for their school, they will want to start crafting their RTI framework. Team members may come to the RTI planning process with varying degrees of knowledge about RTI components. In some cases—such as when a component is already in place, albeit not as an RTI component—team members may have extensive knowledge. In any case, the planning team can benefit from all team members having a solid understanding of the major components as they relate to an RTI framework.

In Part 2, the planning team will learn about the most common RTI framework components. The tools in this section provide team members with numerous ways to develop their understanding through team discussion and exploration of applications in their school. At the end of Part 2, team members should have sufficient knowledge to develop their RTI framework and implementation plan.

The sections in Part 2 correspond to the components that are most often cited in RTI frameworks. A brief description follows.

Multitiered system of support. Most RTI frameworks organize student academic and behavioral interventions and supports in a multitiered approach. The idea is that the first tier of support is appropriate for all students and that each subsequent level reflects interventions that are more intense and available only to those students who require them. See Figure 1 for an illustration of a multitiered system of support.

In Part 2, two sections address the multitiered system of support:

- **Section 1: Understanding Core Instruction**. Strong core instruction (Tier 1) must be in place for the RTI approach to work. Tier 1 addresses the academic and behavioral needs of all students.
- **Section 2: Understanding Tiers 2 and 3**. Some students may need more academic or behavioral support than is available at the core level. Tier 2 and Tier 3 address the needs of a small percentage of students in the school. At Tier 2, an individual student or small group of students may receive individualized interventions. If a student fails to make sufficient or expected progress, the RTI Intervention Team may consider more individualized and intensive interventions at Tier 3.

Problem-solving approach. At the center of RTI approaches is a problem-solving structure. Usually a school-based team—in this tool, that team is referred to as the RTI Intervention Team—addresses student challenges by planning interventions and monitoring student progress. **Section 3** tools provide information about forming an RTI Intervention Team and developing a problem-solving process by which students may receive assistance.

Progress monitoring. RTI frameworks assume that students who are receiving assistance will have their progress monitored. This is done to ensure that the interventions and supports are effective and resulting in improved achievement. **Section 4** tools provide a general introduction to progress monitoring.

Universal screening. In RTI frameworks, universal screening is used to identify individual students and groups of students who are not achieving. Once identified, the RTI Intervention Team may make recommendations for addressing student learning challenges. **Section 5** provides a general introduction to how universal screening can strengthen an RTI approach.

Each tool in the various sections addresses a particular aspect of the component. Although there is always a certain degree of overlap, care has been taken to focus primarily on that particular aspect that is essential for efficient and effective implementation.

The RTI Leadership Planning Team may chose to complete all or some of the tools in a section before moving to the next section. Should a tool not be used, the RTI chair should ensure that team members already have adequate knowledge and skills related to the topic because the content in these sections forms the basis for many of the tools in Part 3. The RTI Leadership Planning team will use the information in the following ways:

- To develop the RTI framework and plan for implementation.
- To conduct professional development for staff members that introduces them to RTI, how the RTI framework will operate, and their role in the process.
- To form the RTI Intervention Team(s) that will receive requests for assistance and complete the problem-solving process.
- To monitor implementation.

At the end of each section is a listing of possible resources for more information. Whenever possible, RTI Leadership Planning Team members might consider reviewing additional resources and doing more in-depth research about a particular aspect of the RTI component.

Figure 1
A Multitiered System of Support

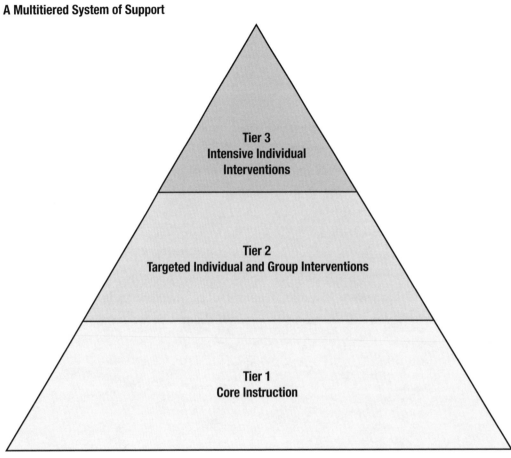

SECTION 1 OVERVIEW: ENSURING EFFECTIVE CORE INSTRUCTION

Ensuring that core instruction is effective for all students is an essential RTI component. RTI assumes that all students have access to highly qualified teachers who recognize the effect of increased student diversity on teaching and learning. Core instruction includes

- **Academics**—Core program and universal academic interventions for all students.
- **Behavior**—Classroom management and universal behavioral interventions (preventive and proactive) that are available to all students.

The RTI triangle generally places core instruction at the first tier. Most RTI frameworks assume that the core program is meeting roughly 80 to 90 percent of students' learning and behavioral needs. From an RTI perspective, schools with fewer than 75 percent of students at or above grade level proficiency have a core program problem. Interventions alone will not solve these students' problems. Further, schools must address core program problems or risk having the same percentage of students requiring interventions year after year.

Many schools have undertaken school improvement and professional development initiatives to ensure that instructional staff members provide effective instruction to all students. Common examples of these include (but are not limited to) the following:

- **Classroom Instruction That Works**. Robert Marzano and his colleagues identified nine research-based instructional practices that have a high probability of improving student achievement across all grade levels and content areas when effectively and systematically used during classroom instruction. These research-based practices are explained in the ASCD book *Classroom Instruction That Works* by Robert Marzano, Debra Pickering, and Jane Pollock. Marzano and colleagues also identified effective classroom management strategies in *Classroom Management That Works: Research-Based Strategies for Every Teacher*. The book describes the action steps for establishing rules and procedures, using effective disciplinary interventions, building positive student-teacher relationships, and developing effective schoolwide management policies.
- **Differentiated Instruction**. Developed by Carol Ann Tomlinson, differentiated instruction seeks to maximize each student's learning progress by offering several different learning experiences in response to students' individual needs. Instructional activities and materials are varied by difficulty to challenge students who are performing at different readiness levels, by topic in response to students' interests, and by students' preferred styles of learning and expression.

- **The Understanding by Design® Framework**. Developed by Grant Wiggins and Jay McTighe, this framework creates more engaging and effective learning through the design of curriculum, assessment, and instruction that is focused on developing and deepening understanding of important ideas. The process enables school teams to determine learning goals; collect, analyze, and summarize evidence from multiple sources of data to determine how well students are performing on accountability tests and the extent to which they really understand what they are learning; and consider the causes of present achievement to increase learning.

- **Universal Design for Learning (UDL)**. UDL provides a framework for creating flexible goals, methods, materials, and assessments that accommodate learner differences. A universally-designed curriculum offers the following elements: multiple means of representation to give learners various ways of acquiring information and knowledge; multiple means of expression to provide learners alternatives for demonstrating what they know; and multiple means of engagement.

- **Positive Behavioral Interventions and Supports (PBIS)**. PBIS provides an operational framework—similar to an RTI framework—for ensuring that all students have access to effective behavioral practices and interventions. Most PBIS models emphasize data-based decision making, measurable outcomes, a tiered system of evidence-based practices, implementation fidelity, and professional development support.

A major task of the RTI Leadership Planning Team is to review the core instruction offered in the school and determine if it is effective for all students.

PURPOSE OF THIS SECTION AND SUMMARY OF TOOLS

The purpose of this section is to provide the RTI Leadership Planning Team with an opportunity to review the strength of the core instructional program. The team will use this information to determine if the core instructional program meets student needs, or if it should be enhanced. The tools in this section present conversation starters and probes that team members may find useful in understanding the core instructional program by

- Looking at how core instruction is currently implemented and its success in addressing student academic and behavioral needs.
- Exploring student data in relation to core instruction.
- Reviewing curriculum standards in relation to core instruction.
- Understanding the role of research-based practices in an RTI framework.
- Identifying instructional resources.

Ensuring Effective Core Instruction

The tools are as follows:

- **Reviewing Student Data in Relation to Core Instruction.** The RTI Leadership Planning Team may use this tool to investigate the success of the core instructional program with subgroups of students. Such inquiry enables team members to decide if the core instructional program is meeting the needs of particular subgroups of students—especially students for whom the school must disaggregate achievement data (e.g., students with disabilities, students from low-income families, students with diverse racial and ethnic backgrounds, and so on).

- **Reviewing Core Instruction in Relation to Standards: Focus Questions.** The planning team will want to review the district curriculum to ensure that it aligns with state standards and accountability assessments and that curricula are implemented consistently so that all students have the opportunity to learn. This tool provides an opportunity to discuss the school's current capacity to offer effective core instruction.

- **Looking at Differentiated Instruction.** The planning team will want to consider the effectiveness of the core program. Differentiated instruction often is cited as one of the ways to guarantee a strong core program. This tool provides team members with an opportunity to determine the extent to which differentiated instruction is being implemented in classrooms.

- **Understanding Research-Based Instructional Practices.** The planning team can use this tool to review the extent to which research-based practices are being implemented in classrooms. The rationale is that if a practice is not effective, then it is impossible to know if a student's lack of progress is a result of a learning difficulty or an ineffective practice (or both).

- **Conducting Observations of Research-Based Instructional Practices.** This tool provides the planning team with a quick strategy for observing whether research-based instructional strategies are being used in classrooms.

- **Considering a Proactive Schoolwide Approach to Behavioral Interventions.** The planning team is concerned with student academic *and* behavioral needs. This tool provides the team with an opportunity to think about student behavior from a schoolwide perspective, identify areas of concern suggested by current school data, and discuss potential ways to positively influence schoolwide behavior changes by strengthening the core program.

- **Strengthening Core Instruction Via Classroom Management Practices.** Strong classroom management practices support student achievement in the core program. This tool provides an opportunity to review current practices and determine if professional development is needed.

- **Ensuring Cultural Responsiveness as Part of the Core Instructional Program.** When reviewing the core instructional program, the planning team may want to focus on how well the needs of students from diverse cultural, ethnic, and linguistic backgrounds are being met. This tool allows the planning team to examine and discuss whether the core instructional program is responsive to diverse groups of learners.

- **Indentifying Curriculum Resources for Tier 1 Interventions—What's Already in Place? What's Needed?** A central task of the planning team is to thoroughly review the core instructional program to determine if it is meeting student needs. This tool helps team members foster a greater understanding of Tier 1 by asking them to identify whether resource needs vary by the curriculum areas of reading and math.

- **Identifying Supplemental Instructional Materials.** This tool provides an opportunity for team members to review the types of supports and resources available and decide if they are adequate.

After completing these tools, the RTI Leadership Planning Team members should be able to consider the strength of the core instructional program. This draft plan should be used in Part 3, Section 1, "Putting It All Together: Developing the RTI Framework and Implementation Plan," when the team actually designs the RTI framework that will be presented to the school.

REFERENCES AND ADDITIONAL RESOURCES

For more information on some of the initiatives mentioned, please see the following resources.

Epstein, M., Atkins, M., Cullinan, D., Kutash, K., 7 Weaver, R. (2008). *Reducing behavior problems in the elementary school classroom: A practice guide* (NCEE #2008-012). Washington, DC: National Center for Education Evaluation and Regional Assistance, Institute of Education Sciences, U.S. Department of Education. Retrieved April 9, 2010, from http://ies.ed.gov/ncee/wwc/publications/practiceguides

Ford, D. Y., & Kea, C. D. (2009). Creating culturally responsive instruction: For students' and teachers' sakes. *Focus on Exceptional Children, 41*(9), 1-16.

Gersten, R., Baker, S. K., Shanahan, T., Linan-Thompson, S., Collins, P., & Scarcella, R. (2007). *Effective literacy and English language instruction for English learners in the elementary*

Ensuring Effective Core Instruction

grades: A practice guide (NCEE 2007-4011). Washington, DC: National Center for Education Evaluation and Regional Assistance, Institute of Education Sciences, U.S. Department of Education. Retrieved April 9, 2010, from http://ies.ed.gov/ncee/wwc/publications/practiceguides

Marzano, R., Pickering, D., & Pollock, J. (2001). *Classroom instruction that works: Research-based strategies for increasing student achievement.* Alexandria, VA: ASCD.

Marzano, R., Marzano, J., & Pickering, D. (2003). *Classroom management that works: Research-based strategies for every teacher.* Alexandria, VA: ASCD.

Marzano, R., Pickering, D., & Pollack, J. (2003) *Classroom instruction that works.* Alexandria, VA: ASCD.

Rose, D., & Meyer, A. (2002). *Teaching every student in the digital age: Universal design for learning.* Alexandria, VA: ASCD.

Strickland, C. A. (2007). *Tools for high-quality differentiated instruction.* Alexandria, VA: ASCD.

Tomlinson, C. (1999). *The differentiated classroom: Responding to the needs of all learners.* Alexandria, VA: ASCD.

Tomlinson, C. A. (2001). *How to differentiate instruction in mixed-ability classrooms* (2nd ed.). Alexandria, VA: ASCD.

Reviewing Student Data in Relation to Core Instruction

PURPOSE

In an RTI framework, effective core instruction addresses the needs of most—usually 80 to 90 percent—students. Students who require additional support receive it in conjunction with the core instructional program. When considering the effectiveness of the core instructional program, it is helpful to determine any commonalities or differences among students who require additional support. Such inquiry enables team members to decide if the core instructional program is meeting the needs of particular subgroups of students—especially students for whom the school must disaggregate achievement data (e.g., students with disabilities, students from low-income families, students from diverse racial and ethnic background, etc.). The purpose of this tool is to provide an opportunity for the RTI Leadership Planning Team to investigate the success of the core instructional program with subgroups of students.

HOW TO USE THIS TOOL

The tool is designed as a conversation starter that the RTI Leadership Planning Team can use in exploring how well the core instructional program meets the needs of subgroups of students. The following steps illustrate how the tool might be used:

- Complete the Demographics form for the school.
- Select an area of inquiry. For example, the second form, Looking at Student Data: Behavior, considers attendance, discipline referrals, suspensions, and expulsions as indicators of student behavioral success. The third form, Looking at Student Achievement Data: Literacy, compares student subgroup results on standardized achievement tests. A fourth form is available for teams who wish to consider other indicators (e.g., graduation rate, tardiness rate, mathematics literacy scores, number receiving special services, and so on).
- Record data for each subgroup, as appropriate.
- Review the results. Is the core instructional program meeting the needs of all student subgroups? Do all students have equal access to an effective core instruction? If not, what are the reasons?

Decision point: At the end of the discussion, decide if the core instructional program is effective across subgroups of students. If not, determine the next steps for strengthening core instruction.

TIPS AND VARIATIONS

1. If it appears that a particular subgroup of students is not achieving, discuss why this might be. For example, there is a body of knowledge concerning the need to make curriculum and instruction culturally responsive. If data show that there is a disproportionate number of students in a subgroup who are not achieving, then consider how instruction might be enhanced to meet their needs. Or, if large numbers of 9th grade students are not advancing to 10th grade on time, then consider how the core instructional program might be enhanced to facilitate their transition.

2. Share this data with school staff. Highlight areas of strength and areas requiring improvement.

Reviewing Student Data in Relation to Core Instruction

REVIEWING STUDENT DATA: DEMOGRAPHICS

Subgroup	Number	Percent of Total Enrollment
African American		
American Indian/Alaskan Native		
Asian/Pacific Islander		
Caucasian		
Hispanic		
Other:		
Economically Disadvantaged		
English Language Learner		
Special Education		
Male		
Female		
Grade:		
Grade:		
Grade:		
Grade:		
Other:		
Other:		

REVIEWING STUDENT DATA: BEHAVIOR

Subgroup	Attendance	Discipline Referrals	Suspensions	Expulsions	Total
African American					
American Indian/ Alaskan Native					
Asian/Pacific Islander					
Caucasian					
Hispanic					
Other:					
Economically Disadvantaged					
English Language Learner					
Special Education					
Male					
Female					
Grade:					
Grade:					
Grade:					
Grade:					
Other:					
Other:					

REVIEWING STUDENT DATA: LITERACY

Subgroups	Above Average	Average Range	Below Average
African American			
American Indian/Alaskan Native			
Asian/Pacific Islander			
Caucasian			
Hispanic			
Other:			
Economically Disadvantaged			
English Language Learner			
Special Education			
Male			
Female			
Grade:			
Grade:			
Grade:			
Grade:			
Other:			
Other:			

Ensuring Effective Core Instruction | Reviewing Student Data in Relation to Core Instruction

SCHOOL TO IDENTIFY OWN FOCUS _____

Subgroups		
African American		
American Indian/Alaskan Native		
Asian/Pacific Islander		
Caucasian		
Hispanic		
Other:		
Economically Disadvantaged		
English Language Learner		
Special Education		
Male		
Female		
Grade:		
Grade:		
Grade:		
Grade:		
Other:		
Other:		

Reviewing Core Instruction in Relation to Standards: Focus Questions

PURPOSE

Curriculum alignment is often cited as one of the most powerful strategies for improving student achievement. The challenge is to ensure that district curriculum aligns with state standards and accountability assessments and that curricula are implemented consistently so that all students have the opportunity to learn. When the content that is taught is not part of a standards-based curriculum, students are not taught what is assessed, which can result in lower achievement scores.

An RTI framework assumes a coherent curricular and instructional program that is aligned with state and district standards. Has your school recently engaged in curriculum alignment, vertical alignment, or other processes to ensure that state and district standards are reflected in the taught curriculum? The purpose of this tool is to provide an opportunity to discuss the school's current capacity to offer effective core instruction.

HOW TO USE THIS TOOL

The tool is designed as a conversation starter that the RTI Leadership Planning Team can use in exploring the strength of the school's core curricular program.

Decision point: At the end of the discussion decide if the core academic program is strong enough to support an RTI approach. If not, determine the next steps for creating better alignment.

TIPS AND VARIATIONS

1. Use this tool as a stimulus to review the core academic program with a focus on how well it aligns with state and district standards. If the school participated in a formal alignment process, review results. Review any significant actions (e.g., restructuring of curriculum, professional development on curriculum mapping, and so on). Consider how teaching and learning has changed since then.

2. Consider any major changes to the school in the time between when the curriculum was last reviewed and now (e.g., changing demographics of students attending the school, a subgroup of students who have not met curriculum standards on statewide assessments, and so on). Discuss how these changes might be addressed by an RTI approach.

3. There are some technology products on the market that support curriculum alignment activities. If your school uses one of these, use this tool as an opportunity to review how well it is working and the degree to which teachers find the data and analyses useful.

Reviewing Core Instruction in Relation to Standards: Focus Questions

The goal of this tool is to stimulate discussion about the strength of the core curriculum and instructional program in relation to state and district standards. It is not intended as a formal review. Rather, it is intended to help RTI Leadership Planning Team members decide if actions need to be taken to strengthen the core program prior to launching an RTI approach.

1. Is content coverage cohesive, consistent, and appropriately linked to standards that have been aligned with state assessments? Has the school reviewed each state standard in relation to the district's written curriculum? Have outcome indicators been identified for each curriculum area and cross-referenced to the district curriculum?

2. Do all students experience the same opportunities to learn valued academic content?

3. What content is emphasized in particular courses? Do teachers know enough about one another's content focus and instruction to ensure that students experience a reasonable progression of content as they advance from grade to grade or course to course?

4. Is the curriculum organized into sequentially focused and manageable content that can be mastered within the time provided? Is content articulated at each grade or course level? Do teachers focus on building skills and knowledge while reducing the need for excess review and repetition? Has a scope and sequence chart been prepared that includes standards, objectives, and performance goals for each content area?

5. Are grade level objectives related to the standards for each curriculum area or course delineated? Have content standards been identified that should be taught and reinforced across several grade levels, as well as those that are prerequisites for others? Do objectives provide a sequential set of steps from one level to the next?

6. Is it clear what students should know and be able to do as a result of mastering the objectives? Has a corresponding list of performance indicators been developed? Have assessment strategies for standards and objectives been developed? Is curriculum aligned with performance or benchmark assessments so that instructional staff can examine differences in instruction, and identify reasons for high and low student performance?

Ensuring Effective Core Instruction

 # Looking at Differentiated Instruction

PURPOSE

Providing all students with access to effective core instruction in Tier 1 is at the heart of an RTI framework. Differentiated instruction often is cited as a mainstay of effective core instruction. In the *Tools for High-Quality Differentiated Instruction: An ASCD Action Tool,* author Cindy Strickland notes that the fundamental philosophy of differentiated instruction is recognizing differences in student readiness, interest, and learning profile and responding to students' varied needs with the intent of maximizing growth, motivation, and efficiency of learning.

The RTI Leadership Planning Team may find it helpful to focus on differentiated instruction as a way to strengthen the core instructional program. This tool provides an opportunity to discuss the school's current capacity to differentiate instruction for all students.

HOW TO USE THIS TOOL

This tool provides a checklist of the major components of differentiated instruction and is intended to serve as a catalyst for the RTI Leadership Planning Team's discussion of current practices within the school and areas where staff members may need more support. In preparation for this discussion, it may be helpful for members of the planning team to reinforce their own understanding of differentiated instruction. For example, team members may want to read one or more articles, such as the ones that follow:

- Huebner, T. A. (2010). Meeting students where they are: Differentiated learning. *Educational Leadership, 67*(5), 79–81.
- Reis, S. M., Kaplan, S. N., Tomlinson, C. A., Westberg, K. L., Callahan, C. M., & Cooper, C. R. (1998). Equal does not mean identical. *Educational Leadership, 56*(3), 74–77.
- Tomlinson, C., & Kalbfleisch, M. L. (1998). Teach me, teach my brain: A call for differentiated classrooms. *Educational Leadership, 56*(3), 52–55.
- Tomlinson, C. A., & Santangelo, T. (2010). *ASCD PD QuickKit: Integrating differentiated instruction and Response to Intervention: From theory to practice.* Alexandria, VA: ASCD.

Decision point: At the end of the discussion, decide if students are receiving differentiated instruction in the core academic program. If not, determine the next steps for strengthening the core instructional program.

TIPS AND VARIATIONS

1. This tool may be reconfigured and used as a self-assessment or team assessment (e.g., grade level team). In this format staff members might be asked to provide feedback regarding their understanding and use of differentiated instruction using the following scale.

   4 = I understand differentiated instruction; I am fully implementing it and can help to support others.

   3 = I understand differentiated instruction; I am implementing it but would like more feedback and practice.

   2 = I understand differentiated instruction but am not yet confident with implementation.

   1 = I do not yet have a clear understanding of differentiated instruction and have not begun implementation.

2. In preparation for the discussion about differentiated instruction, members of the planning team might conduct walk-throughs to observe current practices and gather perceptions of staff comfort levels.

3. The planning team might want to engage faculty members in learning more about differentiated instruction, using the tool as a vehicle for discussing and assessing progress. The following ASCD resources may be helpful in this regard:

   • The Differentiated School: Making Revolutionary Changes in Teaching and Learning by Carol Ann Tomlinson, Kay Brimijoin, and Lane Narvasez

   • *Exploring Differentiated Instruction* by Cindy Strickland

   • *Differentiation in Practice: A Resource Guide for Differentiating Curriculum, Grades K–5* by Carol Ann Tomlinson and Caroline Cunningham Edison

   • *How to Differentiated Instruction in Mixed-Ability Classrooms* (2nd ed.), by Carol Ann Tomlinson

Ensuring Effective Core Instruction

Looking at Differentiated Instruction

Components of Differentiated Instruction	Notes and Questions
Ongoing Assessment • Teachers determine what students know about a topic prior to instruction. • Teachers analyze pre-assessment data to identify students' strengths and needs. • Teachers use varied pre-assessment methods such as pre-tests, KWL charts, demonstration, discussion, show of hands, observations, and checklists. • Teachers use assessments to determine students' interests. • Teachers use assessments to determine students' learning profiles.	
Variation in Content, Process, and Product • Teachers vary what they teach or how students gain access to the content through such methods as interest centers, curriculum compacting, and online extension activities, and independent study options. • Teachers provide varied opportunities for students to process or make sense of the content using such strategies as supportive technology, graphic organizers, and multiple groupings (e.g., opportunities to work alone, in pairs, or in small groups). • Teachers allow students to show what they know, understand, and are able to do in varied ways such as choices of questions on tests and quizzes, varied timelines or check-in points, and product options aligned with varied interests or learning profiles.	

ASCD   87

Part 2

Components of Differentiated Instruction	Notes and Questions
Flexible Grouping • Students experience a range of grouping con-figurations including whole class, working alone or with a partner, and small group. • Teachers use flexible, temporary homogeneous and heterogeneous grouping when there is a need for review, re-teaching, practice, or enrichment. • Flexible groups are based on student readiness, interest, reading level, skill level, background knowledge, and social skills. • Small-group instruction is provided as needed to foster increased opportunities for hearing peer responses, interaction with the teacher and with peers, engagement, and teacher feedback.	
Respectful Learning Activities • Activities are engaging and appropriately challenging for the students for whom they are designed. • Activities are designed, in most cases, to help students achieve the same or very similar learning goals. • Advanced students receive different, more complex work rather than routinely receiving a greater quantity of work. • Both struggling and advanced learners receive appropriate, scaffolded instructional support.	

Ensuring Effective Core Instruction

Understanding Research-Based Instructional Practices

PURPOSE

Research-based, scientifically based, evidence-based—these are all terms that are used when referencing instructional practices that researchers have found to be effective. Research-based practices include scientifically validated curriculum series, instructional practices, programs, and interventions.

Although most educators would want to use practices that have been proven to work, finding such practices is not always easy. For example, the What Works Clearinghouse of the U. S. Department of Education—the federal project that reviews effectiveness data for educational practices—lists only 37 practices that have been reviewed, with fewer than half meeting acceptable research standards. Even in cases in which a practice does have a research base, evidence may be limited to a certain subgroup of students or a specific setting (e.g., implemented in a research facility, implemented by a researcher who is assisted by research assistants, and so on).

RTI frameworks place a premium on using research-based practices at Tier 1 as well as Tier 2 and Tier 3. The rationale is that if a practice is not effective, then it is impossible to know if a student's lack of progress is a result of a learning difficulty or an ineffective practice (or both). The purpose of this tool is to provide an opportunity for the RTI Leadership Planning Team to consider the extent to which research-based practices are currently in use in the school.

HOW TO USE THIS TOOL

Pick a curriculum area (e.g., reading, science, math) or program area (e.g., drop-out prevention). Survey faculty and staff in the school regarding the major practices in use. Use the tool to record information about the practice, including the purpose and characteristics of students for whom there are data (e.g., 4th grade students in a rural school). In the Notes section you can add observations and thoughts (e.g., teachers have received professional development, rarely is the practice implemented with fidelity, success rates, and so on).

ASCD   89

Decision point: After reviewing an area, the planning team should discuss the extent to which research-based practices are being implemented in the school and whether those practices address student needs. The discussion should culminate in a determination of whether the school has sufficient capacity for implementing research-based practices in the core program.

TIPS AND VARIATIONS

1. Develop a coding system for common practices in the school that identifies which of them have the following characteristics:

    - A strong evidence base.
    - An adequate evidence base.
    - A promising evidence base (early results show promise, but too early to tell).
    - An evidence base that is lacking (i.e., use with reservations).
    - No evidence base.
    - Share these with the school staff.

2. Talk with the reading specialist, the team members who participated in the most recent textbook selection committee, or both. Discuss the research-based practices that are embedded in the text as well as textbook company data about the curriculum.

3. Meet with school personnel responsible for monitoring NCLB and IDEA and discuss how requirements for scientifically based instruction in both laws have been implemented.

4. Take a close look at the subject group characteristics. Consider whether the subjects resemble students in your school. If not, discuss whether the practice is appropriate.

5. Use the tool to review research-based interventions representative of Tier 2 and Tier 3 currently in use in the school.

Ensuring Effective Core Instruction

Understanding Research-Based Instructional Practices

Research-Based Practice	Purpose	Students	Notes

Conducting Observations of Research-Based Instructional Practices

PURPOSE

What research-based instructional practices should you be able to observe during core instruction or Tier 1 of a RTI framework based on past professional development and established expectations? This tool is designed to help the RTI Leadership Planning Team address the question by using walk-through teams and providing them with a low-technology format for gathering information and looking for patterns.

A number of research-based instructional practices have been identified as most likely to improve student achievement across all grade levels and content areas when effectively and systematically used during classroom instruction. Nine of these research-based practices are explained in the ASCD book, *Classroom Instruction That Works* by Robert Marzano, Debra Pickering, and Jane Pollock, and are recorded in the tool. The chart may be modified to delete those practices for which professional development has not been provided and to add other research-based instructional practices that have been emphasized in your school.

HOW TO USE THIS TOOL

Prior to initiation, administrators or planning team members should review the walk-through process with staff to provide clarity about the goals, identify walk-through team members and a proposed schedule, discuss plans for feedback, and answer questions. It should be emphasized with the staff that whole-group feedback will be provided rather than individual feedback and that the primary objective of the walk-through process is to help validate instructional practices that seem to be in place, and help them provide input regarding professional development for expansion of selected practices.

This tool serves as a checklist and record-keeping approach to help maintain the observers' focus on looking for the presence or absence of selected research-based instructional practices. Notes are recorded to assist observers in forming overall impressions of current implementation levels and preparing for discussion with other walk-through team members and subsequently the entire staff or identified teams. A separate tool form is recommended for each grade level, teacher, or content area to facilitate subsequent compilation of results.

Decision point: The planning team should determine whether the walk-throughs process has resulted in sufficient information regarding current use of research-based instructional practices. If there is sufficient information, the team should plan to share outcomes with the staff, validate perceptions formed, and obtain feedback regarding professional development needs. If the information is insufficient, the RTI Leadership Planning Team should identify next steps (e.g., conducting additional observations, modifying the observation process, and so on).

TIPS AND VARIATIONS

1. Administrators or designated members of the RTI Leadership Planning Team might use the observation results to engage the whole staff or designated teams (e.g., certain grade levels or content areas) in a discussion. The tool is not intended for use with individual staff members. The discussion with the entire staff might include feedback on observed levels of use of designated instructional practices and identification of professional development needs that would help facilitate expanded implementation.

2. Invite external observers from among your central office staff, educators at institutions of higher education, and those individuals who conducted professional development on selected instructional practices to serve as members of the walk-through team.

3. Engage the entire faculty or designated sections of the faculty to identify those research-based practices that should be the focus of the walk-through.

4. Modify the tool so that it serves as a self-assessment for faculty members as they reflect upon their own practices within a designated time period. The descriptors on the form of Observed and Not Observed might be changed to Used and Not Used.

5. It is essential that walk-through team members are knowledgeable about those research-based instructional practices targeted for the observation process.

6. Prior to conducting the walk-through, read more about the technique in the following article: David, J. L. (2007). Classroom walk-throughs. *Educational Leadership*, 65(4), 81–82.

Conducting Observations of Research-Based Instructional Practices

Observer: _____ **Date:** _____ **Content Area:** _____

Grade Level Observed: _____ **Classroom Teacher:** _____

Research-Based Instructional Practices	Notes and Questions
Identifying Similarities and Differences	__ Observed __ Not Observed Comments/Questions:
Summarizing and Note Taking	__ Observed __ Not Observed Comments/Questions:
Reinforcing Effort and Providing Recognition	__ Observed __ Not Observed Comments/Questions:
Homework and Practice	__ Observed __ Not Observed Comments/Questions:
Nonlinguistic Representations	__ Observed __ Not Observed Comments/Questions:

Cooperative Learning	__ Observed __ Not Observed Comments/Questions:
Setting Objectives and Providing Feedback	__ Observed __ Not Observed Comments/Questions:
Generating and Testing Hypotheses	__ Observed __ Not Observed Comments/Questions:
Cues, Questions, and Advance Organizers	__ Observed __ Not Observed Comments/Questions:
Other Practices:	__ Observed __ Not Observed Comments/Questions:
Other Practices:	__ Observed __ Not Observed Comments/Questions:

Considering a Proactive, Schoolwide Approach to Behavioral Interventions

PURPOSE

Many RTI frameworks emphasize a tiered approach to organizing academic and behavioral interventions. Schools that employ schoolwide, multitiered approaches such as positive behavioral interventions and supports to address student behavior proactively generally expect Tier 1 efforts in the core instructional program to address the needs of 80 to 90 percent of students. These practices, also referred to as primary prevention, are designed as part of the core program to meet the needs of the majority of students.

Although individual teachers may implement variations of positive behavioral support in their classrooms (e.g., rewards, behavioral contracts, self-monitoring, prompts, clear rules and expectations, and so on), schoolwide models may have a greater effect. For example, in schoolwide models, expectations, rules, and procedures are standardized, which helps students navigate through different settings and with different adults. Many of these models also encourage consistency when recognizing and rewarding appropriate behavior.

Unlike a punitive approach to behavior such as suspension, most schoolwide proactive approaches assume that appropriate behavior can be taught to all students. Other components of these approaches that align with RTI academic approaches include:

- Early intervention with an emphasis on prevention.
- Interventions are differentiated so that students receive the appropriate intensity and duration of an intervention.
- Progress monitoring to ensure student success.
- Data-based problem solving and decision making.

When reviewing core instruction, the RTI Leadership Planning Team may find it helpful to review schoolwide approaches for preventing behavioral issues. This tool provides a discussion guide for helping the RTI Leadership Planning Team think about student behavior from a schoolwide perspective, identify any areas of concern suggested by current school data, and discuss potential ways to influence schoolwide behavior changes positively through strengthening the core program.

HOW TO USE THIS TOOL

This tool is designed for the RTI Leadership Planning Team to use as a conversation starter. Through discussion of the questions posed, the team generates additional questions and identifies recommendations and potential next steps.

Decision point: The planning team should decide if the core program provides sufficient support for behavioral issues or if a schoolwide approach to behavioral issues is needed.

TIPS AND VARIATIONS

1. Other school teams (e.g., school counselors, teachers at particular grade levels, etc.) might be given schoolwide data and asked to discuss the questions and share their perspectives and ideas. A designated planning team member or administrator could be asked to join the teams for their discussion and to help with interpreting the data if necessary.

2. Prior to the discussion, consult with schools that are implementing schoolwide proactive behavior approaches.

3. Review additional background on schoolwide proactive models. For example, read the ASCD *Educational Leadership* article, "Safety without Suspensions" (Skiba and Sprague, 2008). In it, the authors discuss a schoolwide rule framework adopted at Kennedy Middle School in Eugene, Oregon. The framework of expectations—Be Safe, Be Respectful, and Be Responsible—was reinforced throughout the school in many different ways: Teachers directly taught lessons on the patterns of behavior related to these expectations, and rules were posted throughout the school as well as in newsletters and in local media. The school implemented a consistent system of enforcement, monitoring, and positive reinforcement. When students were observed following school rules, they received tickets imprinted with the school mascot that could be redeemed for rewards. In addition to their focus on prevention, Kennedy Middle School personnel implemented a multitiered continuum of consequences and supportive reteaching for students with problem behavior. They also implemented data-based decision making through the use of a web-based system for tracking office referrals and discipline patterns.

4. Familiarize yourself with the types of interventions that are associated with proactive schoolwide behavioral approaches. For example, the U. S. Department of Education funds the Center on Positive Behavioral Interventions and Supports which

contains may web-based resources. [*Note*: As of this publication date, information and resources may be accessed at www.pbis.org.]

REFERENCES

Skiba, R., & Sprague, J. (2008) Safety without suspensions. *Educational Leadership*, 66(1), 38–43.

Ensuring Effective Core Instruction

Considering a Proactive, Schoolwide Approach to Behavioral Interventions

Questions	Notes and Ideas
• Are there individual students or subgroups of students who have been referred for more than one disciplinary infraction? • Are the referral levels for these individuals or student subgroups cause for concern?	
• Are there certain disciplinary infractions that occur repeatedly (e.g., disruptive behavior in the hallway during transitions from the cafeteria)?	
• Does the number of students referred for disciplinary reasons suggest that there is room for improvement so that more students will be positively engaged in the instructional program?	
• Do current discipline data suggest the presence of patterns, (e.g., more office referrals on Friday afternoons as compared to other days of the week)?	
• Are there questions that cannot be answered based on current data? • Are there additional data that need to be collected?	
• What practices are currently in place to proactively address behavior on a schoolwide basis?	

• What state and county resources might be available to support exploration and implementation of a proactive schoolwide approach to student behavior?	
• Are there certain behaviors that a number of students exhibit that should be targeted for intervention?	

Additional Ideas, Recommendations, Next Steps, and Individuals Responsible

Strengthening Core Instruction via Classroom Management Practices

PURPOSE

An important part of strengthening the core instructional program is to promote, expect, and support practices that result in effective classroom management. We know that teachers cannot teach and students cannot learn in poorly managed classrooms. We also know that classroom management is viewed as one of the teacher's most important roles. The purpose of this tool is to provide the RTI Leadership Planning Team with a vehicle for discussing current expectations and practices within the school and determining where there is a need for more consistency, reinforcement, targeted professional development, or all three.

HOW TO USE THIS TOOL

This tool may be used by the RTI Leadership Planning Team to consider the use of any practice that promotes classroom management or active student engagement. For example, the concept of "withitness" could be recorded in the first cell of the action tool. This concept, initially identified in a 1970 study by Jacob Kounin, is described by Marzano and Brown in *A Handbook for the Art and Science of Teaching* as one of the most powerful management tools teachers have at their disposal. "Withitness" is being aware of what is occurring in all parts of a classroom at all times by continuously scanning student behaviors and intervening quickly before inappropriate behavior becomes disruptive. Other classroom management practices such as involving students in establishing classroom rules and procedures also might be recorded in the first cell to prompt discussion of current implementation practices within the school. When these types of practices are a part of their repertoire, teachers may be more successful in differentiating instruction and implementing other effective instructional approaches in their classrooms.

Decision point: The RTI Leadership Planning Team should determine if effective classroom management practices are currently in place as part of core instruction. If not, team members should identify actions that might be taken to expand and strengthen the use of these practices.

TIPS AND VARIATIONS

1. This tool might be used by the RTI Leadership Planning Team to prompt follow-up discussion to a walk-through to observe implementation of selected classroom management practices.

2. The form could be modified for use by a grade level team or other designated team. The team could be asked to read about a particular classroom management practice identified by the RTI Leadership Planning Team and to discuss current levels of use and any need for support in refining the practice.

3. Prior to their discussion, the RTI Leadership Planning Team members might want to identify and read a few key articles on classroom management to reinforce their own knowledge and to facilitate a common frame of reference among team members. Downloading the following ASCD articles from the *Educational Leadership* (www.ascd.org/publications/educational_leadership.aspx) publication may be helpful in this regard:

   - DeVries, R., & Zan, B. (2003). When children make rules. *Educational Leadership, 61*(1), 64–67.
   - Gordon, R. L. (1997). How novice teachers can succeed with adolescents. *Educational Leadership, 54*(7), 56–58.
   - Kriete, R. (2003). Start the day with community. *Educational Leadership, 61*(1), 68–70.

REFERENCES AND ADDITIONAL RESOURCES

Epstein, M., Atkins, M., Cullinan, D., Kutash, K., and Weaver, R. (2008). *Reducing behavior problems in the elementary school classroom: A practice guide* (NCEE #2008-012). Washington, DC: National Center for Education Evaluation and Regional Assistance, Institute of Education Sciences, U.S. Department of Education. Retrieved April 9, 2010, from http://ies.ed.gov/ncee/wwc/publications/practiceguides

Marzano, R. J. (2003). *What works in schools: Translating research into action.* Alexandria, VA: ASCD.

Marzano, R. J., & Brown, J. L. (2009). *A handbook for the art and science of teaching.* Alexandria, VA: ASCD.

Ensuring Effective Core Instruction

Strengthening Core Instruction
via Classroom Management Practices

Are Targeted Classroom Management Practices Currently in Use?
Questions and Factors to Consider

Questions and Factors to Consider	Notes
What targeted classroom management practices are currently in place?	
What are the present levels of use in classrooms? ___ High ___ Medium ___ Low ___Absent	
What are the skill and comfort levels with implementing the selected practice(s)? ___ High ___ Medium ___ Low ___Uncertain	
How varied is the use of the classroom management practice(s) across grade levels and content areas? What might be the reason for the variance?	

Ensuring Effective Core Instruction | Strengthening Core Instruction via Classroom Management Practices

What are the perceived barriers to current use?	
What type of targeted professional development is needed to introduce or reinforce the use of selected practices?	
What type of follow-up professional development is needed to review and sustain practices?	
How accessible is the necessary professional development and what is the availability of resources (e.g., time and funding) to support it?	
What other resources could be accessed to deepen understanding of selected practices (e.g., articles, web-based resources, books, visits to other schools).	

What individuals could provide ongoing modeling and coaching of the classroom management practices as needed?	
Which classroom management practices have been emphasized and supported by the central office? What central office supports might be available to support implementation?	
What actions are needed to facilitate staff support or buy-in for implementation of selected practices?	
Other questions and factors to consider:	

Discussion Summary, Action Steps, and Designation of Individual Team Members for Follow-Up

Ensuring Cultural Responsiveness as Part of the Core Instructional Program

PURPOSE

Cultural responsiveness is a term that is often used in the context of looking at classrooms to ensure that students are receiving a respectful, equitable, and appropriate academic experience. When reviewing the core instructional program, the RTI Leadership Planning Team may want to focus on how well the needs of students from diverse backgrounds—cultural, ethnic, linguistic, or a combination—are being met. This is particularly important in schools where

- Demographics have changed recently.
- Subgroups of students who share common backgrounds are not making satisfactory progress.
- There are significant achievement gaps between students from the dominant culture and those from the minority culture.
- Most students are from cultures that are different from those of the instructional staff.

The purpose of this tool is to provide an opportunity for the planning team to examine and discuss whether the core instructional program is responsive to the needs of students from diverse backgrounds.

HOW TO USE THIS TOOL

The tool lists the following aspects of the school experience that may be considered in the context of cultural responsiveness. The team should look for multiple examples in the school.

- **Materials**. Classroom materials can convey cultural responsiveness by acknowledging and respecting diversity. For example, do the learning materials—including texts, posters, supplementary materials, library books, videotapes, etc.—reflect all of the different backgrounds represented in the school? Are tests and assessments bias free?
- **Instruction**. There are many ways that students experience cultural responsiveness from teachers. For example, do teachers interact with students in ways that acknowledge and respect their backgrounds? Do teachers hold high expectations for all

students? Are teachers knowledgeable about social customs (e.g., eye contact may be expected in an Anglo culture, yet would be a sign of disrespect in some Native American cultures)? Is the emotional climate in classrooms inclusive and accepting? Do teachers use instructional strategies that engage students from diverse backgrounds? Are all home-school communications culturally sensitive?

- **School community**. There are many aspects of the total school community that can communicate acceptance. For example, do all school staff members treat students with respect? Do they hold high expectations for all students? Are they knowledgeable about particular social customs? Is the emotional climate warm and inviting? Are home-school communications respectful (e.g., available in languages other than English)?

Decision point: Determine if there is sufficient evidence to suggest that the core instructional program is responsive to all students. If not, consider what actions might be undertaken to enhance the core program.

TIPS AND VARIATIONS

1. As an initial activity, read several recent articles from ASCD's *Educational Leadership* that address issues related to addressing the needs of students from diverse backgrounds. As a group, select one or more articles that appear relevant to your student population. Or, assign each team member a different article to read and to report back to the group. Over the years, ASCD has published numerous articles on the topic of diversity in *Educational Leadership*. The following articles are suggested as a starting place for review as they deal with issues relevant to school improvement efforts.

   - Aleman, D, Johnson Jr., J. F., & Perez, L. (April 2009). Winning schools for ELLs. *Educational Leadership*, *66*(7), 66–69.
   - Bazron, B., Osher, D, & Fleischman, S. (September 2005). Creating culturally responsive schools. *Educational Leadership*, *63*(1), 83–84.
   - Holloway, J. H. (February 2004). Closing the minority achievement gap in math. *Educational Leadership*, *61*(5), 84–86.
   - Howard, G. R. (March 2007). As diversity grows, so must we. *Educational Leadership*, *64*(6), 16–22.
   - Rance-Roney, J. (April 2009). Best practices for adolescent ELLs. *Educational Leadership*, *66*(7), 32–37.

- San Antonio, D. M. (April 2008). Understanding students' strength and struggles. *Educational Leadership*, *65*(7), 74–79.
- Sapon-Shevin, M. (December 2000/January 2001). Schools fit for all. *Educational Leadership*, *58*(4), 34–39.
- Villegas, A. M., & Lucas, T. (March 2007). The culturally responsive teacher. *Educational Leadership*, *64*(6), 28–33.

2. Use the Action Tool as a guide for a walk-through of selected classrooms. Encourage team members to strive to perceive things through the eyes of students from diverse backgrounds.

3. Pick a particular subject area (e.g., mathematics) where there is an achievement gap between students in the dominant culture and those in nondominant cultures. Review the curriculum materials and discuss whether they might be enhanced to be more culturally responsive to students.

Ensuring Effective Core Instruction

Ensuring Cultural Responsiveness as Part of the Core Instructional Program

Examine and discuss the following in terms of cultural responsiveness to students in your school.

	Responsive to Students?	Improvement Needed?
Materials		
Texts		
Posters		
Library books		
Tests		
Instruction		
Teacher interactions		
Teacher expectations		
Response to social behaviors		
Emotional climate		
Instructional strategies		
Home–school communications		
School Community		
Staff interactions		
Staff expectations		
Emotional climate		
Home–school communications		

Identifying Curriculum Resources for Tier 1 Interventions

PURPOSE

A central task of the RTI Leadership Planning Team is to thoroughly review the core instructional program to determine if it is meeting student needs. There are various ways to begin this process. One way is to complete an inventory of practices according to curriculum area. The purpose of this tool is to help team members foster a greater understanding of Tier 1 by asking them to identify whether or not resource needs vary in the curriculum areas of reading and math and to provide a written summary of their discussion.

HOW TO USE THIS TOOL

The following sample questions and actions may be used to facilitate the discussion, self-assessment, and completion of the tool:

- Which curriculum area shall we focus on first—math or reading—and what information do we have that suggests this area as our initial focus? Record the selection in column one. Make notes regarding rationale for the selection.
- What resources are currently available [in the selected curriculum area] that seem consistent with Tier 1? Record responses in column two.
- How widely available are our current resources? How effective are we in using our current resources? Record summary notations in column two.
- What additional resources would help us to improve our instruction at the Tier 1 level (in the selected curriculum area)? Record suggested resources in column three. Upon completion of the listing, engage staff in prioritizing the additional resources recommended.

Upon completion, the discussion leader should request ideas for immediate follow-up action and identify the individual(s) responsible for the action. Possible follow-up actions include the following:

- Arrange for a briefing on current resources that may be unfamiliar to some team members.
- Identify costs associated with some of the recommended resources.

- Determine where the recommended resources are currently in use and arrange to observe and obtain additional information regarding their effectiveness.
- Schedule a follow-up meeting to review actions taken.

Decision point: The planning team should decide if they have sufficient understanding of the core instructional program, or whether they require additional information. Further, team members should decide if there are sufficient curriculum resources in place to address student needs.

TIPS AND VARIATIONS

1. The form might be completed individually by team members and subsequently used during a team meeting to share ideas, generate additional ideas, and reach consensus on current Tier 1 resources and needs.
2. The form may be completed by grade level teams to facilitate self-assessment of Tier 1 resources in reading and math. A planning team member could then review the forms to identify whether the need for additional resources varies by grade level and to begin prioritizing identified needs.
3. Expand the discussion of Tier 1 resources to professional development needs.

Identifying Curriculum Resources for Tier 1 Interventions

Curriculum Focus	Tier 1 Current Resources	Tier I Additional Resources Needed

Follow-up Action and Designated Team Members:

Ensuring Effective Core Instruction

Identifying Supplemental Instructional Materials

PURPOSE

Supplementing the core instructional program by ensuring that staff members have access to a continuum of instructional materials for use with struggling learners can be an invaluable part of an RTI approach. Supplemental instructional materials aligned with the core curriculum may be particularly helpful in providing intensive interventions in identified skills at Tier 2 and Tier 3, and may be in print format, computer software format, or a combination of both. The purpose of this tool is to help the RTI Leadership Planning Team think about factors related to the identification of these materials.

HOW TO USE THIS TOOL

The RTI Leadership Planning Team should identify a content area where supplemental instructional materials are needed. Prior to a team meeting, individual members might access information about potential supplemental materials (e.g., web-based resources, samples provided by publishers, materials borrowed from the central office or other schools, and so on). An example of a web-based resource is the What Works Clearinghouse. Established by the U.S. Department of Education, this website provides information about a number of published materials on which research studies have been conducted that meet their established criteria (http://ies.edgov./ncee/wwc). State department of education websites also may have information to help schools in their identification processes. Intervention Central (www.interventioncentral.org) is another web-based resource with reviews of supplemental instructional materials that schools may find helpful. An example of an information source related to the use of computer-assisted instruction as a way to supplement the core instructional program may be found at The Iris Center of Vanderbilt University (http://iris.peabody.vanderbilt.edu/resources.html).

As team members review information related to supplemental instructional materials, they should complete this tool, using a separate form to record their notes related to each resource under consideration. The planning team members should share their notes either verbally or in writing, during a meeting to discuss the potential use of instructional materials.

Decision point: The planning team should identify supplemental materials that seem to have strong potential for augmenting and extending the core instructional program for struggling learners. Team members also should determine the next steps for further consideration of these materials (e.g., scheduling a presentation by the publisher, meeting with staff members to obtain their input, and so on).

TIPS AND VARIATIONS

1. The planning team members might opt to review supplemental instructional materials under consideration as a team. A recorder could complete the tool forms during a team meeting as each instructional material is considered resulting in one form for each item.

2. The planning team might involve other staff members in the initial process of reviewing supplemental instructional materials. For example, each grade level team could be asked to review materials and submit forms for those materials they consider to be the most viable to the planning team.

3. Prior to beginning to identify and conduct a review of supplemental instructional materials, the planning team could coordinate with the central office, state department of education, or other schools and request recommendations. This assistance could help to narrow the search and help with efficient use of time.

Ensuring Effective Core Instruction

Identifying Supplemental Instructional Materials

Reviewer: _____**Date Reviewed:** _____

Information Source (e.g., publisher's website, sample materials):

Supplemental Instructional Material	Additional Notes
Curriculum Area:	
Name of Material:	
Publisher and Copyright Date:	
Targeted Grade Levels Identified by Publisher:	
Sources of Research and Research Findings:	
Training Required for Implementation (e.g., type, amount, initial and follow-up; education and experience levels recommended for instructors):	

Type and Level of Ongoing Support Needed for Instructors to Help Ensure Fidelity of Implementation:	
Costs of Materials and Funding Needed for Initial Implementation:	
Funding Needed to Sustain Implementation:	
Potential Sources of Funding:	
Recommendations—Use of This Material and Rationale (e.g., not recommended, defer for future consideration, recommend piloting use at one grade level):	

Suggested Next Steps and Designated Individual(s) for Follow-Up

SECTION 2 OVERVIEW: UNDERSTANDING A MULTITIERED RESPONSE TO INTERVENTION APPROACH

Most RTI frameworks organize interventions according to intensity of intervention and frequency of data collection. Typically, interventions are organized into a pyramid. This Action Tool focuses on developing a three-tiered system. [*Note*: Some RTI proponents advocate for more than three tiers, in which case developers would still use the principle of organizing interventions by intensity and frequency of progress monitoring.]

- **Tier 1**. The bottom tier, which generally represents core instruction, addresses the needs of approximately 80 to 90 percent of students and contains accommodations and strategies that general education teachers may use to support struggling students. These interventions should be available to all students who need them and should be implemented within the general classroom framework. On an ongoing basis, teachers assess students to determine instructional strengths and needs.

- **Tier 2.** The middle tier usually addresses the needs of approximately 10 to 15 percent of students and contains supplemental supports that are reserved for students who have more significant challenges, whether academic, behavioral, or both. Tier 2 interventions often include assistance from specialists (e.g., reading), and activities such as tutoring or counseling.

- **Tier 3**. The top tier usually addresses the needs of students with significant academic or behavioral challenges who require the most intensive services in a school. In some schools, Tier 3 supports include individualized services such as special education or related services, mental health counseling, etc. In other schools, special education services are considered Tier 4.

The purpose of organizing resources and supports into a tiered system is to assist the RTI Intervention Team in identifying interventions and instructional strategies and materials that may be effective in meeting the needs of struggling learners. The structure allows the team to see how well the student is responding before recommending a new intervention; for example, one that is more intense. Because staff members do not always know what supports and services are available, the tiered model provides a means for showcasing them. The tiered structure also enables staff members to note where there are gaps in service.

Interventions in an RTI pyramid should be based on research to the extent possible. It is important to ensure that interventions have efficacy (that is, the intervention actually does what it is intended to accomplish) and fidelity (the intervention is implemented as it

ASCD   117

was designed). For example, if an intervention is designed to be delivered for 14 days for 30 minutes, but is only implemented for 15 minutes, then the intervention may not be effective.

The RTI Leadership Planning Team will want to study a multitiered system of interventions so that members may begin building one for the school. To this end, team members will survey interventions and supports that are available in the school and identify any gaps (i.e., where there are student difficulties but no interventions to help them). Team members will organize the interventions and resources into a tiered model that can be shared with school staff, including the RTI Intervention Team.

PURPOSE OF THIS SECTION AND SUMMARY OF TOOLS

The purpose of this section is to provide the RTI Leadership Planning Team with information about interventions at Tier 2 and Tier 3. [*Note*: For information on Tier 1, see the section on core instruction.] The team will use this information to plan how they will organize various interventions and supports for use by the RTI Intervention Team. This section is composed of tools that will help the RTI Leadership Planning Team in

- Discussing and exploring academic and behavioral interventions currently in use in the school.
- Identifying gap services and supports that are needed to address student difficulties.
- Understanding how RTI fits with special education eligibility for learning disabilities.

The tools are as follows:

- **Organizing for Interventions.** The planning team will want to plan carefully for Interventions at Tier 2 and Tier 3 to ensure that they can be implemented efficiently and effectively. This tool provides a blueprint for how intervention assistance will be organized in the school.
- **Creating a Library of Interventions.** Most schools are already using a variety of interventions to address student needs. The planning team can use this tool to catalogue and discuss various interventions that have been used to address student challenges—academic, behavioral, or both.
- **Examining Research-Based Instructional Interventions at Tier 2 and Tier 3.** The planning team should review research-based academic interventions that can be used at Tier 2 and Tier 3. This tool provides a template for reviewing interventions.

- **Identifying Behavioral Interventions at Tier 2 and Tier 3.** The planning team should examine current school practices and determine whether they represent an effective continuum of behavioral supports and interventions for students in Tier 2 and Tier 3. This tool provides a template for reviewing behavioral interventions.

- **Building a Tiered Approach to Intervention: Inventorying Resources and Interventions.** The planning team might begin developing a draft pyramid of supports by inventorying all of the school and district resources currently available to students. The purpose of the tool is to provide a format for the team to compile supports.

- **Identifying Gap Services.** The planning team may find that after completing a draft pyramid of supports and services there are few or no supports or services for certain types of student challenges. The purpose of this tool is to provide an opportunity for the team to review the supports listed in the tiers in relation to student needs and to determine which tiers should be enhanced.

- **Tracking the Success of Interventions.** Some schools may want to track and compile the success of interventions that have been used with students in the school. This tool provides an opportunity to develop a database of interventions that have been implemented successfully.

- **Understanding How RTI Fits with Special Education Eligibility for Learning Disabilities.** The planning team members will want to consider how the specific learning disability eligibility determination may be integrated with the RTI framework that they are developing. The purpose of this tool is to provide a list of suggested steps for considering this component.

After completing these tools, the RTI Leadership Planning Team members should be able to plan the multitiered system of support. This draft plan should be used in Part 3, Section 1, "Putting It All Together: Developing the RTI Framework and Implementation Plan," when the team actually designs the RTI framework that will be presented to the school.

REFERENCES AND ADDITIONAL RESOURCES

Crimmins, D., Farrell, A. F., Smith, P. W., & Bailey, A. (2007). *Positive strategies for students with behavior problems.* Baltimore: Paul H. Brookes.

Duffy, H. (n. d.). *Meeting the needs of significantly struggling learners in high school: A look at approaches to tiered intervention.* Washington, DC: American Institutes for Research,

National High School Center. Retrieved April 9, 2010, http://www.betterhighschools.org/docs/NHSC_RTIBrief_08-02-07.pdf

Gersten, R., Beckmann, S., Clarke, B., Foegen, A., Marsh, L., Star, J. R., & Witzel, B. (2009). *Assisting students struggling with mathematics: Response to Intervention (RtI) for elementary and middle schools* (NCEE 2009-4060). Washington, DC: National Center for Education Evaluation and Regional Assistance, Institute of Education Sciences, U.S. Department of Education. Retrieved April 9, 2010, from http://ies.ed.gov/ncee/wwc/publications/practiceguides/

Gersten, R., Compton, D., Connor, C. M., Dimino, J., Santoro, L., Linan-Thompson, S., and Tilly, W. D. (2008). *Assisting students struggling with reading: Response to Intervention and multi-tier intervention for reading in the primary grades. A practice guide.* (NCEE 2009-4045). Washington, DC: National Center for Education Evaluation and Regional Assistance, Institute of Education Sciences, U.S. Department of Education. Retrieved April 9, 2010 from http://ies.ed.gov/ncee/wwc/

Kamil, M. L., Borman, G. D., Dole, J., Kral, C. C., Salinger, T., and Torgesen, J. (2008). *Improving adolescent literacy: Effective classroom and intervention practices: A practice guide* (NCEE #2008-4027). Washington, DC: National Center for Education Evaluation and Regional Assistance, Institute of Education Sciences, U.S. Department of Education. Retrieved April 9, 2010, from http://ies.ed.gov/ncee/wwc

Sitzmann, B. H., Hightree, B., & Moritz, L. (n.d.). *RtI intervention manual.* Retrieved April 9, 2010, from http://www.esu1.org/dept/sped/RTI/Documents/RtIManual.pdf

Stuart, S. K., & Rinaldi, C. (2009). A collaborative planning framework for teachers implementing tiered instruction. *TEACHING Exceptional Children, 42*(2), 52–57.

Understanding a Multitiered Response to Intervention Approach

Organizing for Intervention

PURPOSE

Interventions at Tier 2 and Tier 3 generally require careful planning. Although each intervention has its own set of requirements, there are some general considerations that the RTI Leadership Planning Team may want to consider to ensure that RTI interventions can be implemented efficiently and effectively in the school. Some of these considerations include the following:

- **Who will implement the intervention?** Most interventions at these tiers require a certain level of proficiency in implementing them. To ensure fidelity of treatment, some may require that educators receive special training. The RTI Leadership Planning Team members will want to consider what interventions are currently available and who has the capacity to deliver them. They also will want to make sure that there are sufficient numbers of intervention specialists to handle forecasted student needs in certain areas. When considering the role of specialists, the team should place an emphasis on how to unify various support services under the RTI umbrella.

- **How will groupings be handled?** Many Tier 2 and Tier 3 interventions are carried out in small groups. If an intervention is delivered by teachers in the general education classroom, then the team should determine teacher comfort and capacity for organizing instruction to accommodate small intervention groups. If a group is conducted outside of the general education classroom (e.g., tutoring groups), then the team should consider implications (e.g., location, what students will be missing, and so on).

- **How will interventions be scheduled?** Time must be scheduled explicitly for interventions; otherwise, there is a risk that the intervention will not be implemented on a regular basis. For example, if the intervention occurs within the general education classroom, teachers may need assistance in organizing the schedule (e.g., schedule the intervention group during a time when other students are at centers). Or, a coteacher or coach (e.g., reading coach, Title 1 teacher, etc.) may be assigned to assist with the intervention during a set time. A walk-to arrangement may be used in which students from several classes participate in a separate class at a scheduled time. At the middle school and secondary school levels, out-of-class interventions may be scheduled during elective periods. Or, in cases where there is block scheduling, a certain time during the block may be assigned for remediation, enrichment, or both. In cases where teachers are expected to collaborate with specialists and other colleagues, sufficient planning time must be made available.

- **How will data be utilized during the intervention?** Progress monitoring is an integral part of implementing interventions. The team should consider the feasibility of having teachers present the intervention as well as the data-tracking procedures. Teachers may vary in terms of their comfort and capacity for collecting, analyzing, and responding to data.

- **How do students move through the intervention system?** There should be an explicit process for placing students in intervention groups. The RTI Leadership Team will want to consider such things as the criteria for placing a student in the group (e.g., benchmark score on a skill), exit criteria, and criteria for moving a student between tiers. Care should be taken to ensure that students are not regrouped so frequently that it has a negative impact on the instructional program.

The purpose of this tool is to provide a blueprint for how intervention assistance will be organized in the school. It assumes that the RTI Leadership Planning Team is familiar with the types of interventions and resources that are available in the school.

HOW TO USE THIS TOOL

Discuss possible interventions that are available at Tier 2 and Tier 3. Identify those that are most likely to be utilized given student needs in the school. For each, complete the questions in the tool.

Decision point: The goal is for the RTI Leadership Planning Team to suggest a beginning infrastructure in which Tier 2 and Tier 3 interventions can be delivered. The team should determine if there is a feasible structure. If not, team members should make a plan for what is needed.

TIPS AND VARIATIONS

1. Talk with other schools about how they have organized Tier 2 and Tier 3 resources for suggestions, such as the following:

- English language arts classes are organized into a 90-minute block three days each week. At 55 minutes in, students who have not reached the benchmark on identified literacy skills walk to the group room to receive Tier 2 interventions.
- Grade level teachers combine their classes into a one-hour block. Students are paired in groups by skill deficits and receive instruction by one of the teachers or a reading specialist. Teachers monitor progress and revisit the groupings after four to six weeks.
- During the first semester, incoming 9th grade students who have not met benchmarks on identified skills are placed into an intervention course instead of an elective.

2. Discuss how the team will make sure that staff members understand that Tier 2 interventions are not a substitute for strong core instruction. Consider how the team will help classroom teachers understand that, in an RTI framework, they still maintain responsibility for student learning.

3. Review how students receive various intensive supports (e.g., speech/language services). What are the pros and cons of how those services are delivered? Are there aspects of delivery that might be helpful when planning RTI delivery? Can these services and supports be incorporated under an RTI umbrella?

Organizing for Intervention

Intervention: _____ **Tier 2** ____ **Tier 3** ____

Who will implement the intervention?
If groupings are used, how will they be organized?
How will the intervention be scheduled?
How will data be used during the intervention?
How do students move through the intervention system?
Can this intervention be delivered in a more intensified way if the student should require more assistance? If so, how will the intervention be organized (e.g., scheduled, delivered by, location, and so on)?

Understanding a Multitiered Response to Intervention Approach

 Creating a Library of Interventions

PURPOSE

RTI Leadership Planning Team members do not need to start from scratch when building a multitiered framework. There will probably be a number of interventions already in use from which they can draw. In some cases instructional staff may have participated in professional development focused on the interventions. The purpose of this tool is to provide an opportunity to catalogue and discuss various interventions that have been used to address student academic or behavioral challenges in the school.

HOW TO USE THIS TOOL

Identify several typical challenges—academic, behavioral, or both—that students in general or a subgroup of students in your school experience. Discuss the different interventions that are used currently in the school to address the challenge. For each intervention, complete the information in the form by identifying

- Resources that may be available (e.g., manuals, professional books, online courses, and so on) and the location (e.g., teachers' work room, counselor's office, and so on).
- Instructional and support staff who have expertise in using the intervention (e.g., have received professional development).
- Tips or notes about the intervention (e.g., more appropriate for beginning readers in 1st and 2nd grades).

Share a draft with instructional staff (e.g., in a meeting, in their professional learning community teams, etc.). Invite them to make additions and provide feedback.

Decision point: The RTI Leadership Planning Team should determine if the school has adequate resources to address student needs. If not, team members should develop a plan for obtaining additional resources.

TIPS AND VARIATIONS

1. Create a virtual intervention library on the school intranet. Post the tool on the school network. Use a blog to encourage instructional staff to comment on how they have used the intervention and the results they experienced.

2. Create a book of interventions for each major student challenge. Make them available in a convenient location. [*Note*: If your school uses a formal RTI referral form, consider referencing them on that form.]

3. Update the library periodically.

4. Engage instructional staff in generating ideas for the tool. For example, invite the entire staff to identify their top academic and behavioral concerns. Have small groups consider the various concerns and complete a first draft. Share drafts among the groups and invite feedback and additions.

Understanding a Multitiered Response to Intervention Approach

Creating a Library of Interventions

Student Challenge:_____

Intervention	Resources/Location	Staff Expertise	Tips for Use

Understanding a Multitiered Response to Intervention Approach

Examining Research-Based Academic Interventions at Tier 2 and Tier 3

PURPOSE

The RTI Leadership Planning Team should consider ways to address the academic skill deficits frequently exhibited by struggling learners. The purpose of this tool is to engage the planning team members in a process of examining and recommending interventions as well as considering many of the practical factors related to implementation. A key implementation factor that the team should consider is planning for targeted professional development. This plan will be essential in helping to ensure that staff members have a deep understanding of the interventions and receive such follow-up support as modeling, coaching, and guided practice to assist them in implementing interventions with fidelity.

HOW TO USE THIS TOOL

The RTI Leadership Planning Team should identify a particular curriculum area and component (e.g., reading comprehension, algebra, and so on) and plan to investigate potential interventions by, for example, reviewing published literature and websites. Prior to a designated meeting, each team member might identify two or three research-based interventions that seem promising based on the needs of the student population and complete a tool form to record information about each intervention. During a subsequent team meeting, team members might report on their recorded information and the chair could help guide the team in determining which practices seem to have the most potential for addressing the needs of their students. These identified practices could then be studied further by the entire team. Each team member might review information sources related to the identified interventions, for example. These interventions also might be shared with other selected staff members (e.g., grade level teams, subject area teams, and so on) for input, involvement, or both in the selection process.

Decision point: RTI Leadership Planning Team members should determine which research-based interventions and strategies could be used to help address the learning needs of their students who require academic interventions at Tiers 2 and 3.

Building Your School's Capacity to Implement RTI | Understanding RTI Components

Understanding a Multitiered Response to Intervention Approach | Examining Research-Based Academic Interventions at Tier 2 and Tier 3

Part 2

TIPS AND VARIATIONS

1. The RTI Leadership Planning Team could invite selected teachers to complete a tool form based on a research-based intervention or strategy with which they already are familiar and that could potentially impact student achievement if used by others on a systematic basis.

2. The planning team might extend this activity by discussing the next step in the identification process (e.g., introducing the intervention or strategy to selected teachers for feedback, observing the strategy in use at another school, providing professional development for those staff members who will use the strategy, and so on).

3. Rather than picking a curriculum area for investigation, the team might select a research-based intervention from the category of cognitive learning strategies. Cognitive learning strategies have been found to be effective in addressing specific skills when used systematically and with fidelity for students requiring instructional interventions at Tier 2 or Tier 3. The University of Nebraska at Lincoln has compiled information related to a significant number of cognitive strategies (www.unl.edu/csi). The What Works Clearinghouse established by the U.S. Department of Education through the Institute for Education Sciences (http://ies.ed.gov/ncee/wwc) might be another source for interventions and strategies.

Team members might also review some of the literature on cognitive learning strategies in a particular curriculum area such as mathematics, such as the following:

- Fuchs, L. S., Fuchs, D., Compton, D. L., Powell, S. R., Seethaler, P. M., Capizzi, A. M., Schatschneider, C., & Fletcher, J. M. (2006). The cognitive correlates of third-grade skill in arithmetic, algorithmic computation, and arithmetic word problems. *Journal of Educational Psychology*, *98*, 29–43.
- Kroesbergen, E. H., & Van Luit, J. E. H. (2003). Mathematics interventions for children with special needs: A meta-analysis. *Remedial and Special Education*, *24*, 97–114.
- Montague, M. (2007). Self-regulation and mathematics instruction. *Learning Disabilities Research and Practice*, *22*, 75–83.

Team members also might find it helpful to familiarize themselves with a general overview of cognitive strategies instruction by viewing the ASCD video-based staff development program, *Teaching Students with Learning Disabilities in the Regular Classroom.*

Examining Research-Based Academic Interventions at Tier 2 and Tier 3

Reviewer(s): _____ **Date:** _____

Intervention: _____ **Curriculum Area:** _____

Information Source(s): _____

Questions and Factors to Consider	Follow-up Questions and Notes
What is the specific purpose of the intervention?	
What are the targeted grade levels?	
What implementation features were employed while researching the strategy (e.g., frequency of instruction, time allocation, and group size)? What research features must be replicated within the school setting to ensure implementation of the intervention with fidelity?	
Which groups of students in the school might benefit from implementation of this intervention?	
What are the initial training requirements for instructors to implement the intervention(e.g., type, amount, training source, education and experience levels of staff, etc.)?	
What types of support will be needed to assist instructors in systematically implementing the intervention with fidelity, and at what level of frequency should they be provided (e.g., onsite coaching on a monthly basis)?	

What materials are needed to support intervention implementation? What are the potential costs and potential funding sources?	
Where is the intervention currently being used? What opportunities are there to observe the intervention and discuss student outcomes?	
In what ways is this intervention similar to or different from other interventions currently in use within the school?	
What planning would be needed to facilitate implementation of the intervention in general education instruction?	
Which staff might be potential candidates to implement the intervention following targeted professional development as needed?	
What types of commitments would be needed by administrative team members and other staff to support intervention implementation (e.g., financial commitment to support staff training, commitment to modify schedules to allocate necessary time for intervention instruction with students)?	

Recommendations for Follow-Up, Targeted Dates, and Individuals Responsible

Identifying Behavioral Interventions at Tier 2 and Tier 3

PURPOSE

Schools that employ schoolwide, multitiered approaches such as Positive Behavioral Interventions and Supports to address student behavior proactively generally expect Tier 1 efforts in the core instructional program to address the needs of 80 to 90 percent of students. Although these practices, also referred to as Primary Prevention, successfully meet the needs of the majority of students, schools can expect that some students will not respond and will need behavioral interventions at the secondary and tertiary levels of a multitiered model.

Secondary level interventions focus on 5 to 15 percent of the student population and may include targeted group or individual behavioral plans. Examples of interventions include: behavioral contracts, restitution, response cost, self-monitoring, social skill instruction, and counseling.

Five to ten percent of the student population may require tertiary level interventions comprising individual behavioral plans based on individual behavioral assessments. These assessments typically include observing and documenting information related to the antecedents and consequences of the problem behavior as well as the setting, time frame, frequency, and duration of the behavior. Using this type of assessment information, RTI Intervention Team members identify behavioral patterns (e.g., determining that the problem behavior occurs more frequently in unstructured settings) and plan an intervention to reduce inappropriate behaviors and replace them with appropriate ones.

Students who need behavioral interventions at either Tier 2 or Tier 3 often benefit from a written behavioral plan that the RTI Intervention Team develops. This plan includes such details as a specific research-based intervention and implementation time frame, a progress monitoring component, frequency of progress monitoring and the staff member responsible, timeline for observing the student, and timeline to review the behavioral plan and make changes as needed.

Building Your School's Capacity to Implement RTI | Understanding RTI Components

Understanding a Multitiered Response to Intervention Approach | Identifying Behavioral Interventions at Tier 2 and Tier 3

Part 2

The purpose of this tool is to help the RTI Leadership Planning Team examine current school practices and determine whether or not they represent an effective continuum of behavioral supports and interventions for students at Tier 2 and Tier 3.

HOW TO USE THIS TOOL

This tool provides a conversation starter to assist the RTI Leadership Planning in discussing questions, ideas, and recommendations for strengthening practices that address student behavior at Tier 2 and Tier 3. For each question, discuss the findings. One option is to answer as many of the questions as possible as a team. For those questions that cannot be readily answered, assign a team member to do further investigation.

Decision point: Decide whether the school currently has the capacity to conduct behavioral assessments, develop behavioral intervention plans as needed, and implement effective Tier 2 and Tier 3 behavioral interventions. Depending on these findings, the team may need to determine the next steps in building or expanding the school's capacity.

TIPS AND VARIATIONS

1. Designated team members might be asked to gather information prior to the discussion. For example, they might check with the central office, state department of education, or other schools for sample forms and other resources (e.g., training opportunities). They also might check the federally-funded website for Positive Behavior Intervention and Support (www.pbis.org), particularly sections related to secondary and tertiary interventions.
2. To establish a common frame of reference, the RTI Leadership Planning Team might request a briefing on behavioral assessments and behavioral intervention plans and review sample documents. The school psychologist or another staff member involved in these processes might be asked to provide the briefing.

Identifying Behavioral Interventions at Tier 2 and Tier 3

Questions	Findings
What types of data might be used to identify students who might require secondary or tertiary interventions (e.g., students who are repeatedly referred to the office based on office referral data)?	
Which staff members are trained to complete individual behavioral assessments? Are individual behavioral assessments currently completed as needed for selected students?	
Which staff members are involved in developing individual behavioral plans for selected students? Is there an established format for the plans to help facilitate consistent best practices throughout the school and to help ensure that plans are comprehensive? Are the plans based on the behavioral assessments?	
Are there procedures in place to help classroom teachers as needed with implementing established behavioral plans?	
How is the effectiveness of the plans assessed? Are behavioral data that would help with determining effectiveness collected for students as part of the plan? What procedures are in place to ensure that behavioral plans are modified as needed for individual students?	

Building Your School's Capacity to Implement RTI | Understanding RTI Components

Understanding a Multitiered Response to Intervention Approach | Identifying Behavioral Interventions at Tier 2 and Tier 3

Is there a need for targeted professional development to assist staff in developing and implementing secondary and tertiary behavioral interventions? If professional development is needed, what resources might be available to facilitate this? What type of follow-up support would help to reinforce the professional development and sustain best practices?	

Additional Ideas, Recommendations, Next Steps, and Individuals Responsible

Building a Tiered Approach to Intervention: Inventorying Resources and Interventions

PURPOSE

Most RTI frameworks organize interventions according to intensity of intervention and frequency of data collection. Typically, interventions are organized into a pyramid:

- The bottom tier (Tier 1) represents core instruction. All students receive instructional and behavioral support to achieve in the core curriculum.
- The middle tier (Tier 2) represents supports for students who require more asistance than is available in the core program. Students whose academic performance or behavior lags behind what is expected receive targeted interventions.
- The top tier (Tier 3) represents more individualized supports and services for students with significant challenges. Students who are unresponsive to research-based practices at the first two tiers receive intensive interventions.

The RTI Leadership Planning Team will develop a draft pyramid of supports. The first step is to inventory all of the resources currently available to students in the school and district. The purpose of this tool is to provide a format for the team to compile supports.

HOW TO USE THIS TOOL

List those supports that are currently in place, such as the following examples:

- Tier 1—Keeping in mind that in Tier 1 supports are available to all students, list those on which instructional staff members have received professional development.
- Tier 2—Consider any supports and services that students receive either in small groups or independently. Depending on the school philosophy and delivery model, these may be delivered in the general education classroom or in separate settings (e.g., tutoring, ninth grade academy, 30 minutes of additional instruction at least three to four times weekly with progress monitoring twice monthly, and so on).
- Tier 3—Review supports and services available in the district and school. These may be more intensive Tier 2 interventions (e.g., 18 weeks of 30-minute intervention sessions with progress monitoring twice weekly). These interventions also may be special education services, related services, mental health services, assignment in specialized

Building Your School's Capacity to Implement RTI | Understanding RTI Components

Understanding a Multitiered Response to Intervention Approach | Building a Tiered Approach to Intervention: Inventorying Resources and Interventions

curriculum, etc. Depending on the school philosophy and delivery model, these services may be delivered in the general education classroom or in separate settings.

For each support or service, note the type of student challenge that is addressed.

Decision point: Reflect on the draft pyramid of supports. Does it include all supports? Are some student challenges addressed more than others? Is this reasonable given the goals of the school?

TIPS AND VARIATIONS

1. Compile the supports into a graphic representation of a pyramid.
2. Review the list. Are some services used frequently? Are some used infrequently?
3. Discuss whether supports and services are research based. Are there sufficient opportunities for students to receive research-based interventions in each tier?
4. If the team cannot decide whether a particular intervention fits best at Tier 1, Tier 2, or Tier 3, keep it on a list for future deliberation. The goal here is to prepare a draft pyramid of supports.

Building a Tiered Approach to Intervention: Inventorying Resources and Interventions

Tier	Supports	Student Difficulty
Tier 1: Core Instruction		
Tier 2: Interventions		
Tier 3: Interventions		

Understanding a Multitiered Response to Intervention Approach

Identifying Gap Services

PURPOSE

After completing a draft pyramid of supports and services, it often becomes apparent that there are few or no supports or services for certain types of student challenges. The purpose of this tool is to provide an opportunity for the RTI Leadership Planning Team to review the supports listed in the tiers in relation to student needs and to determine which tiers should be enhanced.

HOW TO USE THIS TOOL

Make a list of the top 10 challenges that students experience in the core program. Review the results of the tool "Building a Tiered Approach to Intervention: Inventorying Resources and Interventions." Discuss whether there are sufficient strategies available for students with the particular challenges. Continue this process for Tier 2 and Tier 3 types of challenges.

Decision point: Decide if there are gaps in the current RTI tiered offerings. If so, identify the areas in which there are gaps. Share this information with the school administration. Keep in mind that an RTI approach assumes that student challenges can be addressed.

TIPS AND VARIATIONS

1. Restructure the tool to allow you to discuss other challenges (e.g., Top 20 challenges, Top 10 challenges in reading and Top 10 in math, Top 10 challenges for ninth grade students, and so on).
2. Review the RTI pyramid. Are some student challenges and supports better covered than others? Is there a need for this type of coverage? What is the basis for the coverage?
3. Do the gaps reflect insufficient attention to a particular subgroup of students? For example, have demographics changed, resulting in new students who differ in needs from other students?
4. Talk with experts in the various areas where gaps have been identified. Ask if there are research-based strategies that might be available.

Identifying Gap Services

Note: This tool uses the results of the tool "Building a Tiered Approach to Intervention: Inventorying Resources and Interventions" (page 136).

Tier 1

Student Challenges	Tier 1 Strategies	Suggested Strategies
1		
2		
3		
4		
5		
6		
7		
8		
9		
10		

Tier 2

Student Challenges	Tier 2 Strategies	Suggested Strategies
1		
2		
3		
4		
5		
6		
7		
8		
9		
10		

Tier 3

Student Challenges	Tier 3 Strategies	Suggested Strategies
1		
2		
3		
4		
5		
6		
7		
8		
9		
10		

Understanding a Multitiered Response to Intervention Approach

 # Tracking the Success of Interventions

PURPOSE

An issue that often arises when identifying research-based strategies and interventions concerns whether the characteristics of the researchers' subject groups match those of your own students. When subject group characteristics do not match those of your own students, the potential success rate may be reduced. In other words, the evidenced-based intervention may have been researched with students who are different than your students and, thus, may not yield the same results.

One approach to addressing this challenge is to track and compile the success of interventions that have been used with students in your school. In some cases, an intervention will be modified to fit the needs of your students. This information also can be tracked.

The purpose of this tool is to provide a template that the RTI Leadership Planning Team can use to develop a database of interventions that have been implemented successfully.

HOW TO USE THIS TOOL

Complete the tool for every intervention that is selected for a student. Add information to the form if the intervention is used in multiple cases. Complete the following steps:

- Describe the intervention.
- Describe the student's characteristics relative to the presenting problem. For example, is the student an English language learner? Is the student reading at grade level? Is the student motivated to improve?
- Describe the intended goal or result of the intervention.
- Report the dates of use.
- Summarize data that suggest progress.
- Describe modifications that may have been made to the intervention to better meet the student's needs.

Decision point: The RTI Leadership Planning Team should decide if it would be beneficial to track the success of interventions for the school's entire student population.

TIPS AND VARIATIONS

1. Create a virtual intervention library on the school intranet. Post the tool on the school network. Use a blog to encourage instructional staff to comment on how the intervention was used and what the outcomes were.

2. Review the information periodically. Discuss trends (e.g., the intervention tends to be more successful when presented in a small group rather than individually, students who have aggressive/acting out behaviors respond better when the intervention is paired with a behavioral contract, and so on).

3. Analyze the types of modifications that are being made. Determine if similar modifications are being made for various interventions (e.g., assessments are read rather than written).

Part 2

Tracking the Success of Interventions

Intervention: _____

Students	
Goal	
Date	
Data	
Modifications	
Notes	

Understanding How RTI Fits with Special Education Eligibility for Learning Disabilities

PURPOSE

For a number of years, there has been much concern about the over-identification of students with disabilities, particularly students with learning disabilities. There are many reasons. In some cases, the student is struggling and there are no other sources of support from special education. In other cases, student difficulties may result from lack of adequate instruction.

At the same time, concern has been raised about the Discrepancy Model, the identification process for specific learning disabilities, in which students must fail first before they can be evaluated to receive special education services. The 2004 reauthorization of the Individuals with Disabilities Education Improvement Act (IDEA) allows school districts to use an approach other the Discrepancy Model in determining eligibility for learning disabilities services. According to IDEA, in determining whether a student has a specific learning disability, the local education agency may use a process that determines if the student responds to a scientific, research-based intervention as part of evaluation procedures. Further, IDEA also provides that underachievement in a student suspected of having a specific learning disability is not due to lack of appropriate instruction. While the law stops short of defining the evaluation process to be used, it does point out that priority should be given to models that incorporate response to a research-based intervention.

While a typical RTI approach focuses on much more than simply special education eligibility, that purpose can be developed soundly within its framework. An RTI approach has the following advantages when building in the special education component:

- In an RTI framework all students are considered general education students and therefore can receive resources across all programs.
- Students receive effective core instruction, which should reduce the problem of over-identification. Further, research-based interventions are provided quickly, so that the student does not have to wait to fail before receiving help.

Building Your School's Capacity to Implement RTI | Understanding RTI Components

Understanding a Multitiered Response to Intervention Approach | Understanding How RTI Fits with Special Education Eligibility for Learning Disabilities

Part 2

- The use of screening data, data-based problem solving, and progress monitoring provides evidence of the student's difficulty, which may or may not be related to a disability.
- In many RTI frameworks, resources are organized in tiers that are available for all students. Each tier is defined by increasing measurement precision and intervention intensity. This organization helps deploy resources to students as they need them. Special education eligibility often is considered at the third tier.

The RTI Leadership Planning Team members will want to consider how the specific learning disability eligibility determination may be integrated with the RTI framework they are developing. The purpose of this tool is to provide a list of suggested steps for discussing this component.

HOW TO USE THIS TOOL

The first step is to determine if the school district has embraced using an alternative to the Discrepancy Model for determining eligibility for specific learning disability services. The RTI Leadership Planning Team may want to schedule a meeting with the school administrator, at which time it can be decided whether or not to proceed with discussions with central office special education personnel. One question to ask is if the state or the district (or both) has a policy regarding the use of something other than the Discrepancy Model for determining eligibility. For example, some states (e.g., Colorado, Connecticut, Rhode Island, West Virginia) prohibit using the Discrepancy Model.

If a meeting with special education personnel is planned, the questions in the tool may be helpful.

Decision point: The RTI Leadership Planning Team should determine if a special education component will be integrated into the RTI framework. If not, team members should consider how special education will be presented in the RTI framework.

TIPS AND VARIATIONS

1. One of the questions that arises is how does special education referral fit within an RTI framework. For example, does a student have to be referred to the RTI Intervention Team first, or can the student be referred directly for special education evaluation? How are related service personnel used within an RTI approach? These are

Building Your School's Capacity to Implement RTI | Understanding RTI Components

Understanding a Multitiered Response to Intervention Approach | Understanding How RTI Fits with Special Education Eligibility
for Learning Disabilities

questions that should be discussed in collaboration with central office special education personnel and administrators, as these usually are districtwide policy decisions.

2. Consider having select members of the RTI Leadership Planning Team form an ad hoc team with special education personnel to discuss specific issues related to implementing the RTI framework with students who are receiving special education services.

3. Refrain from debating the pros and cons of the Discrepancy Model. This is a policy issue for the district and state.

Understanding How RTI Fits with Special Education Eligibility for Learning Disabilities

QUESTIONS TO CONSIDER:

1. How does the district determine eligibility for students with suspected specific learning disabilities? Does it use a process that determines if the student responds to a scientific, research-based intervention as part of the evaluation procedures?

2. Discuss the philosophy underlying an RTI approach related to special education eligibility decisions. For example, the following conditions may make a case for student referral to special education:

   • Making insufficient progress with Tier 2 and Tier 3 interventions.

   • Continuing to perform well below his or her peers on identified standards.

   • Requiring significant resources that go beyond what can be effectively implemented as part of the general education program. [*Note*: This does not imply that special education services cannot be delivered within the general education program.]

3. Given the RTI framework being developed by the RTI Leadership Planning Team, do special education personnel perceive this as a possible framework for use when determining eligibility? If so, what components appear to be a good fit? What components would not be a good fit?

4. Are there specific special education requirements that must be in place in an RTI framework that incorporates special education? Are there legalities that must be addressed? What is the relationship between RTI and due process?

5. If special education personnel do not see the RTI framework as a good fit, how do they see special education as intersecting with the RTI framework? How should this be communicated to staff and families?

6. If students with IEPs receive Tier 2 and Tier 3 interventions, how should general educators and special educators collaborate?

7. What are the next steps? Who else should be included in this discussion?

SECTION 3 OVERVIEW: ESTABLISHING THE PROBLEM-SOLVING PROCESS AND RTI INTERVENTION TEAM

An essential component of an RTI framework is a problem-solving structure that defines who makes decisions about students and how those decisions are made. This structure is at the heart of RTI frameworks, because it is through the structure that intervention decisions are made for struggling students.

In most RTI frameworks, an RTI Intervention Team is created to accept requests for assistance from instructional staff and others (e.g., guidance counselors). Using a problem-solving process, team members discuss the request, review accompanying student data, identify the intervention(s), and develop the intervention plan that they subsequently will monitor and evaluate for effectiveness.

To plan effectively, the RTI Leadership Planning Team should be knowledgeable about the following components:

- **Problem-solving structure**. Most RTI frameworks suggest that an RTI Intervention Team be established. [*Note*: In some schools, multiple teams are formed.] The purpose of this team is to develop intervention plans for struggling students and to monitor the success of interventions. The RTI Intervention Team also may review screening data and make intervention recommendations as appropriate. The RTI Leadership Planning Team should consider how the RTI Intervention Team will function as well as make team membership suggestions.
- **Problem-solving approach**. Once the RTI Intervention Team has received a request for help—or after the team has reviewed screening data—members will engage in a problem-solving process. Most problem-solving processes involve identifying the problem, gathering additional data, developing an intervention plan, monitoring the plan, and deciding next steps.
- **Documentation**. Most RTI Intervention Teams use various forms throughout the problem-solving process to document progress. Forms may be prepared that address such issues as how to request RTI help for a student, meeting minutes, data analysis, parent notification, etc.
- **Logistics**. Before the RTI Intervention Team begins its work, certain logistics should be addressed, such as identifying meeting space, setting schedules, assigning roles (e.g., who will send out reminders, who will photocopy and distribute the request for assistance forms, etc.), setting agendas, etc.

PURPOSE OF THIS SECTION AND SUMMARY OF TOOLS

This section of the toolkit contains tools that the RTI Leadership Planning Team can use to establish a problem-solving structure for RTI work. Team members will work through the following topics:

- Forming an RTI Intervention Team, including discussing member characteristics and examining current school-based teams that might be reshaped for RTI work.
- Understanding RTI Intervention Team tasks and discussing procedures that may make those tasks more efficient and manageable.
- Establishing an approach to problem solving.

At the conclusion of this section, planning team members should be able to suggest a problem-solving process and set of procedures that can form the basis of the RTI framework.

The tools are as follows:

- **Considering RTI Intervention Team Tasks: Details, Details, Details.** The planning team can use this tool to review the kinds of process tasks that the RTI Intervention Team will need to address. This will help the planning team understand the types of skills intervention team members will need.
- **Forming the RTI Intervention Team: "Must-Have" Characteristics.** The planning team may use this tool to consider the types of skills and characteristics needed on an intervention team.
- **Reviewing Current School-Based Teams: Opportunities for RTI Expansion.** In some cases, the planning team may find that it is more efficient to restructure an existing school-based team for RTI work. This tool provides the planning team with an opportunity to assess current teaming structures with an eye toward expanding, modifying, or otherwise adapting them for RTI work.
- **Establishing a Problem-Solving Process.** To enhance effectiveness, the RTI Intervention Team can benefit from having a formal problem-solving process to use when discussing struggling students. The RTI Leadership Planning Team can use this tool to discuss such a process and create a flow chart to share with the RTI Intervention Team.
- **Creating a Request for Assistance Process.** For documentation purposes, an assistance request form or checklist should be developed. The planning team may use this tool to discuss the types of information that should be included in a request for assistance form.

- **Determining a Problem-Solving Model for Identifying Student Interventions at Tier 2 and Tier 3.** There are three ways that research-based interventions may be identified. This tool provides a guide for helping the planning team discuss which approach to take in crafting the RTI framework.

- **Looking at Data Sources to Document Student Difficulties.** The planning team may want to consider the types of data sources that can be used to support a teacher's request for assistance. The purpose of this tool is to provide an opportunity to discuss various assessments that may be used to gather data on student academic and behavioral challenges.

- **Developing the Intervention Planning Template.** One of the tasks facing the RTI Intervention Team is to develop intervention plans for struggling students. The RTI Leadership Planning Team can assist with this task by following the guidance in this tool.

- **Ensuring Fidelity of Implementation.** A major task facing the planning team is determining how to ensure that interventions will be implemented with fidelity. This tool is intended to serve as a catalyst in prompting planning efforts.

- **Determining Forms.** Most RTI Intervention Teams will use forms for various purposes. In some cases, the school district may require that certain forms be completed. The purpose of this tool is to provide a guide for the planning team in deciding what forms will be recommended and suggesting possible content.

- **Addressing Logistics.** There are certain logistics that must be addressed when establishing an RTI Intervention Team. The purpose of this tool is to provide a list of possible tasks that should be addressed prior to engaging the in student problem-solving activities.

- **Helping the RTI Intervention Team Troubleshoot Possible Challenges.** The planning team may use this tool as a conversation starter when planning for implementation. The ideas that emerge from this discussion may be integrated into the intervention team structure.

After completing the tools, the RTI Leadership Planning Team members should be able to address the problem-solving component of their RTI framework. This draft plan should be used in Part 3, Section 1, "Putting It All Together: Developing the RTI Framework and Implementation Plan," where team members actually design the RTI framework that will be presented to the school.

REFERENCES AND ADDITIONAL INFORMATION

Hamilton, L., Halverson, R., Jackson, S., Mandinach, E., Supovitz, J., & Wayman, J. (2009). *Using student achievement data to support instructional decision making* (NCEE 2009-4067). Washington, DC: National Center for Education Evaluation and Regional Assistance, Institute of Education Sciences, U.S. Department of Education. Retrieved April 9, 2010, from http://ies.ed.gov/ncee/wwc/publications/practiceguides/

Kovaleski, J. F., & Pedersen, J. (2008). Best practices in data analysis teaming. In A. Thomas & J. Grimes (Eds.), *Best practices in school psychology V* (pp. 115–130). Bethesda, MD: National Association of School Psychologists.

Kovaleski, J. F., Roble, M., & Agne, M. (n. d.). *The RTI data analysis teaming process.* Retrieved April 7, 2010, from www.rtinetwork.org/Essential/Assessment/Data-Based/ar/TeamProcess

Marchand-Martella, N. E., Ruby, S. F., & Martella, R. C. (2007). Intensifying reading instruction for students within a three-tier model: Standard protocol and problem-solving approaches within a response to intervention (RTI) system. *Teaching Exceptional Children PLUS, 3*(5).

Marston, D., Muyskens, P., Lau, M., & Canter, A. (2003). Problem-solving model for decision making with high-incidence disabilities: The Minneapolis experience. *Learning Disabilities Research & Practice, 18*(3), 187–200.

Marston, D., Reschly, A. L., Lau, M. Y., Muyskens, P., & Canter, A. (2007). Historical perspectives and current trends in problem solving. In D. Haager, J. Klinger, & S. Vaughn (Eds.), *Evidence-based reading practices in Response to Intervention* (1st ed., pp. 265–285). Baltimore: Paul H. Brookes.

Telzrow, C. F., McNamara, K., & Hollinger, C. L. (2000). Fidelity of problem-solving implementation and relationship to student performance. *School Psychology Review, 29,* 443–461.

VanDerHeyden, A. (n. d.) *Approaches to RTI.* Retrieved April 7, 2010, from www.rtinetwork.org/Learn/What/ar/ApproachesRTI

Part 2

Considering RTI Intervention Team Tasks: Details, Details, Details

PURPOSE

The RTI Intervention Team is charged with identifying the student problem, reviewing and gathering data as appropriate, designing an intervention plan, monitoring progress, and evaluating results. To enhance implementation of these tasks, the RTI Intervention Team may benefit from an operational guide. An operational guide sets forth the process by which tasks are executed. The guide can provide a clearly defined approach that may help team members stay focused as well as help new team members understand the process. Establishing procedures also may help to reduce the risk that certain steps in the process will not be implemented as they should. The purpose of this tool is to provide an opportunity for RTI Leadership Planning Team members to review the kinds of process tasks that the RTI Intervention Team will need to address.

HOW TO USE THIS TOOL

The list of tasks in this tool serves as a starting point for discussion. First, consider reviewing the entire list to get an overall sense of the tasks at hand. Then, discuss each task. Considerations might include:

- Keeping the process simple and doable.
- Defining the process steps.
- Suggesting how RTI Intervention Team members might take responsibility for executing the various steps.

Decision point: Decide if your guide is workable—that is, will it allow for an efficient and effective use of time and human resources? Also, decide if the process is doable, and discuss the types of supports an RTI Intervention Team may need in order to understand and execute these responsibilities.

Building Your School's Capacity to Implement RTI | Understanding RTI Components

Establishing the Problem-Solving Process and RTI Intervention Team | Considering RTI Intervention Team Tasks: Details, Details, Details

TIPS AND VARIATIONS

1. After discussion, consider using selected procedures in a role play scenario to evaluate how the process might work. Tape these role plays for use in future RTI Intervention Team professional development sessions.

2. Write up the process in a series of steps that can be presented to RTI Intervention Team members for feedback. Finalize a guide before rolling out the RTI initiative with staff.

Considering RTI Intervention Team Tasks: Details, Details, Details

The RTI Leadership Planning Team should ask how RTI Intervention Team members will perform the following tasks:

- Select interventions at Tier 1.

- Select instructional interventions that should be used with individual students receiving services at Tier 2 or Tier 3.

- Determine the frequency and duration (number of days per week, number of minutes per day, number of weeks) with which an intervention will be provided (e.g., individual instructor employs intensity designated for pre-established strategy, or a problem-solving team recommends particular intensity).

- Determine who will carry out the intervention for identified students.

- Observe instruction to assess whether or not research-based strategies are being implemented with fidelity.

- Assist instructors who are having difficulty implementing designated interventions with fidelity.

Building Your School's Capacity to Implement RTI | Understanding RTI Components

Establishing the Problem-Solving Process and RTI Intervention Team | Considering RTI Intervention Team Tasks:
Details, Details, Details

Part 2

- Review and interpret the progress monitoring data and identify, based on the data, whether or not instructional changes are indicated.

- Determine when the frequency and duration of a particular strategy should be modified.

- Determine when students should receive more intensive interventions at a higher tier.

- Determine when students should receive less intensive interventions.

- Determine where students will receive Tier 2 interventions (e.g., general education classroom, separate small group in a resource room, and so on).

- Decide how frequently the progress of students receiving Tier 1 and Tier 2 interventions will be assessed.

- Determine how frequently the progress of students receiving interventions at Tier 3 will be assessed.

- Determine how frequently meetings will be held to review the progress of students who are receiving interventions.

Forming the RTI Intervention Team: "Must-Have" Characteristics

PURPOSE

Once the problem-solving structure has been determined, the RTI Intervention Team(s) is developed. Teams may be configured in a variety of ways. The RTI Intervention Team—which is similar to a student support team or student assistance team—receives requests for assistance, reviews data, develops intervention plans, monitors progress, and analyzes results.

The purpose of this tool is to provide the RTI Leadership Planning Team with an opportunity to consider the types of skills and characteristics needed on an RTI Intervention Team.

HOW TO USE THIS TOOL

Review the characteristics in the tool. Consider how you will guarantee that the RTI Intervention Team includes individuals who have these skills, knowledge, and characteristics. Next to each item, discuss whether there are individuals in the school who have the particular attributes. In cases where instructional and support staff may not have particular attributes, discuss what kinds of supports would be needed to build capacity. If a particular individual or individuals are represented repeatedly, discuss ways to protect those individuals from being expected to assume too much responsibility.

Decision point: Decide if the school has the capacity to staff an RTI Intervention Team. If so, how will individuals be chosen to participate? If the school does not have the necessary capacity, suggest a capacity building plan.

TIPS AND VARIATIONS

1. Review the list of supports needed in relation to schoolwide professional development plans and or initiatives. Are there similarities? Could any of the initiatives be expanded to include attention to the RTI attributes?

Building Your School's Capacity to Implement RTI | Understanding RTI Components

Establishing the Problem-Solving Process and RTI Intervention Team | Forming the RTI Intervention Team:
"Must-Have" Characteristics

Part 2

2. Investigate whether there are sources of professional development support available to the school. Look for possible opportunities available from district initiatives, regional resources centers, statewide initiatives, universities, and other sources.

3. If using grade level teams for RTI work, consider how you might deploy expertise on particular topics (e.g., progress monitoring). Consider strategies for engaging instructional staff with particular knowledge and skills in activities to build the capacity of colleagues who do not have these skill sets.

Forming the RTI Intervention Team: "Must-Have" Characteristics

What skills, characteristics, and experiences do you consider to be most important among RTI school leadership team members? The following knowledge, skills, and characteristics have often been referenced as essential for a well-functioning team.

All team members:	Available:	Support needed:
Communication skills		
Collaboration skills		
Belief that all students can learn		
Data-based problem-solving skills		
Planning skills		
Other		

Establishing the Problem-Solving Process and RTI Intervention Team | Forming the RTI Intervention Team: "Must-Have" Characteristics

Represented on the team:	Available:	Support Needed:
Progress monitoring		
Differentiated instruction		
Formative assessment		
Behavioral management		
Instructional and assistive technology		
Research-based interventions		
Implementing research-based interventions with fidelity		
Leadership		
Developing professional skills		
Other		

Reviewing Current School-Based Teams: Opportunities for RTI Expansion

PURPOSE

Many schools use a team structure to implement RTI. The RTI Intervention Team is composed of instructional staff, administrators, and sometimes parents in cases where their child is being discussed. In most cases, schools will not have the resources to hire a new team of professionals for RTI work. Rather, they will rely on the expertise available within their school community.

The RTI Leadership Planning Team may find it useful to consider problem-solving teams that are currently in place to determine if they could be modified or incorporated into an RTI Intervention Team. Consider these examples:

- **Child Study Team**. Many schools have a formal Child Study Teams that reviews information about students who have been referred for special education evaluation. Can this team be restructured with an RTI focus?
- **Professional Learning Communities**. Many schools have implemented Professional Learning Communities. Can the focus expand to include RTI problem-solving activities? Or, can a Professional Learning Community be established schoolwide to implement the RTI process?
- **Grade level or subject area teams**. Many schools afford teachers release time to meet in grade level or subject area teams. Can RTI practices be included as part of such team meetings?
- **Student Support Team**. Some schools use Student Support Teams—which also may be called Teacher Assistance Teams—to solve student difficulties in the core curriculum. While such teams may eventually suggest special education referral for a student, they are not what traditionally are called prereferral teams. Rather, they typically are comprised of general education teachers, administrators, and support staff who respond to requests for help from classroom teachers. In some schools, these teams use data, develop intervention plans, and track progress. These teams may be adapted to incorporate the tenets of an RTI approach.

Building Your School's Capacity to Implement RTI | Understanding RTI Components

Establishing the Problem-Solving Process and RTI Intervention Team | Reviewing Current School-Based Teams:
Opportunities for RTI Expansion

Part 2

The purpose of this tool is to provide an opportunity to assess current teaming structures with an eye toward expanding, modifying, or otherwise adapting them for RTI work.

HOW TO USE THIS TOOL

The tool is designed as a conversation starter that the RTI Leadership Planning Team can use when considering how to establish the RTI Intervention Team structure. Suggested steps for using the tool are as follows:

- Make a list of current teams in the school that, as part of their purpose, address the needs of struggling students.
- For each team, consider any commonalities with RTI components. For example, does the team use data for decision making? What type of data? Does the team monitor student progress?
- Identify individuals on each team who have expertise in RTI components.
- Discuss what it would take to expand the team to incorporate the RTI component.

Decision point: At the end of the discussion decide if one of the school's current team structures may be an option for considering RTI work. If not, determine the next steps for considering a new team structure.

TIPS AND VARIATIONS

1. Visit with teams. Ask them to describe their operations. Ask them to comment on which components are strong and which ones could benefit from additional support. Encourage them to discuss their perceptions of what they might need to embrace certain RTI components (e.g., extend meeting time to accommodate RTI tasks, receive training in progress monitoring, and so on).
2. Consider which teams might be reconfigured and discuss any political ramifications.
3. Make a master list of individuals with expertise relevant to RTI components. Talk with these individuals about how they integrate (or might integrate) their expertise into current teams.

Reviewing Current School-Based Teams: Opportunities for RTI Expansion

Current Team: _____

Date of Team Review: _____

RTI Elements	Similarities/Overlaps with Current Team	Expertise on the Team
Universal screening		
Data-based problem solving		
Focus on enhancing effective core instruction		
Focus on providing interventions to students who are struggling in the core program		
Progress monitoring		
Professional development		
Suggestions for Expansion of Current Team Responsibilities		
Recommendations, Next Steps, and Individuals Responsible		

Establishing a Problem-Solving Process

PURPOSE

Effective problem solving is a major component of RTI. The RTI Leadership Planning Team will want to carefully establish a problem-solving process that the RTI Intervention Team can use.

Typically, the general education classroom teacher—or other concerned individual (e.g., guidance counselor, parent, administrator, etc.,)—consults with the intervention team regarding the difficulties a student is experiencing, whether academic, behavioral, or both. The team considers the needs of the student and develops an intervention plan for the student.

After receiving a request for help for a student—or in cases where the team considers universal screening data to identify students who are struggling—the intervention team typically undertakes a process in which they:

- Review student data and define the problem.
- Plan the intervention by determining research-based interventions that go beyond core instruction.
- Design a plan for assessing the effectiveness of the intervention at designated time periods. Include resources and supports necessary for implementing the plan.
- Implement and monitor the plan.
- Adjust the intervention as needed (e.g., change the intervention, change the frequency with which the intervention is provided, and so on).

The purpose of this tool is to provide the RTI Leadership Planning Team with an opportunity to create a flow chart for the RTI Intervention team to use when solving problems.

HOW TO USE THIS TOOL

The RTI Leadership Planning Team should decide on the stages in the formal problem-solving process that the RTI Intervention Team will use. This process defines how the team operates as well as communicates to others what to expect. Flowcharts are graphic representations of a process and can help provide a solid depiction of a process. The planning team should first discuss the typical stages of problem solving and settle on a flowchart that seems reasonable for their school and then create it.

Decision point: The planning team should determine if the proposed problem-solving approach is efficient (i.e., not burdensome). Team members should ensure that all aspects of the RTI approach have been addressed in the process and that the flowchart communicates the process to others.

TIPS AND VARIATIONS

1. Create a second flowchart that includes references to the forms that are required at each stage.

2. Share the flowchart with others (e.g., teachers, administrators, parents, and so on). Ask for feedback regarding clarity and comprehensiveness. Make modifications as needed.

3. Develop a chart that identifies team responsibilities for each stage in the process. Also determine how the RTI Intervention Team will monitor completion of each stage. Note what skills are needed for each stage.

4. Use the flowcharts when presenting information to school staff members and parents.

5. Check with other teams in the school about the processes they use to solve problems. Compare and contrast.

Establishing a Problem-Solving Process

Once the team has received a request for help—or after the team has reviewed screening data—members will engage in a problem-solving process. Most problem-solving processes involve identifying the problem, gathering additional data, developing an intervention plan, monitoring the plan, and deciding next steps. Draw a flowchart that shows the problem-solving cycle. Consider including the following points:

- Identifiers for each stage of the cycle.
- Amount of time, as appropriate (e.g., the intervention will be implemented with progress monitoring for six weeks; progress monitoring will occur weekly; and so on).
- Decision points.
- Points in the cycle at which certain people, such as parents, are notified.

Creating a Request for Assistance Form

PURPOSE

How will instructional staff request assistance from the RTI Intervention Team? Can others—such as special service personnel, parents, and students as appropriate—request assistance? For documentation purposes, an assistance request form or checklist should be developed. The purpose of this tool is to provide the RTI Leadership Planning Team with an opportunity to discuss the types of information that should be included on a request form.

HOW TO USE THIS TOOL

There are different types of information that the planning team may consider including as part of the request form. Examples are found in the tool. Before developing the actual form, discuss what information is necessary. Keep in mind that there should be a balance between having enough information versus overwhelming the person who is requesting help. Always consider whether the information is essential.

Decision point: Once you have decided on the information to be included, create a draft that shows how the information will be presented. Consider such things as readability, space, ease of use, and so on. Keep in mind presentation techniques:

- Boxes to be checked (e.g., yes or no).
- Checklists.
- Space for descriptions.

TIPS AND VARIATIONS

1. Make sure not to request information that may violate student confidentiality.
2. Review other request and referral forms that the school and district currently use. Are there elements that could be incorporated into the RTI form? Ask individuals who have used these other forms to share their opinions about them (e.g., what they like, do not like, would change, and so on.).

3. Talk with individuals in the school and district who have developed forms. Ask them to share tips (e.g., usability, length, and so on). Find out if there are design templates you might consider adopting for the RTI form.

Creating the Request for Assistance Form

For the following types of information, decide what you will include on the Request for RTI Assistance Form. Also, begin to think about how you might present the information (e.g., checklist, box, other design elements).

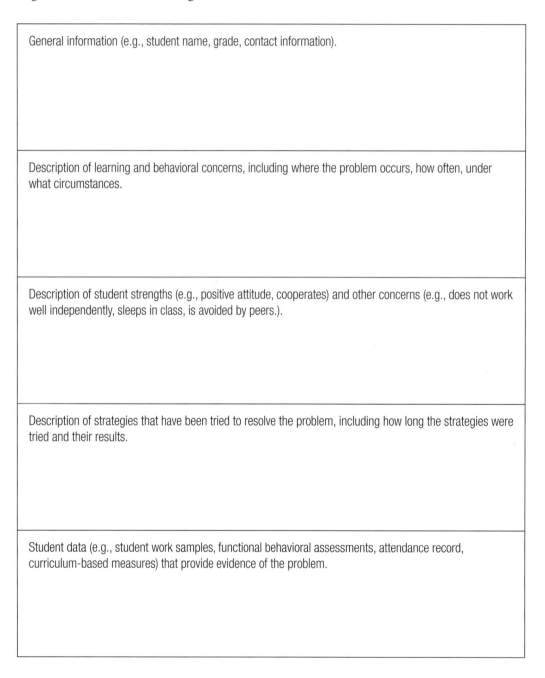

General information (e.g., student name, grade, contact information).

Description of learning and behavioral concerns, including where the problem occurs, how often, under what circumstances.

Description of student strengths (e.g., positive attitude, cooperates) and other concerns (e.g., does not work well independently, sleeps in class, is avoided by peers.).

Description of strategies that have been tried to resolve the problem, including how long the strategies were tried and their results.

Student data (e.g., student work samples, functional behavioral assessments, attendance record, curriculum-based measures) that provide evidence of the problem.

Establishing the Problem-Solving Process and RTI Intervention Team

Determining a Problem-Solving Model for Identifying Student Interventions at Tier 2 and Tier 3

PURPOSE

During implementation of an RTI framework, the RTI Intervention Team typically develops intervention plans for struggling learners. RTI frameworks may provide a standard problem-solving process for this purpose. [*Note*: See the related tool called "Establishing a Problem-Solving Process" on page 165 to help with that component.] In some RTI frameworks, an initial step in developing this problem-solving process is for the RTI Leadership Planning Team to identify an approach that team members will use for determining interventions. Three models that are frequently discussed in the literature are as follows:

- **Standard Protocol Model**. Interventions at Tier 2 and Tier 3 include research-based strategies and instructional materials that have been identified by the central office or a designated school team based on the most common anticipated needs of students in the school. There also may be a designated time period for implementing the intervention and an established system for assessing student progress toward the learning goal at regular intervals. The use of a set range of strategies can result in less variation among instructors and can thereby help to foster instructional quality or fidelity; as a result, it is often favored by researchers. The use of pre-established strategies also can help with planning and managing the professional development needed for staff to learn the strategies. An issue with this model is that the preselected interventions are based on the needs of the majority of students and do not include a feature to address the needs of students who may learn differently or who may be unresponsive to the pre-established interventions.

- **Problem-Solving Model**. The RTI Intervention Team identifies or develops strategies based on the specific needs of individual students. The team recommends these strategies for implementation by designated instructors. This model is sometimes preferred in schools due to the flexibility of the interventions, the attention to the individual needs of students, and the opportunity to use staff expertise. Issues with this model relate to the dependency on strong and positive collaboration between and among team members, the potential need for continuous staff training in interventions and problem solving, and the difficulty of interpreting and summarizing some of the progress data in view of the variability of the interventions and duration.

Part 2

Building Your School's Capacity to Implement RTI | Understanding RTI Components

Establishing the Problem-Solving Process and RTI Intervention Team | Determining a Problem-Solving Model for Identifying
Student Interventions at Tier 2 and Tier 3

- **Combined or Mixed Model**. The combined or mixed model incorporates both the standard protocol model and the problem-solving model. The standard protocol model might be used to address common academic problems such as reading comprehension. The problem-solving model might be used to address the needs of students with behavior problems. Effective use of the mixed model can result in efficient student access to established interventions and greater fidelity of instructor implementation given a limited range of interventions. In addition, the combined model allows for the development of interventions for those students who have different needs.

The purpose of this tool is to provide an illustration of some of the features common to the models, along with a corresponding set of questions for the RTI Leadership Planning Team to discuss as they decide how research-based interventions will be identified for Tier 2 and Tier 3. Team members may find that a particular model seems viable for Year One of implementation and may choose to revisit the decision in subsequent years.

HOW TO USE THIS TOOL

During a planning team meeting, a designated facilitator or meeting chair might facilitate a review and discussion of the individual questions posed in each section to begin generating responses and identifying additional information or actions needed prior to finalizing responses.

Decision point: Upon conclusion of the discussion, the team should reach consensus in selecting an RTI decision-making model to present to the RTI Intervention Team and subsequently to the faculty as a whole.

TIPS AND VARIATIONS

1. Identify other implementation factors related to decision-making models and add them to the tool.
2. Designate a planning team member to investigate how decision-making models are implemented at other selected sites prior to the meeting.
3. Present the three decision-making models to designated teams (e.g., grade level teams) and collect feedback. Consider this feedback as tool questions are pondered.

Determining a Problem-Solving Model for Identifying Student Interventions at Tier 2 and Tier 3

This tool provides an example of how selected features might align with each decision-making model and offers some questions to guide discussion.

Features	Standard Protocol Model	Problem-Solving Model	Combined or Mixed Model	Discussion Questions
Interventions	Standard interventions are pre-established by the central office or school team to address the most common student needs anticipated within specific content areas.	Interventions are developed or identified as needed by an intervention or problem-solving team for individual students; interventions may vary from one student to another.	Interventions are pre-established for selected content areas and developed as needed by a designated team in other areas (e.g., behavior).	• What guidance has been provided by central office regarding a continuum of interventions or tiered interventions? • What are the perceived levels of expertise and comfort among the staff with implementing a pre-established set of standard interventions or with implementing a broad range of interventions that are identified as needed? • How experienced and skilled are staff members, overall, in independently identifying and using research-based strategies to intervene with struggling learners needing support at Tier 2 and Tier 3?

Features	Standard Protocol Model	Problem-Solving Model	Combined or Mixed Model	Discussion Questions
Intensity of Intervention (e.g. frequency, amount of time, duration)	The intensity of interventions is predetermined (e.g., 10-week sessions) and typically corresponds with the intensity identified in the research literature.	Intensity is recommended by the RTI Intervention Team as intervention is identified; intensity may vary depending upon student and team recommendation.	Intensity of academic interventions is the same as in standard protocol; intensity of behavior interventions might vary depending upon student needs and team recommendations.	• What are perceived staff readiness and comfort levels with prescribed levels of intensity based on designated interventions or with varying intensity levels consistent with intervention team recommendations?
Collaboration	A designated school team and central office collaborate to identify menu of pre-established, research-based interventions and materials. The RTI Intervention Team might collaborate as needed to help match a standard intervention to a student need; however, instructional decisions are more often made by the staff member implementing the standard intervention.	A designated RTI Intervention Team collaborates in developing or selecting interventions as the individual needs of struggling learners are identified.	A school team and/or central office collaborates in identifying some standard interventions; a designated school team collaborates in developing others as needed.	• What is the perceived readiness of potential intervention or problem solving team members to collaborate on developing or identifying interventions for students and recommending levels of intensity?

Establishing the Problem-Solving Process and RTI Intervention Team | Determining a Problem-Solving Model for Identifying Student Interventions at Tier 2 and Tier 3

Features	Standard Protocol Model	Problem-Solving Model	Combined or Mixed Model	Discussion Questions
Staff Meeting Time	Initial meeting time is necessary to identify menu of research-based interventions and materials; periodic meetings may be held (for example, on a semester basis) to review the menu of instructional interventions and expand if needed. Meetings should be held as needed if there are questions about matching pre-selected interventions to identified student needs; however, the instructor would typically make the decision using the standard list of interventions.	Regularly scheduled standing meetings are needed by the RTI Intervention Team to identify and develop interventions and to consider needs of individual students.	Same as standard protocol model for academic interventions; standing meetings held to identify and develop behavior interventions for certain students.	• How might the RTI Intervention Team arrange meeting time? • In considering the amount of meeting time that might be needed for each decision-making model, is there a particular model that seems more feasible to implement given the team's current stage of development and practice and given their other responsibilities?
Professional Development Needed for Staff	Staff members are trained on a set range of pre-established interventions and curriculum materials in anticipation of student needs.	Training is needed on a variety of interventions and curriculum materials as they are identified or developed for individual students.	Same as standard protocol for academic interventions; same as problem-solving model for behavior interventions.	• Given the current professional development needs of the staff in the area of interventions and given the current stage of RTI implementation, which decision-making model might be most feasible?

Part 2

Building Your School's Capacity to Implement RTI | Understanding RTI Components

Establishing the Problem-Solving Process and RTI Intervention Team | Determining a Problem-Solving Model for Identifying
Student Interventions at Tier 2 and Tier 3

Recommendations for Identifying Student Interventions at Tier 2 and Tier 3

___ Implement a Standard Protocol Decision-Making Model
___ Implement a Problem-Solving Model
___ Implement a Combined or Mixed Model

Rationale

Next Steps and Individuals Responsible

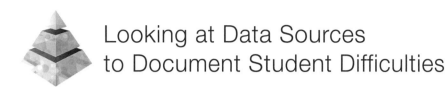

Looking at Data Sources to Document Student Difficulties

PURPOSE

Data-based problem solving is a cornerstone of RTI. When requesting assistance for a student or group of students, teachers should provide the RTI Intervention Team with sufficient data to understand the problem. RTI Intervention Team members are expected to analyze a wide range of data when developing intervention plans.

The RTI Leadership Planning Team may want to consider the types of data sources that can be used to support a teacher's Request for Assistance. The purpose of this tool is to provide an opportunity to discuss various assessments that may be used to gather data on student challenges, whether academic, behavioral, or both.

HOW TO USE THIS TOOL

Discuss each type of assessment on the tool. For each, identify the following:

- Individuals who have expertise in gathering data.
- Individuals who have expertise in analyzing data from each type of assessment.
- How assessments currently are used in the school for decision making.
- Identify assessment tools that require professional development.

Decision point: The planning team should identify those assessment tools that are being used and those that are used infrequently or not used at all. In cases where the assessment tools are not being used, determine the need for professional development on using different assessment tools for decision making. Make a plan for helping instructional staff develop adequate knowledge and skills.

TIPS AND VARIATIONS

1. Prepare an assessment guide for the RTI Intervention Team that includes definitions, purposes, and samples of each type of assessment. Include tips on how to analyze the data.

Part 2

Building Your School's Capacity to Implement RTI | Understanding RTI Components

Establishing the Problem-Solving Process and RTI Intervention Team | Looking at Data Sources to Document Student Difficulties

2. Create a virtual library of classroom-based assessments on the school intranet. Use a blog to encourage instructional staff to comment on how they use the assessments for data-based decision making.

3. Ask grade level teams to share the different classroom assessments they use. Encourage them to use similar assessments across classrooms.

Looking at Data Sources
to Document Student Difficulties

Types of Assessments	Currently in Use? How?	Expertise	Professional Development Needed
Classroom work samples			
Classroom observation			
Instructional assessments			
Curriculum-based measures			
Teacher rating scales			
Parent rating scales			
Student rating scales			
Student self-monitoring charts			
Behavior logs			
Report cards			
Attendance records			
Standardized test results			
Screening results			
Other			

Developing the Intervention Planning Template

PURPOSE

When a student requires more support than is available in the classroom, the RTI Intervention Team will develop an intervention plan. This plan is written and contains documentation of the student's problem and an analysis of the data documenting the problem. The intervention plan also includes the following information:

- Description of the intervention, including measurable outcomes.
- Logistics, including duration, schedule, and setting in which the intervention will be implemented.
- Individuals who are responsible for the implementing the intervention.
- Description of how fidelity will be monitored.
- Description of how progress will be monitored, including a schedule.
- Description of how adjustments will be made, as needed (e.g., under what conditions the intervention might be terminated).
- Resources that will be made available to the student, including who will receive each resource, for how long, and where.

The purpose of this tool is to provide the RTI Leadership Planning Team with an opportunity to develop a prototype intervention plan.

HOW TO USE THIS TOOL

Review the types of components that are typically in an intervention plan. Decide which components will be included. Develop a prototype intervention plan template.

Decision point: The RTI Leadership Planning Team should decide whether the intervention plan provides sufficient guidance for implementing an intervention.

TIPS AND VARIATIONS

1. Make sure the template is easy to use. Ask individuals on existing school teams to review and offer feedback.

2. Determine the type of professional development that RTI Intervention Team members may need to use the template. As part of this activity, make a list of individuals who have these capabilities who might be willing to serve as coaches.

3. Conduct a mock intervention team meeting for a student using the template. Assign one or two people to observe the role play for ease of use, how useful different items were to team planning, and the amount of time needed to complete the process.

4. Ask someone skilled in creating forms to prepare the intervention plan template as it might look in its final format.

Developing the Intervention Planning Template

1. List the components that should be included to document a student's problem. For each, indicate how the information might be presented (e.g., checklist, fill in the blank, check a box, and so on).

2. List the components that should be included to document an intervention. For each, indicate how the information might be presented (e.g., checklist, fill in the blank, check a box).

3. Develop a prototype intervention plan.

Ensuring Fidelity of Implementation

PURPOSE

One of the most challenging aspects that the RTI Leadership Planning Team will undertake in building an RTI framework is ensuring *fidelity of implementation*—a term that often is used to refer to delivering instruction in the way in which it was designed to be delivered.

Here's the challenge. After reviewing student data and identifying the problem, the RTI Intervention Team will select an intervention—preferably research based—to help the student. Team members will need to be sensitive to two potential areas of concern:

- Selecting an intervention that has a high probability of success. If the intervention does not match the problem, then the student may not progress because of the intervention, not because of some innate problem.
- Ensuring that the intervention is delivered to the student as it was intended. If the intervention is not presented appropriately, then lack of progress may not be related to the student's needs.

RTI Intervention Team members should know whether or not an intervention is being implemented as designed to ensure that, if the intervention is unsuccessful with a student, appropriate action can be taken to improve delivery rather than abandoning the intervention altogether. Such knowledge also helps team members understand that unresponsiveness to the intervention may be a result of poor delivery and not something innately problematic with the student.

Further, if it becomes necessary to consider special education eligibility, teams must be able to determine that the student has received appropriate general education instruction. In fact, IDEA (2004) states that a child shall not be determined to be a child with a disability if the determinant factor is lack of appropriate instruction in reading, including the essential components of reading, or lack of instruction in math.

When initiatives are adopted without fidelity to essential program design features, results may not turn out as expected. RTI Intervention Teams also should consider fidelity when implementing other components of RTI, including universal screening, progress monitoring, and decision-making protocols.

The RTI Leadership Planning Team should be cognizant of some of the challenges that might interfere with fidelity. Consider these examples:

- The more complex the intervention, the more difficult it may be to implement. The more difficult it is to implement, the higher the probability that fidelity might be compromised.

- Typically, research-based interventions have been developed by researchers who control for implementation. Sometimes the intervention may have been researched in a lab setting, or delivered by nonteaching staff (e.g., university assistants, researchers, etc.). Also, some interventions may have been implemented with only a few subject groups (e.g., students in the fourth grade with learning disabilities). A particular approach may not exactly fit a particular student in terms of research to support its usage. Or, teachers may not have received sufficient training in the strategy to implement it with fidelity. Thus, a particular intervention may have a strong research base, even though fidelity of implementation may be difficult to achieve.

This tool is intended to serve as a catalyst in prompting the planning team to consider fidelity of implementation.

HOW TO USE THIS TOOL

The planning team should use this tool to guide discussion of topics related to implementing the components of RTI with fidelity.

Decision point: At the end of the discussion, team members should decide what practices can be established that will help to achieve implementation with fidelity and identify those areas where more time and input are needed.

TIPS AND VARIATIONS

1. Talk with other schools about how they are ensuring fidelity of implementation of the RTI components, how they are documenting their efforts, and how they have assigned roles and responsibilities to different staff members in the process.

2. Provide selected parts of this tool to designated teams and request their assistance in planning for fidelity of implementation. For example, a designated grade level team might focus on the content area of reading and decide to develop observation or self-assessment checklists related to the implementation of one specific intervention.

3. As the RTI components are developed, consider fidelity of implementation as it relates to a particular component. For example, as teams are identifying potential interventions, ask teams to generate recommendations for facilitating fidelity of implementation for that particular intervention.

4. Discuss existing practices that can be modified to include a focus on fidelity of implementation (e.g., instructional walk-throughs, feedback provided by mentor teachers or peer coaches).

REFERENCES AND ADDITIONAL RESOURCES

Gresham, F. M., MacMillan, D. L., Beebe-Frankenberger, M. E., & Bocian, K. M. (2000). Treatment integrity in learning disabilities intervention research: Do we really know how treatments are implemented? *Learning Disabilities Research & Practice, 15*(4),198–205.

Individuals with Disabilities Education Improvement Act of 2004 (Public Law 108–446).

Johnson, E., Mellard, D. F., Fuchs, D., & McKnight, M. A. (2006). *Responsiveness to intervention (RTI): How to do it.* Lawrence, KS: National Research Center on Learning Disabilities.

Kovaleski, J. F., Gickling, E. E., & Morrow, H. (1999). High versus low implementation of instructional support teams: A case for maintaining program fidelity. *Remedial and Special Education, 20*, 170–183.

Ensuring Fidelity of Implementation

Questions and Discussion Points	Notes and Ideas
Current Practices	
How does the school currently address issues of fidelity in instruction? How are instructional staff members prepared to embrace fidelity issues? What supports are in place to encourage fidelity of instruction in the school?	
Use of Staff	
Which staff members are qualified or could become qualified to conduct instructional observations of interventions and provide feedback on fidelity (e.g., mentor teachers, teachers with National Board Certification, school psychologists, etc.)?	
What scheduling and role changes might be necessary in order for staff to conduct instructional observations related to fidelity of implementation?	
Which staff members might help to create checklists related to the critical features of specific instructional interventions?	
Which staff members could be used to provide fidelity of implementation feedback related to universal screening and progress monitoring (e.g., school psychologists)?	
What scheduling and role changes might be necessary in order for staff to conduct screening and progress monitoring observations and review data related to fidelity of implementation?	
Which staff members might help to create fidelity checklists related to universal screening and progress monitoring?	

Professional Development	
What initial and follow-up professional development will be needed for staff members to conduct observations of instructional interventions and provide feedback on fidelity of implementation?	
Staff Input	
How can staff be involved in planning strategies to support fidelity of implementation so that it becomes non-threatening and is viewed as part of a positive school culture?	
What approaches can be used to help staff members accept and use the observational feedback related to fidelity of implementation?	
Targeted Areas and Frequency	
What areas should be targeted initially for a focus on implementation with fidelity (e.g., reading, math, universal screening, progress monitoring, etc.)?	
How frequently will observations or other practices to assess fidelity of implementation and provide meaningful and specific feedback be conducted?	
Documentation	
How will observations or other practices related to fidelity of implementation be documented, and who will receive and maintain the documentation?	
Self-Assessment	
What strategies may be used to help staff members assess their own practices related to fidelity of implementation (e.g., watching video-taped lessons, reviewing student work samples with peer colleagues, and obtaining feedback related to implementation of interventions or progress monitoring with fidelity)?	

What ongoing strategies can be used by the RTI Leadership Planning Team to assess schoolwide practices related to fidelity of implementation and to make changes as needed?	
Recommendations, Decisions, Follow-Up Needed and Dates, and Individuals Responsible	

Developing Forms

PURPOSE

Most RTI Intervention Teams will use forms for various purposes. In some cases, the school district may require that certain forms be completed. The purpose of this tool is to provide a guide for the RTI Leadership Planning Team members in deciding what forms they will recommend and in suggesting possible content.

HOW TO USE THIS TOOL

Before beginning this activity, check with the administration to determine if there are required forms. For example, the district may require that all contacts with parents be documented. Or, the district may have a formal Release of Information Form that must be completed when requesting personal information (e.g., assessment scores, counseling files, medical reports, and so on) about a student. As you discuss the need for different forms, keep in mind that sometimes less is more.

The tool lists a variety of possible forms, along with a brief description of their purpose. There is a column to record information about the types of elements you might include in a form, as well as a column for notes.

Decision point: The RTI Leadership Planning Team should decide which forms are essential to fostering the RTI problem-solving process. Prepare prototype versions of those forms. Consider such things as readability, space, and ease of use. Keep in mind presentation techniques like the following examples:

- Boxes to be checked (e.g., yes or no)
- Checklists
- Space for descriptions

TIPS AND VARIATIONS

1. Review other forms that the school and district currently use. Are there elements that might be incorporated into the RTI forms? Ask individuals who have used these

other forms to share their opinions about them (e.g., what they like, do not like, would change, and so on).

2. Talk with individuals in the school and district who have developed forms. Ask them to share tips (e.g., usability, length, and so on). Find out if there are design templates you might consider adopting for one of your RTI forms.

3. Review the suggested forms with the administration. Make sure that the forms are compatible with current district and school policy.

Establishing the Problem-Solving Process and RTI Intervention Team

Developing Forms

For each form type listed below, the purpose and typical elements are provided. As you review this tool, discuss how you will develop forms for the RTI Intervention Team.

Form	Purpose	Typical elements	Notes
RTI Request for Assistance Form	To provide information to the RTI Intervention Team regarding the characteristics of a struggling student.	Student identifiers Description of the problem Student's strengths and weaknesses Interventions tried and results Data or evidence of the problem	
Student Cover Sheet	To provide a list of the steps taken to help the student.	List of forms and completion dates List of meetings and outcomes List of decisions List of data gathered List of progress monitoring intervals Final determination	

Form	Purpose	Typical elements	Notes
Meeting report	To provide documentation for decisions made at the RTI intervention meeting.	Date and time Names of attendees Purpose of meeting Results of meeting Assignments and next steps	
Sample Parent/Guardian Letter	To provide suggested language for corresponding with the family.	Informing the family that their child is receiving RTI assistance Inviting the parents to participate in RTI meeting Asking parents to provide data Informing the parents of the assistance recommended Informing the parents of progress	
Progress Monitoring Form	To document progress.	Monitoring approach Monitoring period Results	

Addressing Logistics

PURPOSE

As part of planning, the RTI Leadership Planning Team should take some time to plan for RTI Intervention Team logistics. This task is twofold: to make sure that the RTI Intervention Team has sufficient resources to operate, and to prepare a logistics plan that can be shared with the RTI Intervention Team during implementation.

There are certain logistics that must be addressed when establishing an RTI Intervention Team. The purpose of this tool is to provide team members with a list of possible tasks that should be addressed prior to engaging in student problem-solving activities.

HOW TO USE THIS TOOL

RTI Leadership Planning Team members can use the tool when working with RTI intervention teams. It is designed as a conversation starter for the RTI Intervention Team to use when considering start-up activities.

TIPS AND VARIATIONS

1. Rotate roles and responsibilities.
2. Once roles have been assigned, prepare a checklist of tasks and responsibilities associated with that role. Make a contingency plan in the event of a team member's absence.

Addressing Logistics

____ Have we identified meeting room space? Will meeting space change during the year? If the room must be requested formally, who has that responsibility? Is the room large enough for guests?

____ Have we identified storage space? Where will student files be kept? Is the location secure yet accessible to team members? Who has access to this space?

____ Have we set schedules? Has a schedule been set for the semester or year? Where is the schedule published? How will meetings be canceled or rescheduled? How long will meetings be?

____ Have we assigned roles? Who will do what (e.g., who will send out reminders, photocopy and distribute the request for assistance forms, invite guests to the meeting, take meeting minutes, and so on)?

____ Have we set agendas? Who will develop the agenda for meetings? Will an agenda be made public prior to the meeting? How will agenda items be handled that do not receive sufficient coverage?

____ Have we interacted with parents? How will the team inform parents that their child is receiving help from the RTI Intervention Team? How will parents be kept informed throughout the process?

Helping the RTI Intervention Team Troubleshoot Possible Challenges

PURPOSE

All new teams experience challenges. As the RTI Leadership Planning Team plans for how the RTI Intervention Team will operate, it is helpful to consider some of the potential challenges that may arise as part of RTI work. This discussion can help the RTI Leadership Planning Team to be proactive in addressing potential challenges:

- **Guaranteeing sufficient meeting time**. The RTI Intervention Team will need to meet regularly in order to address concerns and to monitor student progress. The team also may meet to discuss universal screening results for groups of students. Issues may arise when team meetings are at inconvenient times (e.g., after school, at a time in which some instructional staff can never participate, and so on), are scheduled at infrequent or inconsistent times, or are cancelled or preempted frequently.

- **Providing sufficient professional development time**. RTI Intervention Team members will require different types of professional development to carry out their responsibilities (e.g., implementing the RTI problem-solving process, working together as a team, understanding data-based decision making, being knowledgeable about various interventions, etc). Team members cannot be expected to develop such expertise on their own or without acknowledging the time and effort that is involved.

- **Dealing with noncollaborative team members**. One of the strengths of an RTI Intervention Team is that it brings together professionals who have different areas of expertise to address complex student needs. A potential challenge may occur when some professionals lack collaboration skills and thereby disrupt the process. Examples include individuals who are rigid in their approach to interventions (e.g., favor one approach over other possibilities, criticize team members who think differently), who monopolize group decision making (e.g., jumping to conclusions before all group members have weighed in on a problem), or who do not follow through with their responsibilities (e.g., miss meetings, do not speak up, do not complete assignments). The RTI Leadership Planning Team may want to consider how team members are selected, how team members may be removed, how to provide support when a team is struggling, and how to help teams set ground norms for interacting.

Part 2

Building Your School's Capacity to Implement RTI | Understanding RTI Components

Establishing the Problem-Solving Process and RTI Intervention Team | Helping the RTI Intervention Team Troubleshoot Possible Challenges

- **Having too many requests for assistance**. RTI Intervention Teams may experience an overwhelming number of requests at first. They also may receive a disproportionate number of requests in cases where there are too many struggling students to be accommodated by the number of teams available (e.g., one RTI Intervention Team for an entire high school). Requests may increase as the RTI Intervention Team demonstrates success. To address this challenge, the RTI Leadership Planning Team may find it helpful to consider strategies such as creating building level programs to address common concerns and providing staff development targeted at addressing common concerns as part of the core instructional program.

- **Having too few requests for assistance**. At first, staff may not totally understand how to request assistance from the RTI Intervention Team. Or, they may not perceive that they might benefit from doing so. After the RTI Intervention Team has been operating, requests may decline unless reminders are issued. The RTI Leadership Planning Team may want to consider how the RTI process will be promoted at all stages of implementation.

- **Receiving a disproportionate number of requests for assistance from certain teachers**. Certain teachers may request a large amount of assistance if they lack skills, have a disproportionate number of challenging students, or face other difficulties. In these cases, the RTI Intervention Team may find it helpful to analyze the types of requests it receives and to suggest strategies for helping such teachers (e.g., targeted professional development, reduced caseload, etc.).

- **Dealing with resistance or reluctance to participate from other staff members**. Some teachers may not see a need to participate, while others may view it as a show of weakness if they do. Resistance also has been demonstrated in cases where an administrator or supervisor has instructed a teacher to participate. Some teachers may not agree with the recommendations of the team for philosophical reasons, instructional preferences, or both. The RTI Intervention Team can help teachers feel welcome by respecting them as equal members, responding to their difficulties in nonjudgmental ways, and by engaging them in identifying feasible solutions. Teachers who have participated in the process can be enlisted to share success stories. The RTI Leadership Planning Team may also want to consider ways that the intervention team can receive feedback from participating teachers.

- **Communicating progress and success to the school community**. Sometimes RTI Intervention Team members are so busy solving problems that they neglect to share their progress with the school staff. There should be a regular way in which RTI Intervention Teams communicate with building staff.

The purpose of this tool is to provide a conversation starter for the RTI Leadership Planning Team members to use when planning for implementation. The ideas that emerge from this discussion may be integrated into the RTI Intervention Team structure.

HOW TO USE THIS TOOL

Review the possible challenges included in the tool. Add other challenges that may be particular to your school.

Decision point: The planning team should determine if challenges seem reasonable or overwhelming. If the challenges are too great, the team should develop an action plan to build staff members' capacity to embrace RTI.

TIPS AND VARIATIONS

1. Talk with other problem-solving teams in the school. Ask them to share some of the common types of challenges they face. Add new challenges to the list. Discuss the ways that current teams handle challenges and whether those strategies are effective.
2. Survey the school staff. Ask them how likely and under what conditions they would be to seek assistance from an RTI Intervention Team.
3. Consider designing communication tools—such as an RTI Intervention Team newsletter—that can be distributed to school staff on a regular basis. Create a template. Include information such as meeting schedule for the month, how the process works, how the process is working, successes, challenges, tips for dealing with common problems, and more.

Helping the RTI Intervention Team Troubleshoot Possible Challenges

For each of the following challenges, generate suggestions for preparing for them before they occur:

1. Guaranteeing sufficient meeting time.

2. Providing sufficient professional development time.

3. Dealing with noncollaborative team members.

4. Having too many requests for assistance.

5. Having too few requests for assistance.

6. Receiving a disproportionate number of requests for assistance from certain teachers.

7. Dealing with resistance or reluctance to participate from other staff members.

8. Communicating progress and success to the school community.

SECTION 4 OVERVIEW: ESTABLISHING A PROGRESS MONITORING PROCESS

Progress monitoring—a scientifically based practice of assessing student academic performance on a regular basis—is an essential component of an RTI framework. Progress monitoring can be used to follow the performance of an entire classroom of students or to follow the performance of individual students. Progress monitoring serves the following purposes:

- To determine whether or not students are benefitting from the curriculum and instruction they are receiving and to help develop more effective programs for those who are not.
- To estimate rates of student improvement.
- To help identify appropriate levels of intervention.

According to the National Association of State Directors of Special Education (2005), to be useful in an RTI framework, progress monitoring should

- Assess the specific skills embodied in state and local academic standards.
- Assess marker variables that have been demonstrated to lead to the ultimate instructional target.
- Be sensitive to small increments of growth over time.
- Be administered efficiently over short periods.
- Be administered repeatedly (using multiple forms).
- Result in data that can be summarized in teacher friendly data displays.
- Be comparable across students.
- Be applicable for monitoring an individual student's progress over time.
- Be relevant to the development of instructional strategies and use of appropriate curriculum that addresses the area of need.

In an RTI framework, progress monitoring serves different functions at each tier as follows:

1. **Tier 1**. When progress monitoring is used for all students as a follow-up to universal screening, scores achieved at different points during the year may be compared to identify whether an individual student's performance is increasing, decreasing, or remaining the same. Based on predetermined cut points, students in need of more intensive and extensive interventions can be identified. Reviewing the average results for all students combined and their rate of growth helps teachers and administrators determine whether or not changes are needed in curriculum and instruction at the classroom level.

2. **Tier 2 and Tier 3**. The primary purpose of progress monitoring at these levels is to identify whether or not a specific intervention is successful. Progress monitoring that is based on predetermined decision rules can help address the following questions: Does the specific intervention need to be changed? Is the student no longer in need of services at Tier 2 or Tier 3 and expected to continue making progress in general education (Tier 1)? Should the student be referred for special education services?

FREQUENCY OF PROGRESS MONITORING

The frequency for progress monitoring varies (e.g., biweekly, weekly, and daily) according to the intervention. Recommended frequency levels for progress monitoring also vary depending upon the tier from which the intervention has been chosen. For example, recommendations might call for at least every three weeks for Tier 1, one to three times per week for Tier 2, and three to five times per week or Tier 3. As progress monitoring tools are identified, frequency of use will need to be determined.

TYPES OF PROGRESS MONITORING MEASURES

There are a variety of methods to measure progress (e.g., norm referenced tests, observations, running records, quizzes, rubrics, and so on). Above all, the methods should be reliable and valid. The methods that are chosen should be linked directly to the skill that the intervention is addressing. It is helpful if the method comes in alternate forms so that it can be used on a frequent and regular basis.

Curriculum-Based Measurement (CBM) is one approach to progress monitoring that is found in a number of RTI frameworks. CBM is standardized in that there are prescribed procedures for creating, administering, and scoring the tests and for summarizing and interpreting the results. CBM, when implemented correctly, can produce accurate, meaningful information about students' academic levels and growth. Tasks measured by CBM include the following:

- Prereading (e.g., phoneme segmentation fluency, letter sound fluency)
- Reading (e.g., word identification fluency, passage reading fluency, maze fluency)
- Mathematics (e.g., computation, concepts, and applications)
- Spelling
- Written expression (e.g., correct word sequences)

USEFULNESS OF PROGRESS MONITORING

Progress monitoring results are used to help make decisions about when students may need to receive interventions, with increasing or decreasing levels of intensity resulting in different tiers. Decisions will need to be made about the time periods for movement between the tiers of intervention. RTI frameworks often recommend a six- to eight-week time period for measuring response to Tier 1 instruction before a student moves to Tier 2.

Lack of time can become a barrier for teachers to use progress monitoring effectively, even when they recognize the importance of using it. Therefore, the degree to which progress monitoring can be incorporated into instruction is a factor that must be considered during planning, decision making, and professional development.

As decisions are made about progress monitoring measures, it is important to note that they should be short and easily administered. Further, it will be essential to plan targeted professional development for staff on using the assessments effectively and using the results to quantify rates of progress and adjust instruction.

PURPOSE OF THIS SECTION AND SUMMARY OF TOOLS

The purpose of this section is to provide the RTI Leadership Planning Team with information about progress monitoring. The team will use this information to plan how progress monitoring will be addressed in its RTI framework. This section of the action tool includes tools that will assist school teams in

- Discussing and exploring the school's capacity to implement a progress monitoring component.
- Learning more about progress monitoring assessments currently in use in the school and district.
- Making decisions about the selection of progress monitoring measures.

The tools are as follows:

- **Considering Curriculum-Based Measurement at the Elementary Level.** The RTI Leadership Planning Team members may use this tool to facilitate their discussion regarding the use of Curriculum-Based Measurement as a way to monitor student progress and to identify actions that would be needed to help build the school's capacity for efficient and effective use.

- **Considering Progress Monitoring Measures at the Secondary Level.** The planning team members may use this tool to help them explore the current availability and use of progress monitoring measures; facilitate a discussion about whether there is a need to identify additional measures in selected content areas; and plan ways to build the school's capacity for monitoring student progress.

- **Reviewing Commercial Progress Monitoring Tools.** The planning team members may use this tool to guide their inquiries as they explore the types of progress monitoring tools that are commercially available and that provide might provide an alternative to curriculum-based measurement.

- **Planning for RTI Assessment: Data Sources.** The planning team members may use this tool to think about and develop approaches for assessing the effectiveness of progress monitoring practices by teachers and other instructional staff and to plan for additional professional development and support as needed.

After completing these tools, the RTI Leadership Planning Team members should be able to plan the progress monitoring component of their RTI framework. This draft plan should be used in Part 3, Section 1: "Putting It All Together: Developing the RTI Framework and Implementation Plan," when the team actually designs the RTI framework that will be presented to the school.

REFERENCES AND RESOURCES FOR ADDITIONAL INFORMATION

Deno, S. L. (2003). Developments in curriculum-based measurement. *The Journal of Special Education, 37*(3), 184–192.

Dexter, D. D., & Hughes, C. (n.d.). *Progress monitoring within a response-to-intervention model.* Retrieved April 9, 2010, from www.rtinetwork.org/Learn-About-RTI/Research-Support-for-RTI/Progress-Monitoring-Within-a-Response-to-Intervention-Model

Espin, C. A., & Foegen, A. (1996). Validity of three general outcome measures for predicting secondary students' performance on content-area tasks. *Exceptional Children, 62,* 497–514.

Fuchs, D., & Fuchs, L. S. (2006). Introduction to responsiveness-to-intervention: A blueprint for practitioners, policymakers, and parents. *Teaching Exceptional Children, 38,* 57–61.

Fuchs, L. S. (n.d.). *Progress monitoring within a multi-level prevention system.* Retrieved April 9, 2010, from www.rtinetwork.org/Essential/Assessment/Progress/ar/MutlilevelPrevention

Fuchs, L. S. (n.d.). *Validated forms of progress monitoring in reading and mathematics.* Retrieved April 10, 2010, from www.rtinetwork.org/Essential/Assessment/Progress/ar/ValidatedForms

Hasbrouck, J., & Ihnot, C. (n.d.). Curriculum-based measurement: From skeptic to advocate. Retrieved April 9, 2010, from www.rtinetwork.org/Essential/Assessment/Progress/ar/CBMAdvocate/1

Jenkins, J. R., Hudson, R. F., & Lee, S. H. (n.d.). *Using CBM-reading assessments to monitor progress.* Retrieved April 9, 2010, from www.rtinetwork.org/Essential/Assessment/Progress/ar/UsingCBM/1

Mahdavi, J. N., & Haager, D. (n.d.). *Linking progress monitoring results to interventions.* Retrieved April 9, 2010, from www.rtinetwork.org/Essential/Assessment/Progress/ar/LinkingMonitoring/1

Marzano, R. J. (2009). When students track their progress. *Educational Leadership*, 67(4), 86–87.

National Association of State Directors of Special Education, Inc. (2005). *Response to intervention: Policy considerations and implementation.* Alexandria, VA: Author.

Considering Curriculum-Based
Measurement at the Elementary Level

PURPOSE

A primary way to monitor student progress at the elementary level is through the use of Curriculum-Based Measurement (CBM). These research-based methods are typically used in the areas of math, reading, writing, and spelling. They may be administered to an entire class or to individual students and generally take one to five minutes, depending on the content area. CBM is sensitive to small increments of improvement with scores typically generated by counting the number of correct responses. Results help teachers to compare students' current performance with past performance and determine whether or not they are improving. There are a number of free and commercial CBM instruments available. As in the recommended process for selecting a universal screening assessment, similar factors will need to be weighed in considering CBM. The purpose of this tool is to assist the RTI Leadership Planning Team in discussing different factors related to the CBM selection process.

HOW TO USE THIS TOOL

The tool is designed as a conversation starter that the RTI Leadership Planning Team can use to consider factors related to the selection of CBM tools as a way to monitor student progress.

Decision point: At the end of the discussion, the team members should decide whether CBM can be used efficiently and effectively as a progress monitoring tool, in what content areas it can be used, and what the next steps are in facilitating its use. If CBM is not recommended at this time, determine next steps for preparing to monitor student progress.

TIPS AND VARIATIONS

1. Prior to discussion, check with other schools to determine what types of CBM they are using. Ask questions like these:

    • In what content areas is CBM being used and at what grade levels?
    • How frequently is CBM being administered?

- What sources did they find helpful in identifying potential CBM instruments?
- What types of professional development were undertaken to build staff capacity to use, analyze, and interpret CBM?
- How are CBM findings graphed and how are the results being used to plan instruction?
- What primary factors led to their selection of a particular CBM instrument?

2. Assign different groups (e.g., grade level teams) to review CBM related to different content areas or to review a specific number of measurements in the same content area. For example, 1st grade teachers might be asked to identify and review two or three different CBM instruments in the area of reading.

Considering Curriculum-Based Measurements at the Elementary Level

Curriculum-Based Measurement: _____

Content Area: _____ **Source of Information:** _____

Reviewer(s): _____ **Date:** _____

Questions	Notes and Additional Questions
Staff Preparation and Resources	
What type of initial and follow-up professional development would be needed to prepare staff to administer the CBM and to analyze and interpret the results?	
What level of education is required for staff administering the CBM?	
What technology access is needed as part of staff preparation for administration, scoring, or monitoring?	
What resources are needed for administration or scoring?	
Content	
Is the content aligned with the curriculum for each grade level?	

Establishing a Progress Monitoring Process | Considering Curriculum-Based Measurement at the Elementary Level

Administration	
How frequently can the CBM be administered?	
Are there alternate forms of the CBM?	
Is the CBM administered individually or in a group?	
How much time does it take to administer the CBM?	
Results	
How is the CBM scored (e.g., number of correct responses)?	
What types of individual and group score reports are provided?	
How are results graphed for analysis, comparison, and decision-making purposes?	
What databases are recommended to help with monitoring results across time periods?	

For Commercial CBM	
What are the initial costs per student, and what are the ongoing or future costs?	

Do you recommend further exploration of this assessment for implementation?
_____ Yes   _____ No   _____ Undecided

Why or Why Not?

Next Steps and Individuals Responsible

Considering Progress Monitoring Measures at the Secondary Level

PURPOSE

Monitoring student progress at the secondary level can be challenging because standardized and commercially available Curriculum-Based Measurements are not plentiful. However, there are a number of methods and instruments in the areas of math, reading, writing, spelling, and content area learning that may be used for progress monitoring purposes. For example, many students at the secondary level struggle with reading different types of text and comprehending content-related material. A common CBM approach to monitoring reading progress at the secondary level is the use of maze passages. In a passage of approximately 400 words, every seventh word is replaced with a set of three choices—the correct original word and two incorrect words of about the same number of letters. Based on the context, students must choose the correct word. The score is obtained by counting correct choices. Maze passages may be purchased or constructed using human interest news articles or basal reading materials.

The purpose of this tool is to assist the RTI Leadership Planning Team in exploring tools and approaches for monitoring student progress at the secondary level.

HOW TO USE THIS TOOL

This tool is intended to help guide discussions related to the identification and consideration of progress monitoring tools and approaches. The planning team might begin by focusing on a particular content area, such as writing or algebra. Team members might review instructional materials currently being used and determine whether or not progress monitoring assessments are available as part of the program. The team also should review other sources for progress monitoring tools. For example, the following sites feature resources applicable to progress monitoring in secondary schools:

- The Research Institute on Progress Monitoring: www.progressmonitoring.net
- Intervention Central: www.interventioncentral.org
- National Center on Student Progress Monitoring: www.studentprogress.org
- EdCheckup: www.edcheckup.com

Decision point: At the end of the discussion, the planning team should decide whether there are tools that can be used efficiently and effectively as progress monitoring tools, in what content areas they can be used, and what the next steps are in facilitating use.

TIPS AND VARIATIONS

1. Prior to discussion, check with other secondary schools to determine what types of CBM they are using. Ask questions such as these:

   - In what content areas are progress monitoring measures being used?
   - How frequently are the measures being administered?
   - What sources did they find helpful in identifying potential progress monitoring measures?
   - What types of professional development were undertaken to build staff capacity to use, analyze, and interpret the progress monitoring measures?
   - How are the results of the progress monitoring displayed or graphed, and how are the results being used to plan instruction?
   - What primary factors led to the selection of particular progress monitoring measures?

2. Assign different teams to review progress monitoring measures related to different content areas or to review a specific number of measures in the same content area. For example, selected English teachers might be asked to identify and review progress monitoring measures in the area of reading and writing.

Considering Progress Monitoring Measures at the Secondary Level

Progress Monitoring Measure: _____

Content Area: _____   **Source of Information:** _____

Reviewer(s): _____   **Date:** _____

Questions	Notes and Additional Questions
Staff Preparation and Resources	
What type of initial and follow-up professional development would be needed to prepare staff to administer the progress monitoring tool and to analyze and interpret the results?	
What level of education is required for staff members who will be conducting progress monitoring?	
What technology is needed as part of staff preparation for administration, scoring, or monitoring?	
What resources are needed for administration or scoring?	
Content	
Is the content of the progress monitoring tool aligned with the curriculum?	

Administration	
How frequently can the progress monitoring tool be administered?	
Are alternate forms of the progress monitoring tool available for repeated use?	
Is the assessment administered individually or in a group?	
How much time does it take to administer the assessment?	
Results	
How is the progress monitoring tool scored (e.g., number of correct responses)?	
What types of individual and group data reports are provided?	
Can results be displayed or graphed for analysis, comparison, and decision-making purposes?	
What databases are recommended to help with monitoring results across time periods?	

For Commercial CBM	
What are the initial costs per student and what are the ongoing or future costs?	

Do you recommend further exploration of this assessment for implementation?
_____ Yes _____ No _____ Undecided

Why or Why Not?

Next Steps and Individuals Responsible

Reviewing Commercial Progress Monitoring Tools

PURPOSE

Progress monitoring—formative assessment of student performance on a set schedule—is used to determine if the student is responding to the intervention. One of the tasks of the RTI Leadership Planning Team is to determine if the school has sufficient capacity to implement progress monitoring as part of its RTI framework. The planning team members may wish to familiarize themselves with the types of progress monitoring tools that are available commercially. Examples include, but are not limited to:

- AIMSweb (www.aimsweb.com/) features competency-based measures for early literacy, reading, early numeracy, mathematics, writing, and other skills (K–8).
- Reading A-Z Assessments (www.readinga-z.com/assessment/reading-assessment.php) features progress monitoring tools such as comprehension quick checks for reading skills (K–12).
- Accelerated Math (www.renlearn.com/am/) is a software tool that monitors and manages mathematics skills practice from preschool math through calculus.

The purpose of this tool is to provide questions to help guide the inquiry.

HOW TO USE THIS TOOL

The tool is designed as a conversation starter that the RTI Leadership Planning Team can use in exploring various commercial progress monitoring tools. Team members will want to conduct a search of available progress monitoring tools. It may be helpful to check with school psychologists or the central office staff in charge of assessments for the district, regional resource center staff, or university partners for suggestions.

Decision point: At the end of the discussion, the planning team should decide which progress monitoring tools might be candidates for further study by the administration and school staff.

TIPS AND VARIATIONS

1. Sometimes assessment publishers can direct you to other schools that are using the particular assessment successfully. Talk with educators in those schools who are using the tool. Ask if it is efficient and effective. Find out about the types of resources (e.g., professional development) that were needed to ensure effective implementation and utilization.

2. Invite publisher representatives to present their tools.

3. After you have identified several possible tools, share them with the administration and instructional staff. Encourage teachers to review the tools in grade level teams or professional learning communities. Ask them to answer questions:

   - How would I use data from this tool?
   - How important are these data in terms of monitoring student progress?
   - How difficult would it be to learn to use this tool? Would the costs outweigh the benefits?

4. Team members should select one content area—reading, mathematics, etc.—at a time for inquiry. Content areas should be chosen on the basis of identified needs in the school.

Reviewing Commercial Progress Monitoring Tools

Name of Tool: _____

Skills Assessed: _____

Publisher Information: _____

Considering Commercial Progress Monitoring Tools
What are the initial costs per student, and what are the ongoing or future costs?
What grade levels does this tool address?
What level of education is required for staff administering the tool?
What types of initial and follow-up professional development would instructional staff need?
How frequently can the tool be used and at what intervals (e.g., fall, midyear, and so on)? Are there alternate forms of the tool?
Can the tool be administered to individual students as well as groups of students?

What types of data are generated from the tool? How are the results displayed? What types of reports are provided?
What technology access is needed as part of the staff preparation, implementation, and reporting processes?
Other
Other

Planning for RTI Assessment: Data Sources

PURPOSE

Data-based decision making is a cornerstone of RTI. RTI Intervention Team members are expected to analyze a wide range of data when developing a student's intervention plan. The purpose of this tool is to provide the RTI Leadership Planning Team with an opportunity to discuss various assessments that may be used to gather data on student academic or behavioral challenges.

HOW TO USE THIS TOOL

Discuss each type of assessment. For each, identify the following:

- Individuals who have expertise in gathering data via the assessment tool
- Individuals who have expertise in analyzing data from each type of assessment
- How assessments are currently used for decision making
- Assessment tools that require professional development

Decision point: The RTI Leadership Planning Team should identify those assessment tools that are being used and those that are used infrequently or not used at all. In cases where the assessment tools are not being used, determine the need for professional development resources on using different assessment tools for decision making. Make a plan for helping instructional staff develop adequate knowledge and skills.

TIPS AND VARIATIONS

1. Prepare an assessment guide for RTI Intervention Teams that includes definitions, purposes, and samples of each type of assessment. Include tips on how to analyze the data.
2. Create a virtual library of classroom-based assessments on the school intranet. Use a blog to encourage instructional staff to comment on how they use assessments for data-based decision making.
3. Ask grade level teams to share the different classroom assessments they use. Encourage them to use similar tools across classrooms.

Planning for RTI Assessment: Data Sources

Type of Assessment	Professional Development Needed
Classroom work samples	
Classroom observation	
Instructional assessments	
Curriculum-Based Measurements	
Teacher rating scales	
Parent rating scales	
Student rating scales	

Student self-monitoring charts	
Behavior logs	
Report cards	
Attendance records	
Disciplinary referrals	
Standardized test results	
Screening results	
Other	

SECTION 5 OVERVIEW: ESTABLISHING A UNIVERSAL SCREENING PROCESS

PURPOSE

A universal screening process—also referred to as benchmark assessment—is a frequently cited core component of an RTI framework. The most important outcome of universal screening, regardless of the specific instruments and organizational systems, is using the results to guide instruction and to make changes as needed.

A universal screening process is used to identify students who may be at risk of not making acceptable progress in the standard or core school curriculum and who may require intervention. A universal screening process also is used to

- Identify students' strengths and weaknesses in content areas such as reading and math.
- Compare the performance of individual students with the performance of others and identify those who may need further assessment, intervention, or enrichment.
- Help teachers monitor the performance of students who are struggling.
- Provide a snapshot of classroomwide student performance so that any issues related to curriculum or instruction may be addressed.

Universal screening assessments are typically administered to all students at regular intervals, usually three or four times during the school year. These assessments also may be used for assessing age appropriate critical curriculum skills, such as identifying letters of the alphabet or reading a list of high frequency words.

There are a number of benchmark or screening assessments that might be used. In some cases, the specific assessment instrument might be identified by the state department of education or the school division for designated grade levels. Some school divisions create their own assessments for schools to use, and in some divisions schools might select commercially available tools. For example, some elementary schools have purchased the Dynamic Indicators of Basic Early Literacy Skills (DIBELS), which is comprised of one-minute, individually administered measures.

In addition to selecting a screening assessment, schools will need to identify a prescribed point or score that represents the dividing line between students who are potentially at risk and those who are not at risk. This dividing line score or point, typically referred to as a cut score or cut point, is considered as schools develop guidelines for determining when a student's performance should be investigated further. For example, student performance on the edge of either side of the established cut score could result in progress monitoring with specific assessment for a designated time period (e.g., five weeks).

Using a period of progress monitoring as part of the standard screening procedure for students who are struggling may help prevent them from falling through the cracks due to the inaccuracy of the screening instrument. For example, some students may not be identified initially through screening but later may be identified as at risk for learning. A standard screening procedure also may help schools avoid unnecessary in-depth testing and intensive interventions for students misidentified as being at risk.

To help make the universal screening results useful for teachers and administrators—as well as to allow the results to be monitored over time—schools will need a data base to hold student information and scores. Screening outcomes should result in a visual profile of all students and their comparisons with each other.

PURPOSE OF THIS SECTION AND SUMMARY OF TOOLS

The purpose of this section is to provide the RTI Leadership Planning Team with information about universal screening. The team will use this information to plan how universal screening will be addressed in its RTI framework. This section of the Action Tool comprises tools that will assist the planning team in the following activities:

- Discussing and exploring the school's capacity to implement a universal screening process.
- Learning more about the universal screening assessments currently in use in the school or district.
- Inventorying available supports and services that are directly linked to the skills measured on currently used screening assessments.
- Reviewing commercial screening instruments.

The tools are as follows:

- **Planning for Universal Screening.** The RTI Leadership Planning Team may use this tool to consider the implementation of a universal screening process. It engages team members in a conversation about what is currently in place and what they might need—including professional development for instructional staff—to implement a fully operational universal screening process.

- **Understanding Universal Screening Assessments Currently in Use.** The planning team may use this tool to learn more about the various screening assessments currently in place in their school and district.

- **Reviewing Commercial Screening Instruments.** The planning team may use this tool to learn more about the type of assessments that are commercially available and to discuss whether any of the reviewed assessments might be appropriate for further study and possible adoption.

- **Informing Instruction: Universal Screening in the Classroom.** The planning team may use this tool to identify any screening assessments that teachers are currently using as part of classroom instruction. Such knowledge may help the team plan screening assessments that do not overlap as well as to reflect on teachers' capacity for making data-based instructional decisions.

- **Looking at Screening Results: Are There Sufficient Interventions for Students who Demonstrate Difficulties?** The planning team may use this tool to review universal screening assessments and any interventions that are available to address student needs identified in the assessments. The tool can also be used to identify areas in which students are assessed but where there are not interventions to help those who demonstrate weaknesses.

After completing these tools, the planning team members should be able to plan the universal screening component of their RTI framework. This draft plan should be used in Part 3, Section 1: "Putting It All Together: Developing the RTI Framework and Implementation Plan," when the team actually designs the RTI framework that will be presented to the school.

REFERENCES AND RESOURCES FOR ADDITIONAL INFORMATION

Compton, D. L., Fuchs, D., Fuchs, L. S., & Bryant, J. D. (2006). Selecting at-risk readers in first grade for early intervention: A two-year longitudinal study of decision rules and procedures. *Journal of Educational Psychology, 98,* 394–409.

Davis, G. N., Lindo, E. J., & Compton, D. L. (2007). Children at risk for reading failure: Constructing an early screening measure. *TEACHING Exceptional Children, 39*(5), 32–37.

Dynamic Indicators of Basic Early Literacy Skills [DIBELS]. (n.d.). Retrieved February 11, 2010, from http://dibels.uoregon.edu/index.php

Jenkins, J. R., Hudson, R. F., & Johnson, E. S. (2007). Screening for service delivery in an RTI framework: Candidate measures. *School Psychology Review, 36,* 560–582.

Jenkins, J. R., & Johnson, E. (n.d.). *Universal screening for reading problems: Why and how should we do this?* Retrieved April 2, 2010, from www.rtinetwork.org/Essential/Assessment/Universal/ar/ReadingProblems

Johnson, E., Mellard, D. F., Fuchs, D., & McKnight, M. A. (2006). *Responsiveness to intervention (RTI): How to do it.* Lawrence, KS: National Research Center on Learning Disabilities.

Johnson, E. S., & Pool, J. L. (n.d.). *Screening for reading problems in grades 1 through 3: An overview of select measures.* Retrieved April 2, 2010, from www.rtinetwork.org/Essential/Assessment/Universal/ar/Screening-for-Reading-Problems-in-Grades-1-Through-3-An-Overview-of-Select-Measures

Johnson, E. S., & Pool, J. L. (n.d.). *Screening for reading problems in grades 4 through 12.* Retrieved April 2, 2010 from www.rtinetwork.org/Essential/Assessment/Universal/ar/Screening-for-Reading-Problems-in-Grades-4-through-12

Johnson, E. S., Pool, J., & Carter, D. R. (n.d.). *Screening for reading problems in an RTI framework.* Retrieved April 2, 2010, from www.rtinetwork.org/Essential/Assessment/Universal/ar/Screening-for-Reading-Problems-in-an-RTI-Framework

Pool, J., & Johnson, E. S. (n.d.). *Screening for reading problems in preschool and kindergarten: An overview of select measures.* Retrieved April 2, 2010, from www.rtinetwork.org/Essential/Assessment/Universal/ar/Screening-for-Reading-Problems-in-Preschool-and-Kindergarten

Torgensen, J. (2004). Preventing early reading failure and its devastating downward spiral: The evidence for early intervention. *American Educator, 28*(3), 6–10.

Vaughn Gross Center for Reading and Language Arts. (2005). *Introduction to the 3-tier reading model: Reducing reading disabilities for kindergarten through third grade students* (4th ed.). Austin, TX: Author.

Planning for Universal Screening

PURPOSE

A universal screening process—also referred to as benchmark assessment—is an essential component of an RTI framework because it identifies which students are not making acceptable progress in the standard school curriculum. In an RTI framework, the goal is to identify the roughly 15 to 20 percent of students who are not achieving in the core program and to target to those students who need them. Universal screening is used to

- Identify student strengths and weaknesses in content areas such as reading and math.
- Identify students who are in need of further assessment, intervention, or enrichment.
- Help teachers monitor the performance of struggling learners.

The universal screening process also provides a snapshot of classroomwide student performance so that any issues related to curriculum or instruction may be addressed.

Universal assessments are typically administered to all students at regular intervals, usually three or four times during the school year. There are a number of benchmark assessments that can be used. In some cases, the state department of education or the school division for designated grade levels may identify the specific assessment instrument. For example, in Virginia, many elementary school divisions use the Phonological Awareness Literacy Screening (PALS) assessment in the area of reading. Some school divisions create their own assessments for schools to use, and in other divisions schools may select commercially available tools.

The most important outcome of the screening, regardless of the specific instruments administered, is using the results to guide student instruction and to make changes as needed. The purpose of this tool is to assist the RTI Leadership Planning Team in considering the implementation of a universal screening process within the RTI framework. It engages team members in a conversation about what is currently in place and what they might need—including professional development for instructional staff—to implement a fully operational universal screening process.

Part 2

HOW TO USE THIS TOOL

The tool is designed as a conversation starter that the planning team can use in exploring the school's capacity to implement universal screening.

Decision point: At the end of the discussion, the team should decide if universal screening can be implemented efficiently and effectively as part of an RTI framework. If not, determine the next steps for developing the school's capacity. If yes, answer the following questions:

- What assessments and procedures will be used to generate universal screening results for all students?
- Who will review universal screening results to identify students whose results suggest that that they are not performing at expected levels?
- Who will determine how frequently universal screening will occur?

TIPS AND VARIATIONS

1. Before engaging in discussion, check with other schools to see what types of universal screening approaches and tools they are using. Ask questions such as these examples:

   - What screening instruments are they using?
   - What screening instruments are they using in particular grade levels and content areas?
   - How are they using the results?
   - What types of professional development have they undertaken to build staff members' capacity to use universal screening results to enhance instruction?

2. If your school has universal screening approaches in place, discuss the effectiveness of the results. For example, ask questions such as these:

   - Does the assessment accurately identify students who are at risk for failure and who need additional support to achieve?
   - Is the assessment efficient, or is it too cumbersome to utilize (e.g., costly, time consuming, and so on)? Are there other screening tools that are easier to use and that will yield accurate results?

Planning for Universal Screening

Questions to Address	Notes and Additional Questions
Reviewing Current Screening Practices	
• What screening instruments are required or recommended by the state department of education and central office? • At what grade levels are they recommended, and in what content areas? • How frequently and effectively are these instruments currently used?	
• What self-selected screening instruments are currently used within the school, and in which grade levels and content areas? • What is the frequency of use? • How satisfied are staff members with the current instruments? • How do staff members perceive their knowledge and skills in using screening instruments?	
• How are screening results currently used by teachers? • How are they used by administrators?	
• What professional development practices has the school undertaken to build staff members' capacity for implementing and using screening data? • Are some staff members better prepared than others?	

Understanding Universal Screening Assessments Currently in Use

PURPOSE

What do we know about the assessments that student complete? What more do we want to know about the assessments?

When addressing universal screening as part of an RTI approach, the RTI Leadership Planning Team will want to be well-versed on all aspects of the universal screening assessments currently in use. Usually there are individuals in the district who are experts in the assessments who can be invited to provide information. For example, team members may want to know more about certain points:

- The assessment's purpose and its rationale for use in the district.
- How well norm groups match the characteristics of students in the district.
- Subtests within the assessment and what information can be gleaned from them.
- Why a particular assessment was selected for use.
- How the assessment matches district and state standards and the curriculum.
- How students in the district have performed on the assessment over time.
- Strengths and weaknesses of the assessment.
- Various formats in which the data can be displayed for use.
- Descriptions of how other districts have used the assessment.

The purpose of this tool is to help planning team members learn more about the various screening assessments currently in place in their school and district.

HOW TO USE THIS TOOL

The RTI Leadership Planning Team is encouraged to contact district personnel who are specialists in the various universal screening assessments currently in use. Arrange a meeting when team members can learn more about these assessments. The tool provides a beginning list of questions that might be used for this purpose.

Decision point: The planning team should decide whether the universal screening assessments currently in use provide sufficient information to design interventions and supports for struggling students. Team members also should determine if the universal screening assessments address all of the major areas of concern.

TIPS AND VARIATIONS

1. Assign each team member to investigate a particular screening instrument. Have other team members generate a list of questions about the assessment, or use a standard protocol to elicit information. Report back to the team.

2. Contact the publisher of each assessment. Ask for a sales representative to meet with the team. Find out if there are new versions of the assessment and if the company has updated its findings related to validity and reliability. Ask if the publisher can share how other districts are using the assessment to support teaching and learning.

3. Ask district experts to share information about comparable assessments. Invite them to describe other possible screening assessments that may address specific student needs.

Understanding Universal Screening Assessments Currently in Use

Assessment: _____ **Frequency of Assessment:** _____

Students Assessed: _____

QUESTIONS:

1. What is the assessment's purpose and the rationale for its use in the district?

2. How well do norm groups match the characteristics of students in the district?

3. Are there subtests within the assessment, and if so, what information can be gleaned from them?

4. Why was this particular assessment selected for use?

5. How does the assessment match district and state standards and the curriculum?

6. How have students in the district performed on the assessment over time?

7. What are the strengths and weaknesses of the assessment?

8. What are the various formats in which the data can be displayed for use?

9. Do you have descriptions of how other districts have used the assessment?

10. Other

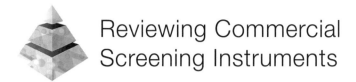

Reviewing Commercial Screening Instruments

PURPOSE

A universal screening process is an essential component of an RTI framework because it identifies which students are not making acceptable progress in the standard school curriculum. Many schools use some form of universal screening to assess students' progress in the standard curriculum

One of the tasks of the RTI Leadership Planning Team is to determine if the school has sufficient capacity to implement universal screening as part of its RTI framework. In cases where there either are no assessments or there are insufficient screening assessments in place, team members may wish to review commercial screening instruments for possible use. The purpose of this tool is to provide questions to help guide the inquiry.

HOW TO USE THIS TOOL

The tool is designed as a conversation starter that the RTI Leadership Planning Team can use in exploring various commercial screening tools. Team members are encouraged to select one content area—reading, mathematics, etc.—at a time for inquiry to help focus the discussion. Content areas should be chosen on the basis of identified needs in the school.

Team members will want to conduct a search of available assessment instruments. It may be helpful to check with other educators, such as central office staff in charge of assessments for the district, regional resource center staff, and university partners, for suggestions.

Decision point: At the end of the discussion, the planning team should decide which universal screening tools might be candidates for further study by the administration and school staff.

TIPS AND VARIATIONS

1. Sometimes assessment publishers can direct you to other schools that are using the particular assessment successfully. Talk with educators in those schools who are using the particular assessment tool. Ask if it is efficient and effective. Find out about the types of resources (e.g., professional development) that were needed to ensure effective implementation and utilization.

2. Invite publisher representatives to present their tools.

3. After you have identified several possible tools, share them with the administration and instructional staff. Encourage teachers to review the tools either in grade level teams or professional learning communities. Ask them to answer questions like the following:

   • How would I use data from this tool?

   • How important are these data in terms of improving student learning?

   • How difficult would it be to learn and use this tool? Would the costs outweigh the benefits?

Establishing a Universal Screening Process

Reviewing Commercial Screening Instruments

Name of Tool: _____   **Skills Assessed:** _____

Publisher Information: _____

Considering Commercial Screening Instruments
What are the initial costs per student and what are the ongoing or future costs?
What grade levels are addressed by the instrument?
What level of education is required for staff administering the screening?
What types of initial and follow-up professional development would be needed for screeners?
How frequently can the instrument be used and at what intervals (e.g., fall, midyear, and so on)? Are there alternate forms of the instrument?
Is the assessment administered individually or in a group?
What types of scores are generated from the screening instrument? How are the results organized for comparison purposes? What types of screening reports are provided?
What technology is needed as part of the staff preparation, screening, or scoring processes?
What databases are used to help with monitoring results across time periods?
Other

Informing Instruction: Universal Screening in the Classroom

PURPOSE

Teachers are increasingly using screening assessments within the instructional program. These measures help them track student progress on benchmark assessments. Typically, these screening assessments differ from standard classroom assessments in that they directly align with district and state standards. They will most likely be found in reading and mathematics.

For example, all 1st and 2nd grade teachers may use a reading screening tool bimonthly to gauge how well students are mastering targeted skills. The screening assessment allows teachers to identify groups of students who may not be advancing at an acceptable rate. Using this information, teachers may choose to conduct additional diagnostic assessments, group students for remediation, seek support from the reading specialist, and so on.

In an RTI framework, this type of screening can enhance the core program as well as engage teachers in routine data-based instructional decision making. As the RTI Leadership Planning Team assesses the school's readiness for using screening data, it is important to survey what teachers are already using. The purpose of this tool is to identify any screening assessments that teachers are currently using as part of classroom instruction. Such knowledge may help the team plan screening assessments that do not overlap as well as to reflect on teachers' capacity for making data-based instructional decisions.

HOW TO USE THIS TOOL

Survey the instructional staff regarding their use of screening assessments within the instructional program. This can be done either by interviewing teachers or soliciting input from department chairs. Use the tool to record the assessment, its purpose, the grade level where it is in use, and any notes (e.g., teachers received professional development in using the assessment, it has only been in use this year, teachers find it burdensome, and so on).

Decision point: Once completed, discuss whether the extent to which teachers are using screening instruments is sufficient. If not, determine what supports might be helpful.

TIPS AND VARIATIONS

1. In cases where grade level or subject area teams are using a screening instrument, explore questions such as the following:

    - Why did they choose to implement an assessment?
    - How did they go about selecting the assessment?
    - How is the assessment helping them improve student achievement?
    - What kind of preparation did they require to use the assessment?
    - Is ongoing support needed to maintain the assessment's use?

2. In cases where grade level or subject area teams are not using a screening instrument, explore questions such as the following:

    - Do you see a potential use for a screening assessment?
    - How do you screen students to assess their progress in meeting district and state benchmarks?

Part 2

Informing Instruction:
Universal Screening in the Classroom

Assessment	Purpose	Grades	Notes

Looking at Screening Results: Are There Sufficient Interventions for Students who Demonstrate Difficulties?

PURPOSE

Universal screening assessments often are designed to identify student progress on certain benchmark skills. It is one thing to know that a population of students in the school has not achieved to the set standard. It is another to be able to address those students' needs to improve their achievement.

The RTI Leadership Planning Team may find it helpful to review universal screening assessments that are in use in relation to the types of supports that are available to help struggling students. For example, in some RTI frameworks, the RTI Intervention Team considers universal screening data in addition to making intervention decisions for individual students. The RTI Intervention Team may review screening results and determine that a subgroup of students could benefit from a particular intervention. In such a case, team members would meet with all teachers involved and design and monitor the intervention plan, just as they do for individual students.

The purpose of this tool is to provide planning team members with an opportunity to review universal screening assessments and any interventions that are available to address student needs identified in the assessments. The tool also can be used to identify areas in which students are assessed but where there are not interventions to help those who demonstrate weaknesses.

HOW TO USE THIS TOOL

RTI Leadership Planning Team members should identify all the universal screening assessments currently in use in the school that are relevant to RTI work. Complete a tool for each assessment. Include the following information:

- Name of assessment
- Date(s) when it is given
- Students who participate in the assessment
- Purpose of the assessment

Building Your School's Capacity to Implement RTI | Understanding RTI Components

Establishing a Universal Screening Process | Looking at Screening Results: Are There Sufficient Interventions for Students who Demonstrate Difficulties?

- School resources. What supports, supplemental materials, services, and so on are available to address any weaknesses identified in the assessment?
- District resources. What supports, supplemental materials, services, and so on are available to address any weaknesses identified in the assessment?
- Notes. What more is needed to address identified student needs?

Decision point: The planning team should decide if there are sufficient interventions—supports, strategies, services, supplemental materials, etc.—available to address any learning, behavioral, and other weaknesses identified in the screening assessments. If not, make a plan for how you might build a satisfactory foundation of offerings.

TIPS AND VARIATIONS

1. Investigate the extent to which the interventions—supports, strategies, services, supplemental materials, etc.—available to address any learning or behavioral weaknesses identified in the screening assessments are successful in helping students achieve.

2. Investigate whether interventions have been made available to students who have not performed adequately on the assessments.

3. Investigate the usage of interventions. Are some interventions used more frequently that others? If so, consider why some interventions are used while others are not.

4. Consider whether there are sufficient interventions linked to the universal screening assessments. If not, make a plan for how you might remedy this situation.

5. As interventions are implemented, keep track of their success in addressing students' identified difficulties.

6. If there are numerous areas assessed by screening assessments, yet there are very few corresponding interventions, discuss why this might be and the implications. For example, are students being measured on assessments that have little relevance to the curriculum? Are student scores not being used to improve instruction and learning? Are there other screening measures that would be more relevant to the curriculum?

Establishing a Universal Screening Process

Looking at Screening Results:
Are There Sufficient Interventions for Students
Who Demonstrate Difficulties?

Name of Assessment:

Screening Assessment: When Given, Students Assessed, and Purpose	Interventions Available Within School	Interventions Available Within District	Suggestions/Notes

Recommendations and Individuals Responsible

PART 3

Developing and Implementing the RTI Plan

◢◢◢◢ About Part 3

The sections in Part 3 help the RTI Leadership Planning Team with developing the draft RTI plan and seeing it through implementation.

Putting It All Together—Developing the RTI Framework and Implementation Plan. The tools in **Section 1** are designed to help the planning team create the proposed RTI framework and RTI implementation plan. The tools address planning topics such as the following:

- **How the proposed RTI framework will be introduced to the staff**. This includes orienting staff to the RTI framework, gaining buy-in and support, and determining next steps in implementation.
- **How the RTI Intervention Team will be formed**. This includes providing professional development for the RTI Intervention Team and ensuring that the RTI problem-solving process is in place.
- **How RTI implementation will be monitored and supported**. This includes assessing how well implementation is going, assessing impact, and planning for enhancements.

After working through the tools in this section, the RTI Leadership Planning Team embers will have completed the following documents:

- RTI implementation plan, including goals, timelines, and required resources
- Communication plan, including a flowchart of the process
- Parent involvement plan
- RTI implementation monitoring plan

Introducing RTI to School Staff Members. The tools in **Section 2** are designed to help the RTI Leadership PlanningTteam introduce RTI to staff members and to assess their buy-in and support for the initiative. These tools are designed as professional development activities that can be presented to the entire staff or to small groups. After completing these activities with staff members, planning team members should be able to finalize roll-out plans for the next phases of the RTI initiative.

Developing the RTI Intervention Team. The tools in **Section 3** are designed to help the RTI Leadership Planning Team form the RTI Intervention Team—including suggestions for providing professional development for the RTI Intervention Team and for helping the team get up and running. The tools in this section can also help the planning team establish the problem-solving process. After completing these tools, team members should be confident that the intervention team is prepared to carry out the RTI problem-solving process. Assuming this is the case, the planning team will be able to initiate the RTI framework in the school.

Monitoring and Supporting RTI Implementation. The tools in **Section 4** provide the planning team with strategies for monitoring implementation, assessing impact, and responding to challenges. The tools also feature ways to gain feedback via self-assessments and focus groups.

After completing these tools, RTI Leadership Planning Team members should be able to review the RTI Implementation Plan and reflect on how well it is being implemented. Team members will want to adjust the plan to address unforeseen challenges and plan enhancements.

SECTION 1 OVERVIEW: PUTTING IT ALL TOGETHER— DEVELOPING THE RTI FRAMEWORK AND IMPLEMENTATION PLAN

Once the RTI Leadership Planning Team members have familiarized themselves with the major RTI components, they will be ready to develop those components into their school's RTI framework. At this time team members also will discuss how the RTI framework with be implemented. For example, the team will consider:

- **Introducing the proposed RTI framework to staff.** This includes orienting staff to the RTI framework, gaining buy in, and determining next steps in implementation.
- **Forming the RTI Intervention Team.** This includes providing professional development to the RTI Intervention Team and ensuring that the RTI problem-solving process is in place.
- **Monitoring and supporting the RTI process.** This includes assessing how well implementation is going, assessing impact, and planning for enhancements.

A major task of the RTI Leadership Planning Team is to provide feedback and support to the staff as the RTI framework is implemented. Team members will serve as resources and coaches as the staff implements the RTI approach.

PURPOSE OF THIS SECTION AND SUMMARY OF TOOLS

The purpose of this section is to provide the planning team members with an opportunity to put all of their planning together into the RTI implementation plan. The tools provide team members with various templates for developing the components of their framework and implementation plan.

The tools are as follows:

- **Preparing a Flowchart of the RTI Process.** A flowchart serves two purposes: to ensure that the planning team has considered all steps in a logical order, and to provide a visual for explaining the process to staff members. This tool provides the planning team with an opportunity to review the RTI process and create the graphic representation of it.
- **Planning for Parent Communication and Involvement.** In planning for RTI implementation, the team will want to consider how parents will be involved in the process. This tool provides the planning team with an opportunity to plan how parents will be informed about RTI, included in the implementation process, and informed in the event that their child's teacher requests assistance.

- **Communicating About RTI.** Planning for communication with all stakeholders is a major task. The purpose of this tool is to provide the planning team with an opportunity to plan major communications.
- **Drafting the RTI Plan and Timeline.** Planning team members can use this tool to record and update their draft goals and objectives for RTI implementation along with estimated timelines.
- **Planning and Monitoring Implementation of the RTI Framework.** The planning team can use this tool to plan how they will monitor implementation.

After working through these tools, the planning team members should have the following documents completed:

- RTI framework, including goals, required resources and a flowchart of the process
- Communication plan
- Parent involvement plan
- RTI implementation plan

Putting It All Together: Developing the RTI Framework and Implementation Plan

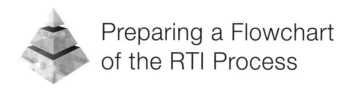

Preparing a Flowchart of the RTI Process

PURPOSE

Once the RTI Leadership Planning Team has determined the RTI process, it is helpful to prepare a graphic such as a flowchart to detail the plan. A flowchart serves two purposes: to ensure that the planning team has considered all steps in a logical order, and to provide a visual for explaining the process to staff members. This tool provides the planning team with an opportunity to review the process and create a graphic representation of it.

HOW TO USE THIS TOOL

The tool provides a sample flowchart. Based on the process that the planning team develops for RTI work, team members will create a flowchart that can be used to illustrate the process for stakeholders.

Decision point: The planning team should determine if the flowchart is logical and meaningful to stakeholder groups. If it is not, team members should rework it until it is clear.

TIPS AND VARIATIONS

1. Include a reference to any forms that are required next to appropriate steps in the process. For example, next to the step "Student learning/behavioral concern is identified," the RTI Request for Assistance Form might be indicated.
2. Include a timeline in the flowchart.
3. Create a flowchart of the entire RTI implementation initiative. Begin by introducing RTI to staff members and end with ongoing monitoring. Include dates and people involved.
4. Share the flowchart with a sample of teachers and family members. Ask for feedback as to whether it is clear and meaningful.

Preparing a Flowchart of the RTI Process

Following is a sample flowchart that the RTI Leadership Team can use as a guide. It focuses on the RTI Intervention Team process.

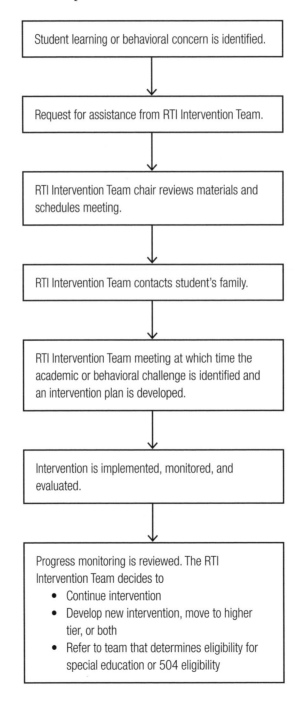

Planning for Parent Communication and Involvement

PURPOSE

In planning for RTI implementation, the RTI Leadership Planning Team will want to consider how parents will be involved in the process. At the very least, parents will need an understanding of RTI. The team also will need to consider parent participation during RTI decision-making processes for their child. The purpose of this tool is to assist the planning team in considering how positive communication with parents might be established and maintained during each phase of the RTI process.

HOW TO USE THIS TOOL

This tool contains questions intended to prompt discussion and ideas among the planning team regarding ways to help parents understand RTI and be involved during different stages of development, particularly when their own child may require interventions.

Decision point: The team should determine if parents have been involved to the extent appropriate, and if they have planned sufficient communication opportunities.

TIPS AND VARIATIONS

1. Invite parent representatives to participate and share their ideas about parent communication and involvement.
2. Consult with other schools to identify their approaches to parent communication and involvement in the RTI process.
3. As decisions are made related to parent communication and involvement, identify parents interested in helping with information dissemination. For example, a parent could be asked to write an article about RTI in the parent newsletter.
4. Using the questions in the tool, generate a frequently asked questions and answers document for parents.

Building Your School's Capacity to Implement RTI | Developing and Implementing the RTI Plan

Putting It All Together: Developing the RTI Framework and Implementation Plan | Planning for Parent Communication and Involvement

5. Review examples of parent communication tools, including those from national organizations, such as the following:

    • Klotz, M. B., & Canter, A. (2006). *Response to Intervention (RTI): A primer for parents*. Bethesda, MD: National Association of School Psychologists. Retrieved April 13, 1010, from www.nasponline.org/resources/factsheets/rtiprimer.aspx

    • Cortiella, C. (2006). *A parent's guide to Response to Intervention: Parent advocacy brief*. Washington, DC: National Center for Learning Disabilities. Retrieved April 13, 1010, from www.ncld.org/publications-a-more/parent-advocacy-guides/a-parent-guide-to-rti

Putting It All Together: Developing the RTI Framework and Implementation Plan

Planning for Parent Communication and Involvement

Questions to Address During Planning	Notes and Ideas
Overall	
What existing parent communication vehicles can be expanded upon to incorporate information about RTI?	
Universal Screening	
How will parents be informed of school plans for universal screening?	
How will parents be informed about the universal screening results for their child?	
Identifying Students with Learning Challenges	
How will you obtain information from parents about their impressions and/or concerns related to their child's academic achievement and/or behavior?	
How will parents be informed and involved as concerns are identified about their child's achievement and/or behavior?	
How will parents be involved as recommendations are being developed to address their child's achievement and/or behavior concerns?	

Part 3

Building Your School's Capacity to Implement RTI | Developing and Implementing the RTI Plan

Putting It All Together: Developing the RTI Framework and Implementation Plan | Planning for Parent Communication and Involvement

Progress Monitoring	
How will parents be informed about the assessment instruments that will be used for monitoring progress?	
How will parents be informed about the frequency of progress monitoring and the expected duration?	
How frequently will parents receive the results of their child's progress monitoring? What parent-friendly format will be used to share the results?	
Interventions	
What role might parents play as interventions are being discussed for their child?	
How will parents be informed about the interventions selected for use with their child at Tier 1?	
How will parents be informed about the interventions selected for use with their child at Tier 2 and Tier 3?	
How will parents be informed about who is providing the interventions?	
What information, materials, and resources can be shared with parents to assist them in furthering their child's progress by helping at home?	

Building Your School's Capacity to Implement RTI | Developing and Implementing the RTI Plan

Putting It All Together: Developing the RTI Framework and Implementation Plan | Planning for Parent Communication and Involvement

Part 3

Other	
What other efforts can be made to ensure that there is positive two-way communication between school staff and parents, particularly as it relates to planning and implementing an RTI framework?	
How will you obtain feedback from parents regarding their views on RTI and the schools efforts to communicate with and involve parents?	
What communication with parents about their child will be documented and in what format?	

Decisions, Recommendations, Next Steps, and Individuals Responsible:

Communicating About RTI

PURPOSE

As with any major school improvement initiative, planning for communication—with administrators, instructional staff, families, the RTI Intervention Team, and, as appropriate, students—is a major task. The RTI Leadership Planning Team should decide what to communicate and to whom, how, and when.

Team members also should determine the types of ongoing communication that will be used. For example, some schools have created an RTI newsletter that is distributed on a regular basis (e.g., bimonthly, monthly, etc.). The newsletter may offer the following information:

- Current activities
- Descriptions of how individuals are implementing RTI
- New materials and supports that are available
- Encouragement from the RTI Leadership Planning Team, administrators, and others as appropriate
- Success stories
- Help with challenges

Some schools have built an RTI page on their school website that includes similar information and is updated frequently.

The RTI Leadership Planning Team also may want to consider assigning point people for daily communication and assistance. These are members of the planning team who are available to answer questions and address any concerns—and to bring back concerns to the team as needed. For example, a team member may be assigned as a point person for 1st and 2nd grade teachers. Another team member may be assigned as a point person for all related service providers in the school.

The purpose of this tool is to provide the planning team with an opportunity to plan major communication strategies.

HOW TO USE THIS TOOL

The tool is organized according to the different phases of implementation. For example, in Phase 1, the planning team will introduce RTI to school staff and families. There may be various communication activities for this phase. Examples include the following

- Family brochure that is sent to each home
- Family meeting to answer questions
- Introduction to RTI at a regular staff meeting
- Flyer describing RTI that is distributed to all instructional staff members
- Staff professional development activities scheduled during teacher work days

For each activity, the RTI Leadership Planning Team should indicate the following:

- Schedule—this includes when it is scheduled and the time frame
- Participants—this includes who will be in attendance
- Intended Outcome—this includes goals for the activity
- Materials—this includes any resources (e.g., handouts, PowerPoint presentations, invitations) that will be used for the activity

Decision point: The planning team should develop a communication plan that includes specific communication activities related to each phase of implementation. Team members also should decide if there will be overarching communication strategies (e.g., newsletter). Roles and responsibilities should be assigned.

TIPS AND VARIATIONS

1. Check out how other schools have designed brochures and web pages.
2. If developing a brochure, consider including these components:
   - Welcome statement
   - Purpose of RTI and rationale
   - Benefits of RTI (i.e., how RTI is intended to benefit students)
   - A flowchart of how the process works
   - Reassurances (e.g., parent notifications, confidentiality, and so on)
   - Contact information

Brochures should be brief (e.g., two pages that can be presented as a tri-fold). Consider developing separate brochures for parents, teachers, service providers, and community members.

The Colorado Department of Education has a sample brochure for stakeholders online (www.cde.state.co.us). It includes the following information:

- Definition
- What you should do if you have concerns about a student
- Core RTI principles
- RTI problem-solving process
- Essential RTI vocabulary

3. Develop an RTI communications handbook. This can be used to brief people who are new to the school about RTI.

Communicating About RTI

Phase 1: Introducing RTI to the Staff				
Activity	**Schedule**	**Participants**	**Intended Outcome**	**Materials**
Phase 2: Establishing the RTI Intervention Team				

Phase 3: Initiating the RTI Process				
Activity	**Schedule**	**Participants**	**Intended Outcome**	**Materials**
Phase 4: Monitoring RTI Implementation and Obtaining Feedback				

Putting It All Together: Developing the RTI Framework and Implementation Plan | Communicating About RTI

Phase 5: Sharing Results and Planning for the Future				
Activity	**Schedule**	**Participants**	**Intended Outcome**	**Materials**

Drafting the RTI Plan and Timeline

PURPOSE

The level of change that may be required as schools implement an RTI framework will depend, in part, on their current culture and practices and how closely aligned these are to recommended RTI components. In many schools, the level of change involved in implementing an RTI approach may require a three- to five-year process. As the RTI Leadership Planning Team expands its understanding of RTI, a logical progression is to continually think about and document plans and ideas for moving towards implementation. This will help team members to ensure that they are progressing in a thoughtful and organized manner that engages stakeholders, facilitates buy-in, and ultimately improves the instructional program for all students. The purpose of this tool is to provide a template that the planning team can use to record and update draft goals and objectives for RTI implementation, along with estimated timelines.

HOW TO USE THIS TOOL

The RTI Leadership Planning Team should use this tool during meetings. It is recommended that the team appoint a recorder. At the end of most, if not all, team meetings, the facilitator should engage team members in a summarizing discussion to identify the relationship between the agenda items discussed and implications for identifying goals and objectives for the recorder to add to the plan. Used in this way, the planning document becomes a vivid touchstone that can help the team and others to understand the direction in which the school is headed.

Decision point: The planning team should determine the goals, objectives, and timelines that will help the school progress toward implementing an RTI framework.

TIPS AND VARIATIONS

1. The planning team might share the draft plan that results from this tool with stakeholders for feedback. For example, once the team members have introduced the faculty to RTI, they might send the draft plan to them electronically, along with a

request for additional ideas. Another option might be to establish an RTI school-based website and use it for posting updated plans following planning team meetings.

2. The planning team might share a copy of the blank planning form with other teams (e.g., grade level teams, the RTI Intervention Team, or others). Each team might use the form to keep a record of its unique plans and actions related to RTI.

3. The planning form may be amended based on the preferences or needs of the users. For example, some staff members might find it helpful to add a status column for use in monitoring their progress along with the planning process. [*Note:* There is a tool called "Planning and Monitoring Implementation of the RTI Framework" on page 266 that may be used along with this tool.]

Drafting the RTI Plan and Timeline

Long-Term Goals:

Year One:

Year Two:

Year Three:

Objectives	Projected Timeline	Resources Needed
Forming the RTI Leadership Planning Team to Launch RTI		
Getting Started: Building Momentum for RTI Initiative		
Planning for Universal Screening Component		

Objectives	Projected Timeline	Resources Needed
Examining and Strengthening Core Instruction Component: Tier 1		
Examining and Planning for Tier 2 and Tier 3		
Planning for Problem-Solving Approach and Formation of RTI Intervention Team		

Objectives	Projected Timeline	Resources Needed
Planning for Progress Monitoring		
Building Consensus Among Stakeholders Regarding RTI Implementation		

Putting It All Together: Developing the RTI Framework and Implementation Plan | Drafting the RTI Plan and Timeline

Objectives	Projected Timeline	Resources Needed
Implementing Job-Embedded Professional Development for RTI Intervention Team and Other Selected Faculty		
Implementing RTI and Sustaining Momentum		

Planning and Monitoring Implementation of the RTI Framework

PURPOSE

Implementing an RTI framework is a multistage process that may take several years, depending on a number of factors such as the connections between RTI and existing school practices. For example, schools where Professional Learning Communities are established as effective vehicles for discussing student achievement may find it appropriate to use these communities for planning implementation of universal screening and progress monitoring for struggling learners.

Wherever schools begin, carefully planning for RTI implementation and reviewing the status of the plans will need to occur in a systematic manner so that essential details are not overlooked and so that plans may be modified as needed. The purpose of this tool is to provide two versions of planning and monitoring formats for the RTI Leadership Planning Team to select from and use when implementing the RTI framework. [*Note*: The action steps reflected in each version of the tool align with the format of this action tool.]

HOW TO USE THIS TOOL

The RTI Leadership Planning Team should establish a cycle to periodically review implementation plans and actions and to identify next steps. This may be accomplished by using either version of the tool as a discussion guide and template during meetings focused on planning and providing status updates. The chair identifies the specific topic on the tool to discuss and solicits comments from team members regarding status, resource needs, and next steps. A designated note taker completes the form to reflect the discussion outcomes. Future status meetings should begin with a review of the form completed at a previous meeting.

Decision point: The planning team should review the plan and determine if it covers all aspects of implementation. Team members will want to share the plan with the administrative team.

Building Your School's Capacity to Implement RTI | Developing and Implementing the RTI Plan

Putting It All Together: Developing the RTI Framework and Implementation Plan | Planning and Monitoring Implementation of the RTI Framework

Part 3

TIPS AND VARIATIONS

1. Members of the RTI Leadership Planning Team might use the tool during meetings with the administration and other teams, such as the RTI Intervention Team and grade level teams, to guide progress and status discussions.

2. The administrative team or planning team might decide to provide periodic updates for the faculty and parents by sharing the results of the planning and monitoring process. This might occur during meetings or in electronic or print publications such as designated RTI newsletters or existing newsletters.

267

Planning and Monitoring Implementation of the RTI Framework: Version 1

Status Key:

1 = Action Not Yet Begun

2 = Work Started; in Beginning Stages

3 = Work Mostly Completed

4 = Completed

Actions	Status	Resources Needed	Next Steps	Projected Timeline
Launching RTI Initiative				
Established RTI Leadership Planning Team				
Planned Support for RTI Leadership Planning Team				
Decided Who to Appoint as RTI Coordinator				
Other:				
Other:				

Putting It All Together: Developing the RTI Framework and Implementation Plan | Planning and Monitoring Implementation of the RTI Framework

Actions	Status	Resources Needed	Next Steps	Projected Timeline
Getting Started				
Identified Roles and Responsibilities among RTI Leadership Planning Team Members				
Examined Implementation Practices at Other Schools via Scenarios and Considered Applicability				
Discussed Historical Roots of RTI and the School's Response to Convergence of Research, Legislation, and Policy				
Reviewed Findings from Web-Based Resources and Considered Potential Applicability				
Developed or Adopted RTI Definition				
Crafted a Vision for RTI in the School				
Explored Connections Between RTI and Other Initiatives				

Part 3

Building Your School's Capacity to Implement RTI | Developing and Implementing the RTI Plan

Putting It All Together: Developing the RTI Framework and Implementation Plan | Planning and Monitoring Implementation of the RTI Framework

Actions	Status	Resources Needed	Next Steps	Projected Timeline
Other:				
Other:				
Establishing a Universal Screening Process				
Examined the School's Capacity to Implement a Universal Screening Process and Identified Subsequent Steps				
Identified Screening Assessments Currently in Use in School and District.				
Determined Effectiveness in Addressing Areas of Student Concern and Applicability to Planning Interventions				
Reviewed Commercially Available Screening Instruments and Made Selections for More Detailed Examination				
Surveyed Staff about Universal Screening Assessments Currently Used as Part of Classroom Instruction				
Determined Linkages Between Skills Measured on Screening Assessments and Availability of Supports and Services for Students				

Putting It All Together: Developing the RTI Framework and Implementation Plan | Planning and Monitoring Implementation of the RTI Framework

Actions	Status	Resources Needed	Next Steps	Projected Timeline
Other:				
Other:				
Ensuring Effective Core Instruction				
Examined Current Implementation of Core Instruction and Its Success in Addressing Student Academic and Behavioral Needs				
Reviewed Student Data and Assessed Effectiveness of Core Instruction Across Subgroups				
Reviewed Curriculum Standards in Relation to Core Instruction				
Determined Extent to Which Differentiated Instruction is Implemented in Classrooms				
Explored the Extent to which Research-Based Instructional Practices are Currently Implemented in Classrooms				

Part 3

Building Your School's Capacity to Implement RTI | Developing and Implementing the RTI Plan

Putting It All Together: Developing the RTI Framework and Implementation Plan | Planning and Monitoring Implementation of the RTI Framework

Actions	Status	Resources Needed	Next Steps	Projected Timeline
Considered a Proactive Schoolwide Approach to Behavioral Interventions				
Reviewed Classroom Management Practices as an Essential Feature of a Strong Core Instructional Program				
Reviewed Cultural Responsiveness of the Core Program to Diverse Groups of Learners				
Assessed Current Tier 1 Curriculum Resources and Identified Needs				
Identified Supplemental Instructional Materials				
Other:				
Other:				

Building Your School's Capacity to Implement RTI | Developing and Implementing the RTI Plan

Putting It All Together: Developing the RTI Framework and Implementation Plan | Planning and Monitoring Implementation of the RTI Framework

Part 3

Actions	Status	Resources Needed	Next Steps	Projected Timeline
Understanding a Multitiered Response to Intervention Component				
Planned Ways to Organize Within the School for Efficient Delivery of Intervention Assistance at Tier 2 and Tier 3				
Developed Library or Catalogue of Interventions, Available Resources, Staff Expertise, and Tips for Using				
Reviewed Research-Based Academic Interventions for Use at Tier 2 and Tier 3				
Examined Current Use of Behavioral Interventions at Tier 2 and Tier 3 and Effectiveness of Continuum of Supports				
Reviewed Student Challenges and Available Supports and Identified Areas in Which There Are Gaps				
Established System for Tracking Success of Interventions				

Part 3

Building Your School's Capacity to Implement RTI | Developing and Implementing the RTI Plan

Putting It All Together: Developing the RTI Framework and Implementation Plan | Planning and Monitoring Implementation of the RTI Framework

Actions	Status	Resources Needed	Next Steps	Projected Timeline
Determined Relationship Between RTI and Learning Disability Eligibility Determination and Determined Representation of Special Education in RTI Framework				
Other:				
Other:				
Establishing the Problem-Solving Approach and RTI Intervention Team				
Assessed Roles of Current School Teams and Examined Feasibility of Modifying for RTI Related Work				
Formed RTI Intervention Team with Representation of Selected Skills and Characteristics				
Addressed Logistics and Established Operational Procedures for Work of RTI Intervention Team				
Established a Problem-Solving Process for Discussing Needs of Struggling Learners				

Putting It All Together: Developing the RTI Framework and Implementation Plan | Planning and Monitoring Implementation of the RTI Framework

Actions	Status	Resources Needed	Next Steps	Projected Timeline
Developed Selected Forms and Templates for Use by Intervention Team				
Selected a Decision-Making Model for Identifying Student Interventions at Tier 2 and Tier 3				
Developed Plans and Procedures to Help Ensure That Interventions Are Implemented with Fidelity				
Other:				
Other:				
Establishing a Progress Monitoring Process				
Explored the School's Capacity to Implement a Progress Monitoring Component of RTI				
Reviewed Progress Monitoring Assessments Currently Used in the School and District				

Part 3

Building Your School's Capacity to Implement RTI | Developing and Implementing the RTI Plan

Putting It All Together: Developing the RTI Framework and Implementation Plan | Planning and Monitoring Implementation of the RTI Framework

Actions	Status	Resources Needed	Next Steps	Projected Timeline
Selected Progress Monitoring Measures				
Other:				
Other:				
Putting It All Together: Developing the RTI Framework and Implementation Plan				
Determined Role of RTI Coordinator and Skills Needed				
Planned for Communicating About RTI with Stakeholders, Including Staff Orientations and Facilitating Buy In				
Planned for Parent Communication and Involvement				
Planned Ways to Address Professional Development Needs of RTI Intervention Team Members				
Drafted the RTI Implementation Plan and Timeline				

Putting It All Together: Developing the RTI Framework and Implementation Plan | Planning and Monitoring Implementation of the RTI Framework

Actions	Status	Resources Needed	Next Steps	Projected Timeline
Planned How to Monitor RTI Implementation				
Other:				
Other:				
Introducing RTI to School Staff Members				
Oriented Staff to Purpose and Rationale for RTI, Including Definition				
Facilitated Staff Understanding of RTI Components, Including Interventions in the RTI Pyramid				
Helped Staff Understand Relationship of RTI to Other School Initiatives				
Presented Proposed RTI Implementation Plan to Staff and Obtained Input				
Helped Staff Members Understand Their Roles in Implementing RTI				

Part 3

Building Your School's Capacity to Implement RTI | Developing and Implementing the RTI Plan

Putting It All Together: Developing the RTI Framework and Implementation Plan | Planning and Monitoring Implementation of the RTI Framework

Actions	Status	Resources Needed	Next Steps	Projected Timeline
Helped Staff Members Gain Knowledge of Selected Web-Based Resources Available to Support RTI				
Other:				
Other:				
Developing the RTI Intervention Team				
Identified Areas for Professional Development to Enhance Work of Intervention Team				
Identified Roles and Responsibilities of Individual RTI Intervention Team Members				
Helped Team Members Develop and Use Protocols to Facilitate Standard and Efficient Meeting Procedures				
Ensured That RTI Intervention Team Members Understand the Problem-Solving Process				

Putting It All Together: Developing the RTI Framework and Implementation Plan | Planning and Monitoring Implementation of the RTI Framework

Actions	Status	Resources Needed	Next Steps	Projected Timeline
Ensured That RTI Intervention Team is Prepared for Using Universal Screening and Progress Monitoring Data During Team Meetings				
Ensured That RTI Intervention Team Uses Procedures to Help Staff Members Implement Interventions with Fidelity				
Other.				
Other.				
Implementing the RTI Plan				
Collected and Analyzed Self-Assessment Feedback from Faculty to Assess Status and Need for Additional Supports				
Conducted Focus Groups to Obtain Implementation Feedback				
Using Monitoring Tools to Assess Progress of Implementation, Review Timelines, and Make Adjustments as Needed				
Using Tools or Strategies to Plan Next Steps and Enhancements				

Part 3

Building Your School's Capacity to Implement RTI | Developing and Implementing the RTI Plan

Putting It All Together: Developing the RTI Framework and Implementation Plan | Planning and Monitoring Implementation of the RTI Framework

Actions	Status	Resources Needed	Next Steps	Projected Timeline
Other:				
Other:				

Putting It All Together: Developing the RTI Framework and Implementation Plan

Planning and Monitoring Implementation of the RTI Framework: Version 2

Status Key:

1 = Action Not Yet Begun

2 = Work Started; in Beginning Stages

3 = Work Mostly Completed

4 = Completed

Goals	Resources Needed	Next Steps	Projected Timeline	Status/Progress
Forming RTI Leadership Planning Team to Launch RTI				

Part 3

Building Your School's Capacity to Implement RTI | Developing and Implementing the RTI Plan

Putting It All Together: Developing the RTI Framework and Implementation Plan | Planning and Monitoring Implementation of the RTI Framework

Goals	Resources Needed	Next Steps	Projected Timeline	Status/Progress
Getting Started: Building Momentum for RTI Initiative				

Building Your School's Capacity to Implement RTI | Developing and Implementing the RTI Plan

Putting It All Together: Developing the RTI Framework and Implementation Plan | Planning and Monitoring Implementation of the RTI Framework

Part 3

Goals	Resources Needed	Next Steps	Projected Timeline	Status/Progress
Planning for Universal Screening Component				
Examining and Strengthening Core Instruction Component —Tier 1				

Putting It All Together: Developing the RTI Framework and Implementation Plan | Planning and Monitoring Implementation of the RTI Framework

Goals	Resources Needed	Next Steps	Projected Timeline	Status/Progress
Examining and Planning for Tier 2 and Tier 3				

Goals	Resources Needed	Next Steps	Projected Timeline	Status/Progress
Planning for Problem-Solving Approach and Formation of RTI Intervention Team				
Planning for Progress Monitoring				

Part 3

Building Your School's Capacity to Implement RTI | Developing and Implementing the RTI Plan

Putting It All Together: Developing the RTI Framework and Implementation Plan | Planning and Monitoring Implementation of the RTI Framework

Goals	Resources Needed	Next Steps	Projected Timeline	Status/Progress
Developing a Proposed Multiyear Plan for RTI Implementation				

Building Your School's Capacity to Implement RTI | Developing and Implementing the RTI Plan

Putting It All Together: Developing the RTI Framework and Implementation Plan | Planning and Monitoring Implementation of the RTI Framework

Part 3

Goals	Resources Needed	Next Steps	Projected Timeline	Status/Progress
Building Consensus Among Stakeholders Regarding RTI Implementation				
Implementing Job-Embedded Professional Development for RTI Intervention Team and Other Selected Faculty				

Part 3

Building Your School's Capacity to Implement RTI | Developing and Implementing the RTI Plan

Putting It All Together: Developing the RTI Framework and Implementation Plan | Planning and Monitoring Implementation of the RTI Framework

Goals	Resources Needed	Next Steps	Projected Timeline	Status/Progress
Implementing RTI and Sustaining Momentum				

SECTION 2 OVERVIEW: INTRODUCING RTI TO SCHOOL STAFF MEMBERS

Once the RTI Leadership Planning Team has developed the RTI Implementation Plan, team members will begin the process of introducing RTI to staff members. In addition to helping staff members become oriented to RTI, planning team members will want to use introductory activities to build buy-in and support for the RTI initiative, encourage participation in activities, and gauge readiness for full implementation.

PURPOSE OF THIS SECTION AND SUMMARY OF TOOLS

The purpose of this section is to provide the planning team with information and professional development activities for introducing RTI to school staff members. The tools in this section are designed as activities that can be presented to the entire staff or used in small groups. In all cases, the activities are only suggestions. The planning team should feel free to revise or change any of the activities to better meet the needs of their staff members, the amount of time, and the availability of resources to carry out the activities.

This section of the action tool contains tools that will assist the RTI Leadership Planning Team in the following

- Orienting school staff to the purpose and rationale for RTI.
- Presenting the proposed RTI framework for the school.
- Making connections between RTI components and current school initiatives and practices.
- Helping staff members understand their role in implementing RTI.
- Directing staff to resources relative to RTI.

The tools are as follows:

- **Starting with an Overview: A PowerPoint Presentation on RTI.** This tool provides a general overview of RTI that team members can share with stakeholders.
- **Using Nonlinguistic Representations to Foster Reflection, Understanding, and Discussion of RTI.** The planning team will want to provide a number of professional development experiences for staff members to receive information about RTI, engage in discussions, and pose questions. This tool is intended for use as a follow-up to a briefing or presentation on RTI.

- **Presenting the RTI Definition.** Definitions help facilitate clear communication about the purpose of the RTI work. This tool is designed for the planning team to use when sharing the RTI definition with staff members and facilitating buy-in.

- **Understanding Changing Roles: Staff Survey.** As part of the orientation phase, planning team members may want to elicit staff members' perceptions. This tool is designed to help staff members reflect on schoolwide RTI goals and to share their ideas regarding their potential roles and responsibilities and the supports or changes that would help to facilitate their participation.

- **Searching Web-Based Resources and Summarizing Findings.** In familiarizing school staff members with RTI—as well as enlisting their help in identifying resources—the RTI Leadership Planning Team may have staff members review several websites and share results. This tool provides a template for recording website content for sharing and future reference.

- **Providing Staff with an Understanding of RTI Components.** The planning team may find it helpful to provide staff members with a summary of the information in written form. This tool provides a brief summary of each of the major RTI components that can be distributed to school staff.

- **Understanding Interventions in the RTI Pyramid.** The planning team should provide staff members with an understanding of the types of interventions found in Tier 1, Tier 2, and Tier 3. This tool provides a professional development activity that can be used to engage staff in thinking about the types of interventions in a tiered system. The planning team can use results from the tool to better understand staff members' perceptions about what constitutes a strong core instructional program.

- **Sharing the Draft RTI Implementation Plan.** The planning team may find it helpful to present the proposed RTI framework implementation plan in a step-by-step fashion. The purpose of this tool is to provide a strategy for engaging staff members in reflecting on what the RTI implementation plan means to them in terms of their roles and responsibilities, additional questions they must have answered, and the types of support they need in order to participate effectively.

- **Showing the Relationship of RTI to Other School Initiatives.** Many ongoing school initiatives already incorporate components of an RTI framework. This tool provides an activity to help staff members explore how RTI connects to—and may complement—initiatives with which they are already involved and committed.

- **Eliciting Ideas, Reactions, and Questions via a Frayer Diagram.** The planning team will want to provide different types of experiences to help to foster staff members' understanding of RTI while at the same time facilitating opportunities for them to share their own ideas, provide feedback, and pose questions. This tool is intended for use as a follow-up to a presentation or briefing on RTI or an article review.

After completing these tools with staff members, RTI Leadership Planning Team members should be able to finalize roll-out plans for the next phase of the RTI initiative—forming the RTI Intervention Team and establishing the RTI problem-solving approach.

In cases where the planning team determines that staff members do not have sufficient readiness to move ahead, team members should reconvene and make adjustments to their RTI implementation plan. Planning team members should keep in mind that change is a process as they revamp or modify their implementation plan. For example, staff may benefit from the following:

- Professional development designed to boost their skills and knowledge with regard to specific RTI components
- Additional time to reflect on RTI and its potential in helping students achieve
- More focused support from the RTI Leadership Planning Team in understanding the roles and responsibilities they are being asked to assume
- Increased administrative support
- Opportunities to discuss perceived challenges and opportunities

Starting with an Overview:
A PowerPoint Presentation on RTI

PURPOSE

The RTI Leadership Planning Team should have a general overview of RTI that team members can share with stakeholders. The general overview should be brief and capture major points:

- What is RTI and what is it designed to do?
- What are the intended benefits of RTI?
- What are the historical and political roots of RTI?
- What are the major components of an RTI framework?

The purpose of this tool is to provide a sample presentation that the planning team may use when introducing RTI to stakeholders.

HOW TO USE THIS TOOL

The RTI Leadership Planning Team members should review the sample PowerPoint presentation for consistency with their school-based RTI plan and make adjustments. See page 7 for instructions on how to download the tool.

- Deciding which slides to include in or omit from their final presentation.
- Determining if additional slides should be added that communicate their school's RTI framework.
- Customizing the PowerPoint presentation (e.g., add the school's vision statement).

After reviewing and adjusting the PowerPoint presentation, planning team members may want to think of strategies to engage the participants during the presentation (e.g., think-pair-share activities in which a question or comment is posed to the participants who first think about it, then share their response with a partner; standard question-and-answer activities; etc.).

The team may want to consider sharing the presentation delivery. For example, one person may welcome the participants, another may provide the overview, another may discuss the history of RTI, and so on.

Decision point: Planning team members should have designed their presentation, including assigning responsibilities to team members.

TIPS AND VARIATIONS

1. After RTI has been initiated, add slides to the PowerPoint presentation that feature instructional staff in the school.
2. Post the PowerPoint presentation on the school's website.
3. Make the PowerPoint presentation available for parents in other languages, as appropriate.
4. Share the PowerPoint presentation with families. Consider hosting a presentation for the PTA/PTO.
5. Add voice to the PowerPoint presentation. Make copies of the PowerPoint presentation available (e.g., in the teacher work room, in the library, or other locations). Share the PowerPoint presentation with staff members who may have been absent on the presentation day, staff members who are new to the school, guests as appropriate, and others.

Using Nonlinguistic Representations to Foster Reflection, Discussion, and Understanding of RTI

PURPOSE

The RTI Leadership Planning Team will want to provide a number of professional development experiences for staff members to receive information about RTI, engage in discussions, and pose questions. These experiences should be designed to help build and enhance knowledge. They also should provide support to staff members during implementation.

This tool is intended for use as a follow up to a briefing or presentation on RTI (e.g., an RTI overview PowerPoint presentation). It provides a vehicle for staff members to think about selected aspects of the presentation in new ways and to help deepen their understanding by representing their learning nonlinguistically. For example, a time sequence pattern organizer might be used to highlight some of the historical underpinnings of RTI.

HOW TO USE THIS TOOL

As part of the advance preparation for introducing RTI to faculty members, the RTI Leadership Planning Team should affix blank chart paper or posters in various locations around the room and provide a set of markers for each small group. The facilitator should explain that upon concluding the presentation, each small group will receive five questions designed to help members think about the applicability of the presentation. Each group will select one of the questions for brief discussion and subsequent decision making about a way to respond to the question nonlinguistically. For example, groups might choose to respond to the question using sketches, pictographs in the form of stick figures or symbols, various types of graphic organizers, flow charts, timelines, etc. The time allocation for this part of the task would be approximately 10 minutes.

After deciding upon the question to address and a way to address it via a nonlinguistic representation, each small group should move to one of the posted charts and create their illustration. The facilitator should end by asking a representative of each group to explain their representation. Time should be provided for those in the audience to ask any clarifying questions. The facilitator should maintain the posters for display in future meetings and discussions as a vehicle for review prior to sharing new information. Further, as faculty

Building Your School's Capacity to Implement RTI | Developing and Implementing the RTI Plan

Introducing RTI to School Staff Members | Using Nonlinguistic Representations to Foster Reflection, Discussion, and Understanding of RTI

Part 3

members continue to expand their understanding of RTI, the facilitator may wish to provide opportunities for groups to modify or enhance their nonlinguistic representations.

Decision point: The planning team should use the illustrations or diagrams to informally assess staff members' understanding and support of creating an RTI framework for the school. Based on this assessment, the team should determine next steps. For example, does the faculty need additional information on a particular topic?

TIPS AND VARIATIONS

1. The facilitator might affix charts around the room that are titled with terms or phrases corresponding with selected key ideas from the presentation. For example, each chart might be titled with one of the main presentation topics, such as definitions, universal screening, core instruction (Tier 1), essential components of reading identified by the National Reading Panel, progress monitoring, or Individuals with Disabilities Education Improvement Act. At the end of the presentation, the facilitator might ask each small group to move to a designated chart and summarize their understanding of the particular title on the chart by adding a corresponding nonlinguistic representation.

2. The facilitator might identify one key component such as core instruction, and ask each group to elaborate on the component by creating a nonlinguistic representation. Another option might be to ask that each small group reach consensus on one topic from the presentation that they found intriguing and create a nonlinguistic representation related to that specific topic.

3. This learning experience might be used at a workshop for parents. The facilitator might choose to provide an example of the task by sharing one or two charts that were created by faculty members.

4. There may be a nonlinguistic representation created by faculty members or parents that might be used in the school's brochure, newsletter, or other literature on RTI.

Using Nonlinguistic Representations to Foster Reflection, Discussion, and Understanding of RTI

Reflective Questions	Ideas for Nonlinguistic Representations
What aspects of RTI seem particularly interesting or promising in terms of benefiting students? How could we summarize one or more of these aspects nonlinguistically?	
If you were asked to convey pertinent information about RTI to a group of stakeholders (e.g., colleagues or parents), what aspect(s) would you focus on and what nonlinguistic representation could you use?	
What nonlinguistic representation could you use to illustrate the relationship between RTI and current practices within our school?	
What nonlinguistic representation could you use to illustrate the component of RTI that might be especially challenging for our school?	

Building Your School's Capacity to Implement RTI | Developing and Implementing the RTI Plan

Introducing RTI to School Staff Members | Using Nonlinguistic Representations to Foster Reflection, Discussion, and Understanding of RTI

Part 3

What nonlinguistic representation would convey one of the challenges currently experienced by a number of our students and a way in which RTI might be helpful?	
Additional Ideas or Notes	

Presenting the RTI Definition

PURPOSE

Definitions can play a significant role in helping to guide the work of schools and facilitating clear communication about the purpose of the work. In previous sections, the RTI Leadership Planning Team drafted a working definition of RTI for its framework that reflected the vision and beliefs of the school and district and emphasized different purposes and components of the RTI framework. This tool is designed for the planning team to use when sharing the RTI definition with staff members and obtaining buy-in.

HOW TO USE THIS TOOL

The RTI Leadership Planning Team should decide who will present the draft definition to the staff. Team members might engage staff in reacting to the definition in various ways:

- Ask staff members to identify key words in the definition. As staff members identify the key words, the facilitator or a note taker should underline them or record them on a separate chart. Use the sample questions in the tool to facilitate discussion.
- Following discussion, the planning team should ask staff members for their endorsement of the definition. The planning team should be prepared with next steps in the event that staff members do not endorse the definition.

Decision point: At the end of the discussion, the planning team should have finalized a definition that can help guide the school's RTI work facilitate clear communication with stakeholders. If staff members have not endorsed the definition, then the planning team should revise the definition and obtain staff input and buy-in.

TIPS AND VARIATIONS

1. In some cases, the school's vision statement may require some modifications in order to embrace the RTI definition. The planning team might want to work with selected school staff members to propose enhancements to the vision statement that incorporate the RTI definition.

2. The planning team might show staff definitions from other organizations. [See "Selecting or Reviewing an RTI Definition" on page 53 for sample definitions from selected organizations.] Staff members might be asked to compare and contrast the definitions with the definition the planning team presented.

3. Begin a two-column chart to highlight what RTI is and what it is not. Discuss the components of the definition and record the discussion points on the chart. The chart might be maintained and expanded in subsequent meetings as the team reviews additional information about RTI. When finalized, the chart can be shared with the broader team as a way to deepen understanding of RTI.

4. Some teams may prefer to use guiding principles in place of a formal definition.

Presenting the RTI Definition

The following sample questions may be used to facilitate and record discussion about the definition or guiding principles:

Sample Questions	Notes
What are the key words or phrases in the definition and guiding principles? (Underline them as they are identified or record them on a separate chart or slide.)	
Which components of the definition and guiding principles do you particularly agree with, disagree with, or have questions about?	
Are any of these components similar to our current practices? How do the components differ from our current practices?	
How do the definition and guiding principles support and enhance our school's vision statement?	
Other Questions	

Understanding Changing Roles: Staff Survey

PURPOSE

Some staff members may find their roles and responsibilities changing as an RTI framework is developed and implemented. For example, the reading coach might be called upon to provide small-group instruction for general education students at Tier 2. School psychologists may be tapped to help instructional staff administer progress monitoring assessments or to provide professional development. A 1st and 2nd grade teacher may receive professional development in specific reading interventions and strategies.

As part of the orientation phase, RTI Leadership Planning Team members may want to elicit the perceptions of staff members. This tool is designed to help staff members reflect on schoolwide RTI goals and share their ideas regarding their potential roles and responsibilities and the supports or changes that would help to facilitate their participation.

HOW TO USE THIS TOOL

During a faculty meeting, the principal or a designated RTI Leadership Planning Team member should explain the purpose of the survey and invite staff members to complete it. Prior to distribution, decide whether staff should complete it at the time or complete it later and return it by a designated date. Planning team members should review completed surveys, compile results, and plan ways to share results with the staff.

Decision point: The planning team should decide if staff members are ready to embrace RTI. They also should decide how best to answer their questions and concerns.

TIPS AND VARIATIONS

1. The principal or designated planning team member might use the survey as a conversation starter with selected staff in lieu of the full staff.
2. Members of school-based teams (e.g., grade level) might be asked to respond as a group to the survey rather than individually.
3. The survey might be customized by adding or deleting goals.

Understanding Changing Roles: Staff Survey

As our school moves forward with planning for RTI implementation, we are asking staff members to share their experiences, expertise, and interests with colleagues and students in some new and different ways. This survey provides an opportunity for you to

- Think about some of our RTI goals.
- Share your ideas to help us achieve them.
- Share ways in which you might be able to contribute.
- Note changes and supports that you would need.

RTI Goals	How You Can Help	Changes and Supports You Would Need
Assisting in review of core instructional program in reading or math. Helping to identify research-based practices to help strengthen the core program as needed. *Ideas:*		
Reviewing accommodations and modifications within Tier 1 to ensure that targeted students receive the necessary supports. *Ideas:*		
Selecting universal screening instruments. *Ideas:*		

Part 3

RTI Goals	How You Can Help	Changes and Supports You Would Need
Helping to provide training on universal screening instruments. *Ideas:*		
Administering, scoring, and interpreting universal screening instruments. *Ideas:*		
Providing small-group instruction for students who require more intensive instructional support. *Ideas:*		
Helping develop plans for at-risk students moving from Tier 2 or Tier 3. *Ideas:*		
Selecting progress monitoring instruments. *Ideas:*		

RTI Goals	How You Can Help	Changes and Supports You Would Need
Becoming an early user of progress monitoring instruments and data systems and helping to train others. *Ideas:*		
Helping to determine when a student requires more intensive instructional support (including determining cut scores on progress monitoring instruments). *Ideas:*		
Reviewing progress monitoring data and helping to determine when changes are needed in strategy, materials, intensity, or tier level. *Ideas:*		
Observing selected instructional strategies and materials usage and providing feedback regarding fidelity of implementation. *Ideas:*		
Responding to teacher requests for assistance with instructional strategies. *Ideas:*		

Introducing RTI to School Staff Members | Understanding Changing Roles: Staff Survey

RTI Goals	How You Can Help	Changes and Supports You Would Need
Developing materials to foster parent understanding of RTI. *Ideas:*		
Additional Ideas, Questions, and Concerns		

Searching Web-Based Resources and Summarizing Findings

PURPOSE

Type "Response to Intervention" in a search engine, and literally hundreds of URLs will be cited. Some of these websites may contain valuable resources and downloadable tools that school staff can use in their RTI work.

In familiarizing staff members with RTI, the RTI Leadership Planning Team may want to have them review several websites and share their findings. It also is helpful to document aspects of each website that may serve as future resources. Examples of websites on RTI include:

- National Center on Response to Intervention: www.rti4success.org
- RTI Action Network: www.rtinetwork.org
- The Colorado Department of Education: www.cde.state.co.us/RtI/ToolsResources RtI.htm

The purpose of this tool is to provide a template for recording website content for sharing and future reference. It also can serve as a form of professional development for staff.

HOW TO USE THIS TOOL

The amount of information found on websites is extensive. Because individuals could literally spend weeks reviewing all of the available websites, it is helpful for the planning team to streamline the process. For example, a completed tool could be shared with staff members as an example when exploring web-based resources. Or, selected planning team members could model the process by perusing a website and summarizing their findings on the tool. Next, staff could be invited to explore various websites, preferably in small groups, and to discuss their findings with the total group. The planning team could engage staff in discussing the usefulness of websites in providing useful resources. Their completed tools could be posted online or in notebooks for future reference.

Decision point: The planning team should determine the level of staff member interest in learning about RTI by observing the extent to which they benefitted from the activity and by the questions they raised.

TIPS AND VARIATIONS

1. If the planning team members have already surveyed websites as part of their learning about RTI, they might direct staff members to those websites that they found to be most useful.

2. The planning team might ask staff members to review web-based resources related to specified topics (e.g., graphing progress monitoring data, using universal screening data, implementing positive behavioral support as part of effective core instruction, and so on). Here are some examples:

Data Use: Curriculum-Based Measurement, Universal Screening, and Progress Monitoring

- National Center on Student Progress Monitoring (funding for site has ended but resources still available): www.studentprogress.org
- National Center on Response to Intervention (see updated progress monitoring tools chart): www.rti4success.org/chart/progressMonitoring/progressmonitoring toolschart.htm

Screening Tools

- AIMSweb: http://aimsweb.com
- DIBELS data system: http://dibels.uoregon.edu
- Yearly Progress Pro (McGraw Hill): http://www.mhdigitallearning.com
- Intervention Central (RTI section): http://www.interventioncentral.org

Academic Interventions

- The Access Center (funding for site has ended but resources are still available): www.k8accesscenter.org
- Florida Center on Reading Research (characteristics of effective supplemental and intensive instruction): http://www.fcrr.org
- Review of core reading programs: www.fcrr.org/FCRRReports/reportslist.htm

- University of Oregon (see Big Ideas in Beginning Reading for early literacy): http://reading.uoregon.edu/
- University of Nebraska at Lincoln (information on cognitive strategy instruction): www.unl.edu/csi
- Vaughn Gross Center for Reading and Language Arts (information on reading interventions): www.texasreading.org/utcrla
- What Works Clearinghouse through the Institute for Education Sciences: http://ies.ed.gov/ncee/wwc

Behavioral Interventions

- Positive Behavioral Interventions and Supports: www.pbis.org
- Florida's Positive Behavior Support Project http://flpbs.fmhi.usf.edu/resources_newsletter.asp

3. Selected websites might be assigned to pairs of staff members, to school-based teams (e.g., grade level teams), or to departments based on content areas. The summary information compiled might be shared and discussed within the context of team or department meetings. Or, staff members might be invited to share their report summaries electronically with designated colleagues.

Searching Web-Based Resources and Summarizing Findings

Name of Website and URL: _____

Staff Reviewer: _____ **Date Reviewed:** _____

Overall Focus of Website:

Types of Resources (e.g. articles, PowerPoint presentations, and so on):

Pertinent Findings for Our School and Potential Ways to Use:

Suggestions for Further Exploration:

Follow-Up Recommendations:

Providing Staff with an Understanding of RTI Components

PURPOSE

When introducing RTI components to the staff, the RTI Leadership Planning Team may find it helpful to provide staff members with a written summary of the information. This helps to ensure that staff members have consistent information to which they can refer when implementing the RTI framework. This tool provides a summary of each of the major RTI components that can be distributed to school staff.

HOW TO USE THIS TOOL

The briefs in the tool contain a summary about the particular RTI component and a series of reflection questions. See page 7 for instructions on how to download the tool.

1. A Tiered Response to Intervention Approach
2. The RTI Problem-Solving Process and RTI Intervention Team
3. Progress Monitoring
4. Universal Screening as Part of RTI

The briefs can be used in several ways:

- After a presentation on the component, have staff members form small groups of four members and discuss the reflection questions. Debrief with the entire group.
- After a presentation, ask staff members to discuss the reflection questions at a later time in one of their collaborative groups (e.g., Professional Learning Community, grade level team, subject area team).
- Provide staff members with the briefs before the presentation (e.g., attach to the meeting agenda).

Decision point: At the end of the presentation(s) on RTI components, the RTI Leadership Planning Team should determine if school staff members have sufficient knowledge of the topics. If not, team members should plan additional professional development activities for staff.

TIPS AND VARIATIONS

1. Before presenting the handout brief to staff members, the RTI Leadership Planning Team might conduct an activity to tap into prior knowledge. For each component, ask staff members:

    - What do you *know* for sure about the RTI component?
    - What do you *think you know* about the RTI component?
    - What do you *want to know* about the RTI component?

2. Ask staff to respond in writing to the reflection questions. Tally results and share. Use the information to plan professional development.

3. Before introducing the RTI component, ask school staff to generate questions about the component. After a presentation on the topic, ask staff members to review the questions and identify any that have not been answered. Add additional questions to the list that the planning team can answer at a future time.

4. Using the information found in the briefs, create a shorter brief for parents. Consider using a question-and-answer format.

Understanding Interventions in the RTI Pyramid

PURPOSE

When introducing RTI to staff members, the RTI Leadership Planning Team may find it helpful to spend time explaining the types of interventions found in Tier 1, Tier 2, and Tier 3. The key is to provide staff members with sufficient understanding without creating a debate in which the focus is on assigning an intervention to a tier for its own sake.

The purpose of this tool is to provide an activity that can be used to engage staff in thinking about the types of interventions in a tiered system. Results from the tool can be used to better understand staff members' perceptions about what constitutes a strong core instructional program.

HOW TO USE THIS TOOL

The RTI Leadership Planning Team can use the activity in Part 1 of the tool as a springboard for discussing the difference between interventions at Tier 1 and higher. Explain to staff members that interventions found in Tier 2 and Tier 3 differ from accommodations and supports that normally occur in the core instructional program. *Their challenge*: To determine which of the activities listed qualify as a Tier 1, Tier 2, or Tier 3 intervention, given this definition. [*Note for facilitator*: All of the activities listed would be considered components of a core program and, therefore, not a Tier 2 or Tier 3 intervention.]

Provide five to seven minutes for participants to complete the tool. Tally and discuss results. Pay particular attention to those activities that participants believe should be considered as Tier 2 or Tier 3 interventions.

Move into a discussion of how interventions at Tier 2 and Tier 3 differ from those used in Tier 1. Use the RTI pyramid graphic in Part 2 of the tool for this activity. Ask staff to think about various interventions currently available in the school. With a partner or small group, ask participants to think about the types of interventions currently available in the school and to plot them on their pyramid. Debrief with the entire group. The planning team can share additional interventions that staff members have not identified.

Decision point: Before moving ahead, the planning team should determine whether staff members understand the types of accommodations and practices that are part of core instruction. Team members also should assess staff members' familiarity with Tier 2 and Tier 3 interventions.

TIPS AND VARIATIONS

1. Discuss the extent to which teachers use various practices as part of core instruction. Ask staff to describe how they decide when and how to use these various instructional activities.

2. Discuss the types of student challenges that the activities listed in the tool address.

3. Have participants generate a list of additional accommodations and modifications that they employ as part of the core instructional program.

4. Meet with the RTI Intervention Team and discuss the extent to which school staff members are familiar with various interventions. Sort the interventions by levels of staff familiarity. Decide which supports and interventions might be good candidates for schoolwide professional development.

5. After the meeting, send out a final version of the RTI pyramid to the entire staff.

6. The planning team might use the completed RTI Pyramid to gauge professional development needs by asking staff members to circle the top five instructional and behavioral supports or interventions on which they would like to receive professional development.

7. The planning team might invite small groups of instructional staff members to volunteer to learn more about a particular support or intervention. Schedule a follow-up meeting when the group can present their findings.

Part 1: Understanding Interventions in the RTI Pyramid

For each of the following instructional activities, indicate whether or not it most likely would be considered a Tier 1, Tier 2, or Tier 3 intervention.

____ 1) Suspension

____ 2) Parent conference

____ 3) Homework

____ 4) Preferential seating

____ 5) Extra time to complete an assignment

____ 6) Manipulatives in mathematics

____ 7) Drill and practice

____ 8) Guided practice with teacher feedback

____ 9) Independent practice

____ 10) Differentiated instruction

____ 11) Graphic organizers

____ 12) Student choice

____ 13) Curriculum aligned with standards

____ 14) Learning contracts

____ 15) Proximity control

___ 16) Active learning

___ 17) Activity modified for difficulty

___ 18) Explicit instruction of basic skills

___ 19) Formative assessment

___ 20) Reinforcement and recognition

___ 21) Summarizing main points

___ 22) Cooperative learning

___ 23) Advance organizers

___ 24) Note taking

___ 25) Modified directions

___ 26) Peer and cross-age tutoring

___ 27) Additional instructional time in a deficit area

___ 28) Consistent clear expectations

___ 29) Predictable classroom routines

___ 30) Smooth transitions

Part 2: Understanding Interventions in the RTI Pyramid

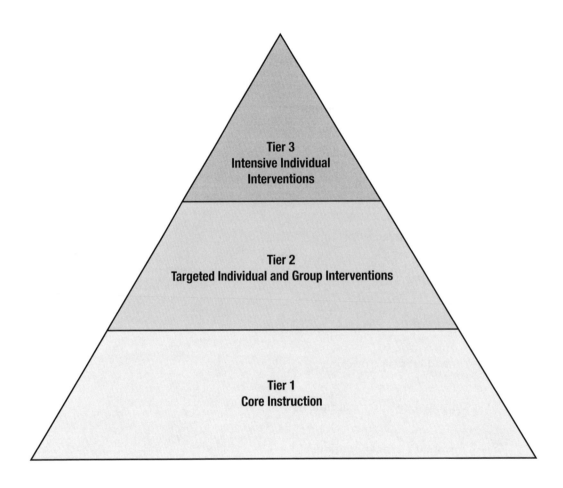

Sharing the Draft RTI Implementation Plan

PURPOSE

Once the RTI Leadership Planning Team has provided an overview of RTI and the major RTI components to staff, team members should share the draft RTI implementation plan. The implementation plan presents the RTI framework that the planning team developed in Part 3, Section 1.

It is helpful to present the implementation plan in very concrete terms. Think in terms of walking staff members step-by-step through the process. If the planning team completed a flowchart of the RTI process in Part 3, Section 1, then it could be used as a visual representation. The purpose of this tool is to provide a strategy for engaging staff members in reflecting on what the RTI implementation plan means to them in terms of their roles and responsibilities, additional questions they need answered, and the types of support they believe they need in order to participate effectively.

HOW TO USE THIS TOOL

The tool is designed as a worksheet for individual staff members. The planning team will share how the RTI initiative will be implemented. Staff members are encouraged to use the tool to record their thoughts. Here are some possible strategies to follow:

- Ask staff members to form small groups. These can be grade level groups, subject area groups, or random groups. Invite staff members to share their perceptions related to roles and responsibilities. Encourage the groups to raise any issues that might undermine implementation. Make note if any of these issues might necessitate changes or tweaks to the implementation plan.
- Ask staff members to share their questions and requests for support at the end of the session. Use the results for planning future professional development activities.
- Probe the group to ascertain their buy-in for the process. Ask them to rate their level of commitment to RTI. For example, a typical Likert scale could be used (e.g., strongly committed, committed, somewhat committed, somewhat not committed, not committed). Or, staff could be asked to respond to feedback questions (e.g., 3

means totally committed, 2 means positive but still need more information, 1 means not convinced this is right for our school).

Decision point: The planning team should determine whether staff members have sufficient understanding of the implementation plan, as well as their capacity and commitment to carrying it out. If there appear to be significant challenges or resistance to the plan, the planning team should revise the plan.

TIPS AND VARIATIONS

1. Write each aspect of the plan on separate piece of chart paper that is taped to the wall. Invite staff members (e.g., during break, as part of a museum walk activity, etc.) to write their questions and requests for support on the appropriate chart paper.
2. Present a timeline and review next steps in implementation.
3. In cases where staff members' questions reflect requests for more information on a topic, form study groups. Assign the groups several questions related to the topic. Ask the groups to research the questions. Provide the groups with resources (e.g., websites, books, articles, etc.). Invite the groups to report their findings.

Sharing the Draft RTI Implementation Plan

Ensuring Effective Core Instruction	
My role and responsibilities:	
Questions I need answered:	
Support I need to excel:	
Participating in the RTI Problem-Solving Process	
My role and responsibilities:	
Questions I need answered:	
Support I need to excel:	
Implementing Interventions for Struggling Students	
My role and responsibilities:	
Questions I need answered:	
Support I need to excel:	

ASCD 319

Conducting Progress Monitoring and Using Data to Inform Instructional Decisions	
My role and responsibilities:	
Questions I need answered:	
Support I need to excel:	
Using Universal Screening Data to Inform Instructional Decisions	
My role and responsibilities:	
Questions I need answered:	
Support I need to excel:	

Showing the Relationship of RTI to Other School Initiatives

PURPOSE

A question that often arises is, "How will RTI fit with our other initiatives?" In most cases, schools are involved in one or more major initiatives that have elements of RTI embedded. For example:

- **Professional Learning Communities** may emphasize data-based decision making, enhancing instruction, supporting struggling learners, and developing new skills and knowledge.

- **P–16** and **21st Century Skills** may emphasize strengthening the core instructional program, monitoring progress at each transition point, and providing support to struggling students as they need it.

The school also may have been involved in adopting comprehensive approaches to teaching and learning. For example, ASCD's Whole Child Initiative emphasizes ensuring that students are fully prepared in an effective core instructional program, in which all of their needs—academic, emotional, and physical—are addressed. Students receive the support they need to achieve.

Many schools have undertaken school improvement and professional development initiatives to ensure that instructional staff members provide effective instruction to all students. Common examples of initiatives that are designed to strengthen the core instructional program and to incorporate data-based decision making include (but are not limited to):

- **Classroom Instruction That Works**. Robert J. Marzano and his colleagues explain research-based instructional practices that have a high probability of improving student achievement across all grade levels and content areas when effectively and systematically used during classroom instruction in the ASCD book, *Classroom Instruction That Works*. Marzano and colleagues also identified effective classroom management strategies in another ASCD book, *Classroom Management that Works: Research-Based Strategies for Every Teacher*.

- **Differentiated Instruction**. Developed by Carol Tomlinson, differentiated instruction seeks to maximize each student's learning progress by offering several different learning experiences in response to students' individual needs.
- **The Understanding by Design® framework**. Developed by Grant Wiggins and Jay McTighe, this framework creates more engaging and effective learning through the design of curriculum, assessment, and instruction that is focused on developing and deepening understanding of important ideas.
- **Universal Design for Learning (UDL)**. UDL provides a framework for creating flexible goals, methods, materials, and assessments that accommodate learner differences.
- **Positive Behavioral Interventions and Supports (PBIS)**. PBIS provides an operational framework—similar to an RTI framework—for ensuring that all students have access to effective behavioral practices and interventions. Most PBIS models emphasize data-based decision making, measurable outcomes, a tiered system of evidence-based practices, implementation fidelity, and professional development support.

In addition to strengthening instruction in general, some schools have launched specific initiatives in subject areas (e.g., reading or mathematics) and at certain transition points (e.g., 9th grade academies for struggling students entering high school).

In some cases, schools have organized their initiatives according to state and federal mandates such as NCLB, IDEA, or statewide universal screening. As with other initiatives, components of RTI may be inherent (e.g., considering responsiveness to intervention when identifying a student as having a specific learning disability, using research-based practices to address student difficulties with reading, etc.).

The purpose of this tool is to provide the RTI Leadership Planning Team with an activity to help staff members explore how RTI fits with—and may complement—initiatives with which they are already involved and to which they are already committed.

HOW TO USE THIS TOOL

The planning team should identify the various initiatives with which staff members are engaged. For each initiative, the planning team should engage staff in exploring how that initiative may use or embed RTI components. The tool lists essential elements that are found in an RTI approach:

- Universal screening.
- Data-based problem solving.

- Effective core instruction.
- Supports and interventions, preferably research based, that are organized in levels or tiers reflecting their intensity.
- Progress monitoring.
- Professional development.

For each initiative, conduct a crosswalk with RTI. Discuss the following points:

- Similarities between RTI and the initiative.
- How the initiative might incorporate RTI concepts.
- How an RTI framework could help enhance work on related issues and goals.

At the end of the discussion, invite staff members to share their analysis of how RTI aligns with their current work.

Decision point: The planning team should determine whether staff members see links between RTI and other initiatives. Team members also should probe to determine staff members' receptiveness to RTI in light of these other initiatives. In cases where there are few initiatives or practices that align with RTI, the planning team should discuss the implications and what that might mean in terms of the school's readiness for RTI.

TIPS AND VARIATIONS

1. Convene meetings with leaders and supporters of the various initiatives (e.g., transition to ninth grade, dropout prevention, English as a second language, inclusion of students with disabilities in the general education curriculum, etc.). Present an overview of RTI. Invite participants to identify similarities between RTI and the initiative. Explore how the two approaches might be used in conjunction to support students.
2. Ask staff form small groups to complete the tool. Have each group debrief with the entire group.
3. In cases where staff does not think that RTI is a good fit with a particular initiative, ask for suggestions for eliminating the barriers. Brainstorm what kinds of changes or adjustments might be undertaken to make it a better fit.
4. Acknowledge that RTI may not fit with every initiative.
5. Ask for volunteers to work with the planning team to discuss ways that RTI could enhance the initiative. Share those findings with the entire staff.

Showing the Relationship of RTI to Other School Initiatives

Initiative: _____

RTI Component	Similarities and Overlaps	Suggestions
Universal Screening		
Data-Based Problem Solving		
Effective Core Instruction		
Tiered Supports and Interventions		
Progress Monitoring		
Professional Development		

Analysis: Is RTI a "Good Fit" with This Initiative?

_____ Excellent Fit—Many possibilities for enhancing our work

_____ Okay Fit—Will need to reflect on the types of changes and/or adjustments needed to make this workable.

_____ Not a strong fit—Elements of RTI appear in opposition to our current work.

_____ Not sure—Will need more information.

Introducing RTI to School Staff Members

 # Eliciting Ideas, Reactions, and Questions via a Frayer Diagram

PURPOSE

The administration and the RTI Leadership Planning Team will want to provide different types of experiences that help to foster the faculty's understanding of RTI while at the same time facilitating opportunities for them to share their own ideas, provide feedback, and pose questions. This tool is intended for use as a follow-up to a presentation or briefing on RTI or an article review. Given this sequence, the tool serves as a vehicle for engaging faculty members in a follow-up discussion and helps generate their views and suggestions related to developing an RTI framework for the school. The results of discussions through use of this tool should be recorded, analyzed, and reviewed by the planning team members to assist them in identifying next steps in building faculty support for implementing an RTI framework.

HOW TO USE THIS TOOL

A facilitator should be assigned to guide the faculty through this learning experience. It may be helpful for the principal or another member of the administrative team to serve as the primary facilitator. This may help to convey administration interest and commitment. Another option is for the planning team to designate a facilitator from among its membership. A recorder should be assigned to take notes and capture the staff's discussion, questions, and ideas.

The facilitator should have the following materials: timer, a copy of the Frayer Diagram chart for each participant, a copy of the Frayer Diagram for each small group, and writing implements. *Note*: It might be helpful to enlarge the charts for the small groups or print them on colored paper as a way to distinguish them from those used by individual participants.

As a follow up to a presentation on RTI or an RTI article, the facilitator might conduct the activity as follows:

- Ask staff members to form small groups. These groups may be self-selected or the facilitator may organize them.

- Disseminate a Frayer Diagram chart to each participant and request that they individually spend a total of approximately eight minutes responding in writing to the question printed in each of the four quadrants. Allow approximately two minutes per question prompt. The facilitator should ask participants to write directly on their chart. Explain that a timer will be set for eight minutes, and that at the end of the designated time period staff members will be requested to share their responses with others in their small group.

- If there are multiple small groups, consider quietly circulating around the room, assessing the effectiveness of the time allocation and encouraging participants as needed (e.g., to move to the next quadrant).

- At the end of the eight-minute individual work period, ask that each small group assign a discussion leader and note taker. Disseminate the small-group version of the Frayer Diagram to the note takers. Explain that the role of the discussion leader is to help the group focus on one quadrant at a time and to help ensure that each person in the group has the opportunity to share. [*Note*: The purpose of the color-coded version of the chart is to differentiate it from those completed individually.]

- Share that upon concluding the small-group discussion, each discussion leader or note taker should be prepared to share with the large group one item from each quadrant that was discussed in their small group. Tell the staff that the small-group charts will be collected and incorporated into a compilation of results for the planning team.

- Designate 10 minutes for members of each small group to share their individual ideas and questions and for the note taker to record a summary of their feedback in preparation for large group sharing.

- Guide participants to take turns sharing their individual responses with others in their small group and request that the note taker record individual responses on the color coded or enlarged diagram. Request that temporary role switching occur within the small group to provide an opportunity for the note taker to share. Ask note takers to signal duplication of comments from group members by adding check marks at the end of a statement rather than restating the remarks.

- Request that the leader or note taker for each small group report out to the larger group by sharing an example of one statement from each quadrant. Ask clarifying questions as needed. The note taker should record notes to capture the discussion during this segment of the discussion. At the end of the meeting, collect the charts from each small group for further compilation and analysis.

After the meeting, the facilitator or note taker should compile the responses from all the small groups to create a single document reflecting the ideas generated by each question. The facilitator or note taker should present the summary document during a follow-up meeting with the planning team, at which time team members will consider the feedback and plan for future actions—including the possibility of sharing the summary results with the faculty members who participated in the discussion.

Decision point: The planning team should assess the effectiveness and productivity of this experience for the faculty and determine whether it has resulted in meaningful and helpful feedback related to developing an RTI framework. The team should also determine the feasibility of using this activity in the future with a modification of the questions and procedures. Finally, the team should decide how to communicate final outcomes with the faculty. For example, a summary of the faculty discussion might be posted on the school's website or published in the school's newsletter.

TIPS AND VARIATIONS

1. The facilitator might omit asking participants to complete the Frayer Diagram individually and, instead, ask that each small group discuss the questions, record responses, and share examples with the larger group. The facilitator might arrange to have large chart paper available so that the work of each small group could be posted as a visual reference during discussion. The facilitator also might opt to print the diagram or questions on the large chart paper.

2. The facilitator might modify the questions in the quadrants and adjust the amount of time allocated for this process. For example, the diagram might be modified to relate only to one component of RTI such as universal screening.

3. The Frayer Diagram tool might be used with parents or other stakeholders (e.g., parent teacher organization). Another alternative might be to use the tool with small teams, such as Professional Learning Communities or grade level teams, in lieu of the full faculty.

4. This tool might be used more than once. Repeated use might be planned for different time periods consistent with school's progress toward implementation of an RTI framework.

Eliciting Ideas, Reactions, and Questions
via a Frayer Diagram

Response to Intervention

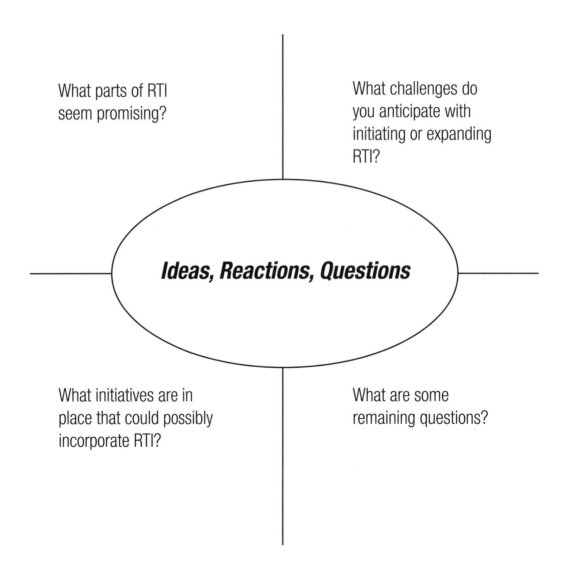

What parts of RTI
seem promising?

What challenges do
you anticipate with
initiating or expanding
RTI?

Ideas, Reactions, Questions

What initiatives are in
place that could possibly
incorporate RTI?

What are some
remaining questions?

PART 3, SECTION 3 OVERVIEW: DEVELOPING THE RTI INTERVENTION TEAM

Many schools use a team structure to implement RTI. In this Action Tool, we refer to that team as the RTI Intervention Team. In some cases, the RTI Leadership Planning Team will have recommended that a new team be established for this purpose. In other cases, the planning team may have decided that it was more efficient to expand the role or reconfigure existing problem-solving teams in the school to carry out intervention team work. In "Reviewing Current School-Based Teams: Opportunities for RTI Expansion" (page 161), the planning team had the opportunity to consider expanding the roles of other problem-solving teams:

- **Child Study Teams**. Some schools have restructured Child Study Teams that review information about students who have been referred for special education evaluation to have an RTI focus.
- **Professional Learning Communities**. Some schools have expanded their Professional Learning Communities to focus on RTI issues. Others have established a schoolwide Professional Learning Community to implement the RTI process.
- **Grade level or subject area teams**. Some schools have increased teacher release time to address RTI issues within grade level or subject areas teams.
- **Student Support Teams**. Some schools have adapted their Student Support Teams to incorporate the components of an RTI approach (e.g., data-based decision making, progress monitoring, etc.).

Regardless of how the intervention team is configured, the planning team will need to prepare the team members for RTI work:

- Forming the team (e.g., identifying roles and responsibilities).
- Understanding the problem-solving process.
- Using data for decision making.
- Identifying and monitoring the implementation of interventions.
- Ensuring that interventions are implemented with fidelity.

The planning team may also want to consider planning professional development for intervention team members, especially in cases where the majority of team members require additional knowledge and skills related to a major component such as universal screening or progress monitoring.

Note: In cases where there is more than one intervention team in the school (e.g., several Professional Learning Communities or teams at each grade level), the planning team may want to assign one or more of its members to each intervention team. For professional development purposes, they may want to combine the teams for some activities. In schools that have an RTI coordinator, this individual may be assigned to the intervention team as both a coach and a liaison with the planning team.

PURPOSE OF THIS SECTION AND SUMMARY OF TOOLS

The purpose of this section is to provide the planning team with information about establishing the RTI Intervention Team. This section of the Action Tool contains tools that help the planning team guide intervention team members as they

- Discuss their roles and responsibilities.
- Understand their role in the problem-solving process, including identifying interventions, developing an intervention plan, ensuring that the intervention is implemented with fidelity, monitoring student progress, and determining success.
- Handle housekeeping tasks, such as setting agendas and meeting dates, storing data, and corresponding with family members.
- Identify areas for professional development.

The tools are as follows:

- **Orienting the RTI Intervention Team: A Team-Building Activity.** When members of new teams come together for the first time, time should be allotted for initial team-building activities. The planning team can use this tool to engage intervention team members in sharing their expertise and personal commitment to RTI work.
- **Developing the RTI Intervention Team: Roles and Responsibilities.** Once the intervention team members are identified, the planning team works with them to assign roles and responsibilities. The planning team can use this tool to help intervention team members determine their roles and responsibilities.
- **Reviewing RTI Intervention Team Tasks Related to Identifying and Monitoring Interventions.** The planning team's orientation to the RTI Intervention Team should include a discussion of the various tasks that are part of the RTI process related to identifying and monitoring interventions. This tool provides an outline of tasks for discussion.
- **Planning Professional Development for the RTI Intervention Team.** Intervention team members should receive ongoing professional development in the

problem-solving model and in the other components of RTI, particularly research-based strategies and progress monitoring. This tool provides a foundation for discussing the types of skills and knowledge that will be needed for the intervention team to be effective.

- **Using a Protocol for RTI Intervention Team Meetings.** The planning team may find it helpful to provide a protocol that can be built into meeting agendas. A protocol provides team members with a standard approach to completing their business. The purpose of this tool is to provide a stimulus for helping the intervention team develop meeting agendas.

- **Organizing for Data Use During RTI Intervention Team Meetings.** The intervention team must organize and maintain progress monitoring and, sometimes, universal screening data. This tool focuses on identifying managerial tasks related to handling data that the planning team can use as they build the intervention team's capacity to use data for decision making.

- **Facilitating Fidelity of Implementation.** Fidelity of implementation refers to delivering instruction in the way in which it was designed to be delivered. The planning team and intervention team can use this tool to plan how fidelity of implementation of RTI will be handled.

After completing these tools, the planning team members should be confident that the intervention team is prepared to carry out the RTI problem-solving process. If so, the planning team will be able to initiate the RTI framework in the school. As is the case when any new activity is rolled out, the planning team will initially want to provide support to the intervention team to ensure that the process is going smoothly. Prior to initiating the process with actual students, the planning team may find it helpful to have the intervention team practice implementing the process using a case-study scenario.

Orienting the RTI Intervention Team— A Team-Building Activity

PURPOSE

When members of new teams come together for the first time, time should be allotted for initial team-building activities. Even in cases where an existing team is used for RTI intervention work, such as a Professional Learning Community team, taking time for members to orient themselves personally to the new focus can be helpful. The purpose of this tool is to provide an opportunity for RTI Intervention Team members to share their expertise and personal commitment to RTI work.

HOW TO USE THIS TOOL

A planning team member may want to facilitate this activity. The goal is for intervention team members to share their knowledge and skills related to the various components of RTI and to acknowledge the level of expertise within the team.

This activity can be organized in different ways:

- Ask intervention team members to complete the tool before the meeting.
- Give the tool to intervention team members and allow time to complete it.
- Consider one item in the tool at a time (i.e., complete progress monitoring, discuss, complete differentiated instruction, discuss, and so on).

Ask the intervention team members to share their results. Record the results. One suggestion is to use a semantic web to organize team members' responses on each RTI component. A semantic web provides participants with a visual summary of results. To complete a semantic web, draw a circle and write the topic in the center (e.g., progress monitoring). As team members share their results, cluster similar answers on spokes (e.g., "five years of experience using progress monitoring in reading" may be an offshoot of a "practical experience" spoke and "participated in a professional development webinar on progress monitoring this year" may be an offshoot of a "knowledge" spoke). The facilitator should draw attention to the degree of expertise in the group and encourage team members to utilize each others' skills.

Decision point: The facilitator should decide if there is sufficient expertise in the group and a beginning feeling of camaraderie. The facilitator also should note any areas in which the expertise of team members should be enhanced. If the facilitator determines that there are areas of inadequate expertise—or areas where only one individual has expertise—then a plan should be made for reconstituting the team and/or building the team's capacity.

TIPS AND VARIATIONS

1. Offer examples of the types of expertise members possess. For example, a team member might have the following types of expertise related to behavioral management:

    -   Classroom experience in managing behaviors of diverse students at the middle school level
    -   Participation on the Positive Behavioral Intervention and Support Team, which was charged with identifying schoolwide rules and interventions
    -   Attendance at a professional development workshop on writing functional behavioral plans for students with significant behavioral difficulties
    -   Professional interest in nonpunitive disciplinary techniques, such as alternatives to suspension and expulsion
    -   University coursework focused on helping students with emotional and behavioral disorders

2. Consider having individuals share their expertise with a teammate before sharing with the entire group.
3. Ask team members to rate their perceived level of expertise for each RTI component. Ask them to pick one area in which they would like to receive professional development. Consider using the scale on page 334.

Orienting the RTI Intervention Team—A Team-Building Activity

Directions: Enter a number from the following scale to reflect your current level of understanding of selected RTI components. Please use the comment section to share additional information, questions, and needs.

4 = I understand this RTI component; I am fully implementing it and can help support others.

3 = I understand this RTI component; I am implementing it but would like more feedback and practice.

2 = I understand this RTI component but am not yet confident with implementation.

1 = I do not yet have a clear understanding of this RTI component and have not begun implementation.

What I Bring to the Team	Comments
Progress Monitoring	
Differentiated Instruction	
Formative Assessment	
Behavioral Management	
Instructional and Assistive Technology	

What I Bring to the Team	Comments
Research-Based Interventions	
Implementation of Research-Based Interventions with Fidelity	
Leadership	
Developing Professional Skills	
Data-Based Decision Making	
Collaboration Skills	
Other	

Developing the RTI Intervention Team: Roles and Responsibilities

PURPOSE

Once the RTI Intervention Team is identified, the RTI Leadership Planning Team works with members to assign roles and responsibilities. The purpose of this tool is to help intervention team members identify their roles and responsibilities.

Meeting roles typically include the following:

- **Chair**. It should be clear how the chair will be chosen. In some schools, the chair is appointed, perhaps by the RTI coordinator. Or, the responsibility for chairing the team may rotate; this can be one way to help build the capacity of the team to function effectively in the absence of an individual member. Usually, the chair is responsible for facilitating the meeting, organizing the agenda, making sure all forms are in order, making initial contact with families, providing feedback to the administration, inviting additional people to the meeting, and assigning case manager roles for individual requesting teachers. Some chairs may choose to delegate some of these responsibilities to other team members. Or, if the school provides support staff for assistance, the chair may delegate some tasks to them.

- **Note taker**. Documentation is a must in all RTI frameworks. Keeping meeting minutes is necessary for documenting student intervention and progress. In some schools, the note taker is assigned for a period of time to ensure consistency of recorded information. The individual may be a team member or a support staff member. Sometimes, this individual also carries out the role of filing paperwork, sending out meeting reminders, and organizing Request for Assistance Forms.

- **Time keeper**. This role is necessary for helping the team stay on track in order to cover the agenda. This role may rotate from meeting to meeting.

- **Case manager**. Different intervention team members may serve in this role. The purpose of this role is to be the point person for a designated teacher who seeks intervention team assistance. This person may oversee intervention implementation, progress monitoring, and fidelity of treatment. The case manager may also act as a peer coach for the teacher who has requested assistance.

- **Intervention specialist**. Core intervention team members usually serve in this role at all meetings. Sometimes, other individuals who have special expertise, such as a school psychologist, a social worker, or the chair of the mathematics department may be invited to the team to fulfill this role.
- **Data specialist**. Intervention team members should have an understanding of screening and progress monitoring data. Sometimes, other individuals who have special expertise may be invited to the team to fulfill this role.

Depending on the particular team composition, the same member may serve in multiple roles.

HOW TO USE THIS TOOL

A designated member of the planning team should meet with the intervention team. The tool should be used to help guide the discussion about potential roles and responsibilities and to engage intervention team members in providing input and finalizing plans for the team's functioning. For example, the team members might be asked their views about rotating some of the responsibilities or if they would prefer to maintain the same role for a designated period of time. This meeting also could be an opportunity for individual team members to share their comfort level with assuming one or more specific roles and to indicate any additional training needs in preparation for the role. In addition, team members should identify other practices and procedures that may not align with specific roles, but would contribute to their ability to operate effectively and efficiently. The note taker or the planning team member guiding the discussion should record agreements or decisions about the roles and responsibilities.

Decision point: The planning team should help the intervention team members determine specific roles and responsibilities that will be represented on the team and which members will assume them. The planning team should also identify other processes that will help the intervention team function effectively and efficiently.

TIPS AND VARIATIONS

1. Prior to the meeting, the planning team might give the tool to intervention team members and ask them to record some of their ideas about specific roles and assigned responsibilities. The planning team might collect this information before the meeting and analyze it to identify commonalities and differences. The chair could begin

the meeting with a summary of the views and lead a discussion to help reach consensus and make final decisions regarding designated roles and responsibilities and other meeting and support processes.

2. The chair could use this time to discuss the importance of engaging in processes that help the intervention team assess its effectiveness and efficiency, recommend changes, and identify the need for additional support. An additional section could be added to the form and intervention team members could be asked to complete it on a periodic basis (e.g., bimonthly) as a way to report on their team's overall functioning and their views about the effectiveness of the roles and responsibilities. This added section of the form might be titled "Self-Assessment of Effectiveness and Efficiency and Recommended Changes or Supports."

3. The RTI planning team might help the intervention team by conducting an observation of how each role is being implemented during a meeting and providing feedback. The feedback may be provided on the same form in another added section.

Developing the RTI Intervention Team:
Roles and Responsibilities

Roles	Responsibilities	Designated Individuals
Chair		
Note taker		
Timekeeper		
Case Manager		
Intervention Specialist		
Data Specialist		
Other Roles:		

Other agreements regarding team functioning

Reviewing RTI Intervention Team Tasks Related to Identifying and Monitoring Interventions

PURPOSE

The RTI Leadership Planning Team's orientation for the RTI Intervention Team should include a discussion of the various tasks that are part of the RTI process related to identifying and monitoring interventions:

- Selecting an intervention.
- Selecting the method for monitoring progress.
- Assigning responsibility for implementing the intervention and assessing student progress.
- Determining when to reconvene the intervention team to review progress and make adjustments as needed.

At the very least, the intervention team should discuss how they will engage in these tasks. Having a clear process has several advantages:

- Helping team members to stay focused on the process.
- Discouraging individual team members from unintentionally monopolizing the conversation.
- Helping to convey that the intervention team is a formal group that is invested in carrying out serious tasks.

Optimally, it would be helpful to have a guide that describes how the team carries out these tasks. A guide provides the team with an agreed upon process that can be shared with new members, guests, and family members who might attend. The purpose of this tool is to provide an outline of tasks for discussion.

HOW TO USE THIS TOOL

The list of tasks in the tool can serve as discussion points for intervention team members. Discussion may be facilitated by adhering to the following steps:

- Discuss the task purpose.
- Brainstorm possible steps to carrying out the task.

Building Your School's Capacity to Implement RTI | Developing and Implementing the RTI Plan

Developing the RTI Intervention Team | Reviewing RTI Intervention Team Tasks Related to Identifying and Monitoring Interventions

Part 3

- Discuss the pros and cons of each possibility.
- Decide which process steps will be adopted.
- Record.

Decision point: The planning team should determine whether intervention team members have a sound process in place to guide their work. If not, determine next steps for helping them build capacity.

TIPS AND VARIATIONS

1. Before engaging in the discussion, consider this example for the task of selecting interventions at Tier 1:

    The intervention team receives the Request for Assistance form and reviews the case materials. If the problem is identified as requiring interventions at Tier 1 (core instruction), then the team (including the teacher requesting assistance)

    - Reviews the list of suggested accommodations or interventions developed by the school or district and discusses whether any of these might support student achievement.
    - Discusses interventions that have been used successfully with other students with similar academic or behavioral challenges and emphasizes those with an evidence base.
    - Brainstorms which interventions appear to have high probability of success.
    - Evaluates interventions for ease of implementation (e.g., cost, availability, teacher preparation, etc.).
    - Decides which intervention to implement and with what support.

2. In Part 2, Section 3, the RTI Leadership Planning Team may have worked through the "Considering RTI Intervention Team Tasks: Details, Details, Details" tool. As part of that tool, the planning team may have developed a guide. If that is the case, then use this tool as an opportunity to familiarize intervention team members with the guide. Engage them in a discussion about each task, share the rationale for each set of process steps, and seek their feedback regarding any task descriptions that might be enhanced with modifications. To provide a clearer understanding of process steps, the planning team may want to role-play the tasks. These role-plays may be videotaped for future reference and professional development.

Building Your School's Capacity to Implement RTI | Developing and Implementing the RTI Plan

Developing the RTI Intervention Team | Reviewing RTI Intervention Team Tasks Related to Identifying and Monitoring Interventions

3. Identify additional tasks that should be addressed in this way.

4. The intervention team might be asked to role-play a meeting using the identified process steps. The planning team may observe and provide feedback.

RTI Intervention Team Tasks Related to Identifying and Monitoring Interventions

IDENTIFYING AND MONITORING INTERVENTIONS, TIER 1

Select interventions at Tier 1.

Determine who will carry out the interventions for identified students.

Determine the frequency and duration (number of days per week, number of minutes per day, number of weeks) with which an intervention will be provided.

Determine how student progress will be monitored. Assign responsibility.

Observe instruction to assess whether or not research-based strategies are being implemented with fidelity.

Assist instructors who are having difficulty implementing designated interventions with fidelity.

Review and interpret the progress monitoring data and identify, based on the data, whether or not instructional changes are indicated.

Determine how frequently meetings will be held to review the progress of students who are receiving interventions

IDENTIFYING AND MONITORING INTERVENTIONS, TIER 2 AND TIER 3

Select instructional interventions that should be used with individual students receiving services at Tier 2 or Tier 3.

Determine who will carry out the interventions for identified students.

Part 3

Building Your School's Capacity to Implement RTI | Developing and Implementing the RTI Plan

Developing the RTI Intervention Team | Reviewing RTI Intervention Team Tasks Related to Identifying and Monitoring Interventions

Determine the frequency and duration (number of days per week, number of minutes per day, number of weeks) with which an intervention will be provided (e.g., individual instructor employs intensity designated for pre-established strategy or a problem-solving team recommends particular intensity).

Observe instruction to assess whether or not research-based strategies are being implemented with fidelity.

Assist instructors who are having difficulty implementing designated interventions with fidelity.

Review and interpret the progress monitoring data and identify, based on the data, whether or not instructional changes are indicated.

Determine when the frequency and duration of a particular strategy should be modified.

Determine when students should receive more intensive interventions at a higher tier.

Determine when students should receive less intensive interventions.

Determine where students receive Tier 2 and Tier 3 interventions (e.g., general education classroom, separate small group in a resource room, or other setting).

Decide how frequently the progress of students receiving Tier 2 and Tier 3 interventions will be assessed.

Determine how frequently meetings will be held to review the progress of students who are receiving interventions.

Planning Professional Development for the RTI Intervention Team

PURPOSE

Members of the RTI Intervention Team should receive ongoing professional development in the problem-solving model and in the other components of RTI, particularly research-based strategies and progress monitoring. The purpose of this tool is to provide the RTI Leadership Planning Team with a foundation for discussing the types of skills and knowledge that will be needed for an effective intervention team.

HOW TO USE THIS TOOL

Invite intervention team members to complete the survey. Tally the results and share them with the intervention team.

Decision point: The planning team should decide if school staff members have sufficient knowledge and skills to initiate an intervention team and problem-solving approach. Team members should also identify needed supports and interventions. If staff members require professional development before launching an RTI framework, develop the stages of this intermediary plan.

TIPS AND VARIATIONS

1. Encourage survey participants to prioritize areas for professional development. For example, have them note the items for which they would like more information or training. From that list, have them prioritize the areas in which they would like immediate assistance.
2. Encourage survey participants to identify areas in which they have strong knowledge and skills. Invite them to suggest ways they might be willing to support colleagues in developing skills in those areas.
3. Identify areas that might be addressed within the entire school, as well as areas in which small teams might work together to expand their skills and knowledge.
4. Research district and other resources (e.g., universities, state, regional resource center, online course offerings) for professional development assistance.

5. Make a three-year plan for developing skills in the various areas.
6. Use the survey with the entire staff.

Planning Professional Development for the RTI Intervention Team

The purpose of this tool is to identify areas for professional development to enhance the RTI Intervention Team's work. Respond to each item using a Likert scale in terms of how skilled and knowledgeable you are:

- 4 = Very Skilled/Knowledgeable

- 3 = Somewhat Skilled/Knowledgeable

- 2 = Not Very Skilled/Knowledgeable

- 1 = Not Skilled/Knowledgeable

- N/A = Not applicable to my current assignment

CORE INSTRUCTION

1) ____ Differentiated Instruction

2) ____ Classroom Management

3) ____ Positive Behavioral Support

4) ____ Research-Based Strategies: Literacy

5) ____ Research-Based Strategies: Math

6) ____ Accommodations

7) ____ Universal Design for Learning

8) ____ Curriculum Standards

9) ____ Data-Based Decision Making

10) ____ Other

INTERVENTIONS FOR STRUGGLING STUDENTS

1) ____ Research-Based Strategies: Challenging Behavior

2) ____ Research-Based Strategies: Challenging Academic Problems

3) ____ Mental Health and Other Agency Supports and Services

4) ____ Special Education and Related Services

5) ____ Title 1 Services

6) ____ Specialized Services (District and School)

7) ____ Other

PROGRESS MONITORING

1) ____ Monitoring Progress

2) ____ Curriculum-Based Measurement

3) ____ Interpreting Data

4) ____ Other

TEAMING

1) ____ Collaboration Skills

2) ____ Communication Skills

3) ____ Problem-Solving Process Skills

4) ____ Data-Based Decision Making

5) ____ Team Facilitation Skills

6) ____ Coaching and Providing Feedback

7) ____ Observing Classroom Instruction

8) ____ Other

Developing the RTI Intervention Team

Using a Protocol for RTI Intervention Team Meetings

PURPOSE

Often, RTI Intervention Teams must conduct their meetings under very strict time frames. As a result, a typical challenge for team members is to stay focused on the problem-solving process during meetings.

The RTI Leadership Planning Team may find it helpful to provide a protocol that can be built into meeting agendas. A protocol gives team members a standard approach to completing their business. It also shows new members (e.g., teacher requesting assistance, parent, specialist) a clear format for how the meeting will proceed.

The purpose of this tool is to provide a stimulus that the planning team can use to help the intervention team develop meeting agendas.

HOW TO USE THIS TOOL

The planning team may use the tool to stimulate conversation. Begin by reviewing the tasks for different types of meetings. Pose this challenge: If you have 45 minutes to complete these activities, how will you allot your time? Draft an agenda for several types of meetings—the initial meeting, the review meetings in which progress is discussed, and the meeting in which a final determination is made (e.g., whether the student requires additional interventions, interventions at a higher tier, etc.).

Decision point: Determine if intervention team members have sufficient understanding of the RTI process to develop agendas. If not, make a plan for providing them with support.

TIPS AND VARIATIONS

1. Expand the activity to discuss strategies for keeping intervention team members on track. For example:

- Having a time keeper who monitors the time and alerts the team when they have taken more time than was allotted.
- Using facilitation strategies such as stopping to reflect on whether the agenda needs to be modified, summarizing the discussion and asking for permission to move ahead, gently reminding team members of the time, etc.
- Having a back-up plan for unexpected occurrences (e.g., the parents and an advocate attend and want to address the team, the person assigned to monitoring progress has not analyzed the data sufficiently and is taking too much time sharing raw data, a teacher becomes extremely emotional and requires time to process feelings, etc.).

2. Role-play a meeting using the agenda times to get a feel for how much time different activities might take.
3. Review agendas from other schools.
4. Make the distinction between process and product. For example, the product goal may be to arrive at a plan for student, whereas the goal of the process by which that goal is achieved may be to build a collaborative culture or to ensure parity among team members. Discuss strategies that facilitate both (e.g., active listening and summarizing people's statements is a process strategy; taking notes and periodically summarizing where the team is in the agenda supports the product goal).

Developing the RTI Intervention Team

Using a Protocol for RTI Intervention Team Meetings

Initial Meeting Tasks	Time Allotted
1) Welcome	
2) Introductions and Roles	
3) Review Purpose and Goal	
4) Review Agenda	
5) Invite Discussion of Problem	
6) Share Data	
7) Decision Point: Identify Problem	
8) Discuss Interventions	
9) Decision Point: Identify Intervention	
10) Develop Intervention Plan	
11) Summarize Meeting	
12) Identify Next Steps	
13) Ask for Feedback or Questions	
14) Adjourn	

Progress Review Meeting Tasks	Time Allotted
1) Welcome	
2) Introductions and Roles (optional)	
3) Review Purpose and Goal	

4) Review Agenda	
5) Share Data	
6) Discuss Progress	
7) Decision Point: • Continue Intervention • Modify Intervention • Develop New Plan	
8) Summarize Meeting	
9) Identify Next Steps	
10) Ask for Feedback and/or Questions	
11) Adjourn	

Final Determination Meeting Tasks	Time Allotted
1) Welcome	
2) Introductions and Roles (optional)	
3) Review Purpose and Goal	
4) Review Agenda	
5) Share Data and Discuss Outcomes	
6) Decision Point: Next Steps • No More Action Needed • Revise Plan • Develop New Plan • Other:	
7) Summarize Meeting	
8) Identify Next Steps	
9) Ask for Feedback and/or Questions	
10) Adjourn	

Organizing for Data Use During RTI Intervention Team Meetings

PURPOSE

The RTI Intervention Team must organize and maintain progress monitoring and universal screening data. To facilitate the use of progress monitoring data during meetings, certain managerial issues should be addressed.

The purpose of this tool is to provide the stimulus for a discussion focused on identifying managerial tasks related to handling data. RTI Leadership Planning Team members may wish to use this tool as they build the intervention team's capacity to use data for decision making.

HOW TO USE THIS TOOL

The planning team should familiarize itself with the items in the tool. In some cases, the team may want to suggest procedures that the intervention team will adopt. For each question, discuss and record notes to indicate next steps in planning for data use during and after meetings.

Decision point: At the end of the discussion, determine if there is a plan for using data as part of RTI Intervention Team meetings. If not, develop an action plan.

TIPS AND VARIATIONS

1. Ask intervention team members to review each step. Discuss the challenges inherent in addressing each task.
2. Encourage team members to have a back-up plan in the event that someone is absent.
3. Use the tool to periodically monitor overall effectiveness of the intervention team's data use.
4. Encourage intervention team members to use the tool periodically to check on how well they are managing data.

Organizing for Data Use During RTI Intervention Team Meetings

Discussion Questions	Notes, Ideas, Recommendations
Making Data Available to the Team	
Who maintains a compilation of the data? Who is responsible for making sure that reports are readily accessible at team meetings? For example, some schools have designated a staff member to serve as the RTI coordinator, whose responsibilities include compiling and maintaining the data and meeting with teachers during discussions of the data. Who makes sure that both current and historical data reports are available to help maintain a big picture focus (e.g., designated percentage of students achieving at benchmark) and current year's progress compared to same time period of previous year?	
Creating Meeting Structures to Facilitate Use of Data	
How will data be presented at meetings? Who is responsible for summarizing and/or organizing data for presentation (e.g., creating displays such as graphs)?	
Communicating with Parents	
What progress monitoring data will be shared with parents and how frequently? Is there a standard process for sharing progress monitoring data with parents?	

Keeping Records	Notes, Ideas, Recommendations
What types of record keeping will occur to document outcomes of meetings and next steps? What types of record keeping will occur to document communication with parents? How will the team ensure the confidentiality of student data?	
Other Questions	

Final Recommendations, Actions, Individuals Responsible, and Timelines

Facilitating Fidelity of Implementation

PURPOSE

After reviewing student data and identifying the problem, the RTI Intervention Team will select an intervention—preferably research based—to help the student. Team members will need to be sensitive to two potential areas of concern:

- Selecting an intervention that has a high probability of success. If the intervention does not match the problem, then the student may not progress because of the intervention, not because of some innate problem.
- Ensuring that the intervention is delivered to the student as it was intended. If the intervention is not presented appropriately, then lack of progress may not be related to the student's needs.

In relation to the latter, the term fidelity of implementation is often used to refer to delivering instruction in the way in which it was designed to be delivered. Staff members should know whether or not an intervention is being implemented as designed so that if the intervention is unsuccessful with a student, appropriate action can be taken to improve delivery rather than abandoning the intervention altogether. Such knowledge also helps team members understand that unresponsiveness to the intervention is a result of poor delivery and not something innately problematic with the student.

Further, if it becomes necessary to consider special education eligibility, teams must be able to determine that the student has received appropriate general education instruction—in fact, the Individuals with Disabilities Education Improvement Act of 2004 states that a child shall not be determined to be a child with a disability if the determinant factor is lack of appropriate instruction in reading, including the essential components of reading, or lack of instruction in math. Results can be poor when initiatives are adopted without fidelity to essential program design features. RTI Intervention Teams also should consider fidelity when implementing other components of RTI including universal screening, progress monitoring, and decision-making protocols.

The RTI Leadership Planning Team should be cognizant of some of the challenges that might interfere with fidelity. Consider these examples:

- The more complex the intervention, the more difficult it may be to implement. The more difficult to implement, the higher the probability that fidelity might be compromised.
- Typically, research-based interventions control for implementation. Sometimes the intervention may have been researched in a lab setting, or delivered by non-teaching staff (e.g., university assistants, researchers, etc.). Also, some interventions may have been implemented with a only few subject groups (e.g., students in the fourth grade with learning disabilities). A particular approach may not fit a particular student exactly in terms of research to support its usage. Or, teachers may not have received sufficient training in the strategy to implement it with fidelity. Thus, a particular intervention may have a strong research base, even though fidelity of implementation may be difficult to achieve.

This tool is intended to serve as a catalyst in prompting the planning team to consider how fidelity of implementation of RTI will be handled.

HOW TO USE THIS TOOL

The planning team should use this tool to guide discussion of topics related to implementing the components of RTI with fidelity.

Decision point: At the end of the discussion, decide what practices can be established that will help to achieve implementation with fidelity and identify those areas where more time and inputs are needed.

TIPS AND VARIATIONS

1. Talk with individuals from other schools about how they are ensuring fidelity of implementation of the RTI components, how they are documenting their efforts; and how they have assigned roles and responsibilities to different staff members in the process.
2. Provide selected parts of the tool to designated teams and request their assistance in planning for fidelity of implementation. For example, a designated grade level team

could focus on the content area of reading and decide to develop observation or self-assessment checklists related to the implementation of one specific intervention.

3. As the RTI components are developed, consider fidelity of implementation as it relates to a particular component. For example, as teams are identifying potential interventions, ask them to generate recommendations for facilitating fidelity of implementation for that particular intervention.

4. Discuss existing practices that can be modified to include a focus on fidelity of implementation (e.g., instructional walk-throughs or feedback provided by mentor teachers or peer coaches).

Facilitating Fidelity of Implementation

Questions and Discussion Points	Notes and Ideas
Current Practices	
How does the school currently address issues of fidelity in instruction? How are instructional staff members prepared to embrace fidelity issues? What supports are in place to encourage fidelity of instruction in the school?	
Use of Staff	
Which staff members are qualified or could become qualified to conduct instructional observations of interventions and provide feedback on fidelity (e.g., mentor teachers, teachers with National Board Certification, school psychologists, etc.)?	
What scheduling and role changes might be necessary in order for staff to conduct instructional observations related to fidelity of implementation?	
Which staff members might help to create checklists related to the critical features of specific instructional interventions?	
Which staff members might be used to provide fidelity of implementation feedback related to universal screening or progress monitoring (e.g. school psychologists)?	
What scheduling and role changes might be necessary in order for staff to conduct screening and progress monitoring observations or review data related to fidelity of implementation?	
Which staff members might help to create fidelity checklists related to universal screening and progress monitoring?	

Professional Development	
What initial and follow-up professional development will be needed for staff members to conduct observations of instructional interventions and provide feedback on fidelity of implementation?	
Staff Input	
How can staff members be involved in planning strategies to support fidelity of implementation so that it becomes nonthreatening and is viewed as part of a positive school culture?	
What approaches can be used to help staff members accept and use the observational feedback provided related to fidelity of implementation?	
Targeted Areas and Frequency	
What areas should be targeted initially for a focus on implementation with fidelity (e.g., reading, math, universal screening, or progress monitoring)?	
How frequently will observations or other practices to assess fidelity of implementation and to provide meaningful and specific feedback be conducted?	
Documentation	
How will observations or other practices related to fidelity of implementation be documented, and who will receive and maintain the documentation?	

Self-Assessment	
What strategies may be used to help staff members assess their own practices related to fidelity of implementation (e.g., watching video-taped lessons, reviewing student work samples with peer colleagues, and obtaining feedback related to implementation of interventions or progress monitoring with fidelity)?	
What ongoing strategies can be used by the RTI Leadership Planning Team to assess schoolwide practices related to fidelity of implementation and to make changes as needed?	

Recommendations, Decisions, Follow-Up Needed and Dates, and Individuals Responsible

SECTION 4 OVERVIEW: MONITORING AND SUPPORTING RTI IMPLEMENTATION

Once the RTI Intervention Team and problem-solving process are established, the RTI Leadership Planning Team will turn its attention to ensuring that staff members use the RTI process efficiently and effectively. To this end, planning team members may find themselves engaged in the following types of activities:

- **Monitoring implementation**. This includes checking on how well the RTI process is working by considering such things as student performance data and intervention team workload.

- **Assessing staff members' participation in the RTI process**. This includes seeking staff feedback, ascertaining their perceptions, and tracking staff use.

- **Supporting staff members.** This includes providing professional development, making resources available, and coaching.

- **Reflecting on next steps and planning enhancements**. This includes asking staff for input, identifying areas for further focus, and planning enhancements to the RTI process.

PURPOSE OF THIS SECTION AND SUMMARY OF TOOLS

The purpose of this section is to provide suggestions for monitoring and supporting RTI implementation. The tools in this section are designed to help the planning team monitor implementation, assess impact, and respond to challenges. The tools also feature ways to gain feedback via self-assessments and focus groups.

The tools are as follows:

- **Understanding and Implementing RTI: Self-Assessment and Identification of Additional Supports.** As part the RTI implementation and monitoring process, the planning team may find it helpful to seek feedback from faculty members and other stakeholders on a systematic basis. This tool provides a structured self-assessment approach for obtaining feedback from faculty members.

- **Assessing RTI Implementation Progress via Focus Groups.** The planning team will want to keep participants engaged and moving forward. One strategy is to convene focus groups. This tool provides procedures for conducting a focus group.

- **Monitoring Implementation: Looking at Program Data.** The planning team may want to consider program data—e.g., data on student performance, intervention team

Monitoring and Supporting RTI Implementation

workload data, professional development outcomes, use of resources, and number of interventions successfully implemented—as part of monitoring RTI implementation. The purpose of this tool is to provide the RTI Leadership Planning Team with a strategy to begin this discussion.

- **Reflecting on Next Steps and Planning Enhancements.** After the RTI process has been implemented for some time, the planning tem may find it helpful to reconvene the team to reflect on progress. This tool provides a planning sheet for reviewing areas that might be enhanced.

The planning team members can reuse these tools as they continue to monitor and refine the RTI initiative.

Understanding and Implementing RTI: Self-Assessment and Identification of Additional Supports

PURPOSE

As part the RTI implementation and monitoring process, the RTI Leadership Planning Team may find it helpful to seek feedback from faculty members and other stakeholders on a regular basis. Such information will enable the team to determine the success and impact of its communication and professional development efforts and facilitate the identification of areas requiring further emphasis.

This tool provides a structured self-assessment approach for the planning team to use in obtaining feedback from faculty members regarding their level of understanding of RTI components and their identification of needs (e.g., additional information, additional time to practice implementation of selected components). Such a feedback process also helps to communicate the intent of the administration to support and help sustain an RTI approach.

HOW TO USE THIS TOOL

The planning team should identify an appropriate time frame for administering the survey to faculty members based on the amount of time that has lapsed since initiating the RTI framework and providing professional development in selected areas. For example, if RTI was launched in the fall and faculty members have already been implementing selected components, mid-year may be an appropriate time to survey the faculty and identify additional actions that can be taken in response to the survey results. In planning for administering the survey, the planning team will also need to develop a plan for compiling and reviewing the results and planning next steps, including sharing survey outcomes with the faculty.

Decision point: The planning team should determine the appropriate time for administering the self-assessment to faculty members and plan next steps upon reviewing the compiled results.

Building Your School's Capacity to Implement RTI | Developing and Implementing the RTI Plan

Part 3

Monitoring and Supporting RTI Implementation | Understanding and Implementing RTI: Self-Assessment and Identification of Additional Supports

TIPS AND VARIATIONS

1. The administrative team or planning team might decide to disseminate the self-assessment survey only to selected faculty members. For example, if RTI were phased in starting with selected grade levels, the team may elect to survey only faculty members at those grade levels.

2. The survey might be modified to reflect only those RTI components that have been the focus of implementation.

3. Rather than surveying individual faculty members, the administrative team or planning team might request that teams discuss the survey items and submit responses reflecting consensus points of view (e.g., grade level teams, RTI Intervention Team members).

Understanding and Implementing RTI: Self-Assessment and Identification of Additional Supports

Directions: Enter a number from the following scale to reflect your current level of understanding of selected RTI components; please use the comment section to share additional information, questions, and needs.

4 = I understand this RTI component; I am fully implementing it and can help support others.

3 = I understand this RTI component; I am implementing it but would like more feedback and practice.

2 = I understand this RTI component but am not yet confident with implementation.

1 = I do not yet have a clear understanding of this RTI component and have not begun implementation.

_____ **Universal Screening:** Administering assessments, interpreting results, and identifying struggling learners.

_____ **Monitoring Student Progress:** Using and interpreting selected progress monitoring measures and discussing results with colleagues to help identify next steps (e.g., identifying interventions, changing level of tiered instruction).

_____ **Core Instructional Program (Tier 1):** Implementing strong core program that reflects such practices as effective classroom management, proactive behavioral interventions, cultural responsiveness, differentiated instruction, research-based instructional strategies, and supplemental instruction for struggling learners.

_____ **Tier 2 Interventions:** Implementing intensive individual or small-group instruction using selected research-based interventions and instructional materials for students in ____ reading, ____ math, ____ written expression, ____ other.

Building Your School's Capacity to Implement RTI | Developing and Implementing the RTI Plan

Monitoring and Supporting RTI Implementation | Understanding and Implementing RTI: Self-Assessment and Identification of Additional Supports

Part 3

_____ **Tier 3 Interventions:** Implementing very intensive individual or small-group instruction using selected research-based interventions and instructional materials for students in ___ reading, _____ math, _____ written expression, _____ other.

_____ **Participating in Data-Based Problem Solving Processes Related to Student Assessment and Instructional Planning:** Presenting universal screening and progress monitoring data and brainstorming with colleagues to help identify ways to modify instruction to facilitate increased student learning.

Assessing RTI Implementation Progress via Focus Groups

PURPOSE

Most major initiatives require support to keep participants engaged and moving forward. Once RTI implementation has begun, the RTI Leadership Planning Team will want to sustain the momentum by systematically engaging stakeholders in assessing progress and recommending additional actions. One strategy is to convene focus groups. This tool provides procedures that the planning team may use to obtain stakeholder feedback within a focus group format.

HOW TO USE THIS TOOL

The planning team, with input from the administration as appropriate, should identify the specific topic or topics for which they would like feedback on how well implementation is going, such as progress monitoring, effective core instruction, or the problem-solving process. These topics form the basis for discussion. At this time, the planning team should identify a facilitator for the focus group and make arrangements for recording the discussion.

Next, the team should determine the desired stakeholder composition of the focus group. Team members may want to vary the focus group's composition depending on certain factors. Examples include varying by

- Level of involvement in helping to implement RTI. If RTI has been implemented only at the primary grade levels, then it may be appropriate to convene a group comprising only faculty members who work with those students.
- Number of available participants. Multiple groups may be needed to ensure that they are manageable (e.g., 2 focus groups of primary grade level and resource faculty members with 10 to 12 participants in each group).
- The need for feedback on a specific topic may target certain individuals for participation (e.g., staff who have been involved in using positive approaches to schoolwide discipline).

The planning team should also develop a process for sharing focus group outcomes and subsequent actions with focus group participants (e.g., in a follow-up meeting) as well as with the entire staff (e.g., in an RTI newsletter, at a regular staff meeting).

To conduct the focus group, the facilitator may want to prepare by posting chart paper labeled with headers such as those found on the tool:

- What's Working Well
- What We Can Do Better—Suggestions
- Questions and Concerns

When focus group members are assembled, the facilitator should express appreciation for their attendance, review the meeting purpose, and outline procedures. Following is an example of opening remarks:

> Thank you for accepting the invitation to participate in today's focus group meeting. The purpose of this meeting is to obtain your views on the implementation of RTI in the area of universal screening. [*Note*: other components of RTI may be selected.] As you know, our school began implementing universal screening in September. As we prepare for another round of screening, the RTI Leadership Planning Team has requested specific feedback about what has worked well; suggestions that would help to facilitate a more effective and efficient process for the next screening; and the identification of questions and concerns. This is intended to be a process where I hope you can share what comes to mind comfortably. I am asking that we each respect confidentiality and not attribute comments and questions to any individual focus group participant. To generate the most ideas, it is important that we refrain from expressing agreement or disagreement with remarks. We want to be open all points of view.
>
> Thirty minutes has been allocated for this meeting. I would like to start with a round-robin approach, but please feel free to pass if you have not yet generated an idea. As you share, our colleague will take notes on the chart paper. We want to capture as many ideas and questions as possible. Once each person has had an opportunity to share in a round-robin format, I will seek additional input and anyone in the group may contribute additional ideas.
>
> After the meeting, I will transcribe the meeting notes for submission to the RTI Leadership Planning Team and to you. Statements and questions will not be attributed to any individual and, as previously stated, we will each need to respect confidentiality.

Decision point: The planning team should decide how to respond to the ideas and questions generated during the focus group. For example, does the focus group format provide an effective vehicle for involving stakeholders and for providing information that help in assessing the status and progress of selected RTI components? Should the focus group format be used in the future, and if so, for which topics?

TIPS AND VARIATIONS

1. Identify an outside facilitator, such as a central office staff member or experienced facilitator from another school who has experience implementing RTI.
2. Use a computer and projector to record notes in a manner that will be visible to the focus group participants.
3. Convene multiple focus groups to address the same topic and subsequently compile and analyze all of the ideas and questions.
4. Convene multiple focus groups with each group providing input on a different topic.

Assessing RTI Implementation Progress via Focus Groups

Focus Group Ideas and Questions

Specific Topic: _____

What's Working Well	
What We Can Do Better— Suggestions	
Questions and Concerns	

Monitoring Implementation: Looking at Program Data

PURPOSE

In addition to surveying staff members' perceptions of how well RTI is being used, the RTI Leadership Planning Team may want to consider program data (e.g., data on student performance, RTI Intervention Team workload data, professional development outcomes, use of resources, number of interventions successfully implemented) as part of monitoring RTI implementation. The purpose of this tool is to provide a guide to reviewing program data.

HOW TO USE THIS TOOL

The planning team should consider various types of data that provide insights into how the program is working. The content in the tool corresponds to different program aspects for which data may be available. It should be used as a starting point for a discussion focused on how well the RTI program is serving student and staff needs. Consider these examples:

- Data showing a large number of requests for assistance from the RTI Intervention Team may signal a burdensome caseload for the team. In this case, the planning team may want to consider establishing a second intervention team. Or, team members may do an analysis of the types of requests to determine if there is a pattern of the same teachers requesting assistance for the same student difficulties. In this case, the planning team may want to consider targeted professional development.

- The planning team may look at student data showing the number of referrals out of the classroom for behavioral infractions and compare these numbers with the number of referrals prior to RTI, as well as the number of requests for assistance that focus on behavioral difficulties. The intervention team will want to analyze why that is so (e.g., core instructional program could be enhanced by professional development in behavioral management, a subgroup of students are responsible for 80 percent of the infractions, and so on).

- Data showing how often instructional resources and technology are used may be considered when assessing the strength of the core instructional program. For example, if the planning team determines that more than half of the instructional support tools are not being used regularly, then they may want to investigate why (e.g., no training in how to use the materials, the materials are too cumbersome to use).

The planning team should determine which data points they will review. For each data point, they should indicate what data are available, their analysis (i.e., what it tells them about how well RTI is being implemented), and future actions that should be undertaken.

Decision point: The planning team should decide if there is sufficient program data to monitor implementation. If so, team members should develop action plans to address any deficiencies or to bolster success. If there are insufficient data, team members should plan how to identify various data sources.

TIPS AND VARIATIONS

1. Some data will be available immediately (e.g., number of requests for assistance), whereas other data may not be available for several months (e.g., student progress data). The planning team might want to plan data review sessions to accommodate these realities.
2. The planning team might invite representatives from the district program evaluation office to offer insights and suggestions when reviewing program data.
3. The planning team might want to assign responsibility for certain data sources to individual members. Responsibilities may include such tasks as gathering data and organizing it for analysis.

ASCD
373

Monitoring Implementation: Looking at Program Data

Program Data Source	Describe Data Available	Analysis/ Results	Future Actions
Student Performance			
Progress Data			
Screening Data			
Behavioral Data			
Attendance Data			
Other			
Professional Development Outcomes			
Number of Sessions Offered			
Attendees			
Classroom Observations			
Other			

Program Data Source	Describe Data Available	Analysis/ Results	Future Actions
RTI Intervention Team Workload			
Number of Meetings			
Number of Students Served/Disposition			
Number of Staff Requesting Assistance			
Parent Participation			
Other			
Other			
Resources Used			
Number of Requests			
Other			
Other			

Reflecting on Next Steps and Planning Enhancements

PURPOSE

After the RTI process has been in place for some time, the RTI Leadership Planning Team may find it helpful to reconvene the team to reflect on progress. Team members may use this time to discuss successes and identify areas that might benefit from enhancements or additional efforts. Consider these examples:

- The RTI Intervention Team usually selects from the same five interventions when developing student support plans. The planning team may see this as an opportunity for engaging the intervention team in professional development on other interventions.

- English language arts teachers use the RTI process for students who have difficulty with reading and writing. However, the RTI process is rarely used for students who have difficulty with science, social studies, or other academic areas. The planning team may see this as an opportunity to engage staff in those subject areas in self-assessment and focus groups to determine how best to expand support to students with difficulties in these content areas.

- The school has been involved in universal screening, but results are never discussed as part of the RTI process. The planning team might use this as an opportunity to meet with the administration to discuss how screening results might be integrated into the RTI process and develop an action plan.

- Classroom teachers have embraced the concept of core instruction. However, there are few resources for them to use when differentiating instruction and providing accommodations to students. The planning team may use this as an opportunity to review the inventory of resources and meet with staff members to identify additional resources that would be helpful.

- Data indicate that a subgroup of students continue to perform below grade level. The planning team may use this as an opportunity to form a task force of staff and experts to make recommendations.

The purpose of this tool is to provide a planning sheet for reviewing areas that might be enhanced.

HOW TO USE THIS TOOL

The planning team might use the planning sheet in the following ways:

- Each team member should complete the first three questions. This includes talking to staff members and gathering data. The entire team discusses what might be done to address issues.
- The team identifies one or more areas for study. Team members volunteer to interview staff members and gather data to bring back to the group for further discussion.
- The first three questions are presented to various teams in the school, such as the intervention team or the grade level team, and they are asked to discuss the questions and share their results with the planning team.

Decision point: Once the focus areas have been analyzed thoroughly, the planning team should determine if the action plan can be implemented. This involves getting approval from the administration as well as outlining implementation activities, time schedules, team member responsibilities, and monitoring procedures.

TIPS AND VARIATIONS

1. Share draft action plans with staff. Ask for their input.
2. As appropriate, query parents of students who have received support from the intervention team about their perceptions. Ask them to identify things that they perceive to be helpful and things they perceive should be improved.
3. Invite selected staff to join the planning team when discussing possible focus areas.

Reflecting on Next Steps and Planning Enhancements

Focus Area: _____

Discussion Questions	Notes
What data do we have about the focus area?	
How do staff members perceive the focus area, and what do they suggest we should consider when addressing it?	
What might we do to enhance the RTI process to address these issues?	

Action Plan, Individuals Responsible, and Timelines

▶▶▶▶ About the Authors

Patricia Addison is president of the Addison Leadership Group, LLC, and an assistant professor at George Mason University. With more than 34 years of experience in public education, Addison has held a number of public school teaching and administrative positions including director of special education for Fairfax County Public Schools in Fairfax, Virginia, the 12th largest school division in the nation. In this role, Addison led a variety of school improvement efforts and districtwide change processes, including an initiative to foster inclusive schools. Addison's experience in forming positive relationships and working effectively with all stakeholders—including superintendents, school board members, principals and other school-based administrators, general education teachers, special education teachers, support staff, parents, community members, and higher education faculty— serves as a foundation for her approach to coaching others in how to facilitate change.

Addison's practical experience and expertise in leadership have culminated in her conducting workshops nationally; teaching graduate classes; and consulting, particularly in the areas of leadership assessment and development and Response to Intervention. She is currently directing an Aspiring Special Education Leaders Academy for the Virginia Department of Education.

Addison earned her Doctor of Education degree from the University of Virginia in the area of educational leadership. She has served on a number of national, state, and local committees and boards, including the Board of Directors for the Council of Administrators of Special Education. She was president of the Virginia Council of Administrators of Special Education (VCASE) for a two-year term and member of its Executive Board for six years. Her awards include several Above and Beyond the Call-of-Duty Awards from Fairfax County Public Schools and the VCASE James T. Micklem Award in 2008 for outstanding contributions in the field of special education in the Commonwealth of Virginia.

Cynthia L. Warger is president of Warger, Eavy and Associates, an educational and communications consulting firm. Before forming WEA in 1989, she taught in the public schools, directed education training programs at the university level, and was in charge of program and professional development for ASCD. As editor of *TEACHING Exceptional Children*, she received two Educational Press Association of America's Distinguished Achievement Awards. She has published extensively on topics such as curriculum, effective instructional practices, instructional and assistive technology, and positive behavioral support. She coauthored the guide *Early Warning, Timely Response: A Guide to Safe Schools*, which then-President Clinton distributed to every school in the United States. She also wrote and produced the companion documentary *Promising Practices for Safe and Effective Schools*, which received four national awards, including the prestigious CINE Award for excellence. She has worked in numerous school districts helping educators implement systemwide changes and initiatives, including schoolwide positive behavioral support, effective core instruction, and data-based problem-solving teams. In addition, she has presented numerous professional sessions in school districts and at conferences nationwide.